# Dreams of Difference, Songs of the Same

## The Musical Moment in Film

Amy Herzog

University of Minnesota Press
Minneapolis • London

Portions of the Introduction were published in "Images of Thought and Acts of Creation: Deleuze, Bergson, and the Question of Cinema," *In Visible Culture* 3 (Fall 2000), http://www.rochester.edu/in_visible_culture/; and in "Affectivity, Becoming, and the Cinematic Event: Gilles Deleuze and the Futures of Feminist Film Theory," in *Conference Proceedings for Affective Encounters: Rethinking Embodiment in Feminist Media Studies,* ed. Anu Koivunen and Susanna Paasonen (Turku, Finland: University of Turku and the Finnish Society for Cinema Studies, 2001), http://media.utu.fi/affective/proceedings.html. An earlier version of chapter 1 was published as "Illustrating Music: The Impossible Embodiments of the Jukebox Film," in *Medium Cool: Music Videos from Soundies to Cellphones,* ed. Roger Beebe and Jason Middleton (Durham, N.C.: Duke University Press, 2007), 30–58; copyright 2007; all rights reserved; reprinted by permission of the publisher, Duke University Press. A section of chapter 1 also appeared in "Discordant Visions: The Peculiar Musical Images of the Soundies Jukebox Film," *American Music* 22, no. 1 (Spring 2004): 27–39. Portions of chapter 2 appeared in "The Dissonant Refrains of Jean-Luc Godard's *Prénom Carmen,*" in *"Carmen": From Silent Film to MTV,* ed. Chris Perriam and Ann Davies (Amsterdam: Rodopi Press, 2005), 135–50. An earlier version of chapter 4 was published in *Afterimages of Gilles Deleuze's Film Philosophy,* ed. D. N. Rodowick (Minneapolis: University of Minnesota Press, 2010).

Published by the University of Minnesota Press
111 Third Avenue South, Suite 290
Minneapolis, MN 55401-2520
http://www.upress.umn.edu

Library of Congress Cataloging-in-Publication Data

Herzog, Amy.
    Dreams of difference, songs of the same : the musical moment in film / Amy Herzog.
    p. cm.
    Includes bibliographical references and index.
    ISBN 978-0-8166-6087-2 (hc : alk. paper) — ISBN 978-0-8166-6088-9 (pb : alk. paper)
    1. Motion picture music—History and criticism. I. Title.
    ML2075.H478 2009
    781.5'42—dc22

                                    2009030839

Printed in the United States of America on acid-free paper

The University of Minnesota is an equal-opportunity educator and employer.

17 16 15 14 13 12 11 10    10 9 8 7 6 5 4 3 2 1

# Dreams of Difference, Songs of the Same

# Contents

# Introduction

And at that very moment, on the other side of existence, in this other world which you can see in the distance, but without ever approaching it, a little melody began to sing and dance: "You must be like me; you must suffer in rhythm."

—JEAN-PAUL SARTRE, *Nausea*

Jean-Paul Sartre ends his novel *Nausea* with a single moment of aesthetic transcendence. Roquentin, the narrator-writer whose existential dissolution the novel follows, sits in a café, asking the barmaid to play again and again the same record. He contemplates a small skip in the recording: "Someone must have scratched the record at that spot because it makes an odd noise. And there is something that clutches the heart: the melody is absolutely untouched by this tiny coughing of the needle on the record."[1] The untimeliness of the record overwhelms Roquentin, a fragment whose duration, caught within the imperfect grooves of the disk, somehow takes on an impersonal life beyond the will or knowledge of its creators. Sartre isolates music in this novel, and specifically popular music, as having a unique relation to time and space. Roquentin's brief moments of happiness in *Nausea* are triggered by his encounters with jazz and trips to the cinema. It seems that the pleasure gleaned from these practices is inextricably bound to their repeatability: the anticipation of a particular passage, the familiar nuances of the voice, the precise speed of the projector, or the phonograph ticking off the unstoppable passage of time. Yet the comforting sameness of each repetition, for Roquentin, is charged with a liberating brush with a time and space distant from one's own existence, the adventure of leaping outside of one's self to connect with a force that is immaterial yet bears the physical weight of the sounds, lights, and lives that created it.

Film and recorded music are media marked by their manipulations of time and space, their emotional affect arising from the space between the reproducibility of the material form and the seeming etherealness of the aesthetic experience. While the transcendent nature of the encounter that Sartre describes demands interrogation, his discussion of popular music points to many of the contradictions that are central to this book: the repeatability of the identical recording versus the changing contexts in which it is heard; the singularity of the moment recorded versus its preservation in a reproducible form; the distance of the bodies that perform versus the intimacy with which that performance is experienced; and the mass-produced commodity versus the intensely personal experience of the audience. The transcendence that Roquentin experiences is but a facet of yet another contradiction: How is it that popular music and popular film, two media produced by heavily conglomerated commercial industries, defined by their formulaic structures and marred by culturally repressive modes of representation, are nevertheless experienced as forces that propel us elsewhere, outside ourselves?

This book examines the relations between popular music and images in the cinema, focusing on the operations of what I call the "musical moment." Drawing on the work of Gilles Deleuze and Henri Bergson, I argue that music and film, as media composed of time and movement, demand a mode of analysis focused on those qualities. The peculiarity of the musical moment, and of the musical as a genre, further complicates the theoretical frameworks we typically draw on when studying cinema. The musical film is a "mongrel" format, evolved from diverse traditions of vaudeville and the stage and encompassing a hugely varied range of styles.[2] In nearly all its incarnations, and particularly within its production sequences, the musical is driven by a sonic, as opposed to a visual, logic. Unfettered by the demands of causality, the sensorial spectacles in the musical often subsume the narrative framework, creating configurations of time and space completely unlike those found in other filmic works. At the same time, there is a penchant for repetition in musical cinema that suggests a certain conservatism. The musical is marked by both structural repetitions (of format, of narrative, of songs, of characters, of melodic structures) and cultural repetitions (e.g., persistent representations of gender, race, and class); these recurring refrains often work to prescribe and reinforce meanings according to the dominant rationale of a particular historical moment.

This contradiction, between the sameness of the identical repetition and a movement toward transformation, difference, and excess, provides the foundation for my inquiry. I should establish from the outset that my project is not a genre study and that I am not interested in establishing firm distinctions between musical and nonmusical films. Instead, my analysis centers on the musical moments that erupt within all manner of cinematic (and, indeed, video) forms, exploring their philosophical, cultural, and political implications. Because these moments are often most fully realized within the musical genre, several of the examples included here are drawn from "classical" Hollywood musicals. The majority of the films I reference, however, push the boundaries of the musical canon. I have arrived at these selections for a number of reasons. Some, like Esther Williams's films, are admittedly clumsy or strange, and the transitions between musical and narrative portions are abrupt and unconvincing. Others, like Soundies jukebox films from the 1940s, moved along paths of circulation and drew on musical traditions very different from narrative films. Finally, variations on the musical from outside the United States, such as Jacques Demy's *Les parapluies de Cherbourg (The Umbrellas of Cherbourg)* (1964) and Tsai Ming-liang's *The Hole* (1998), reflect and expand on the conventions of the genre in significant ways.

My decision to structure this project around such a diverse selection of films is fourfold. First, the philosophical problematic that drives my inquiry—the tension between difference and repetition that arises within the musical moment—needs to be grounded within highly specific contexts to avoid verging into abstract musings. Second, this specificity requires a further demonstration of the diverse ways in which these larger theoretical questions will resonate in different contexts; my case studies, as such, are drawn from disparate historical and national points of origin. Third, the complex nature of much of the theory I work with here presents a challenge in terms of shifting between the registers of abstract philosophical concepts and readings of individual films. This is a difficulty that I would argue plagues Deleuze's own writing on cinema and much of the literature that follows in his footsteps. I have organized my project into four sets of case studies with the goal of exploring the connections between the general and the particular in as much detail as possible.

Finally, I have found a recurring theme in the films that captured my attention as I began researching the connections between Deleuze and musical film. The most marginal musical films continually spoke the most forcibly about the tension between difference and repetition. While many canonical musicals retain a sense of smoothness and closure, these more obscure films are marred by failure, noise, clumsiness, rupture, and perversity. Glitches, accidents, and discontinuities serve as types of differences that interrupt the sameness of the reproduction of image and sound.[3] The low fidelity of the jukebox film, for example, screams with this kind of noise, and this, I argue, is the source of that medium's affective power. The discomfort that the failed musical image produces opens up into a realm of indeterminacy and unfixed meaning, which in turn allows for the generation of critical readings and creative thought. These failings also tell us something about how the elements of film and music work in general, pointing to a certain representational logic that may lie hidden beneath the surface in more seamless, polished works.

I further suggest that social differences (race and gender, in these examples) create a similar type of noise. The degree of rupture or discomfort that a stereotypical representation causes is of course contingent on the cultural context of the viewing event; a representation may not be interpreted as stereotypical during different time periods or by different audiences. By exploring the nuances of this dynamic, I hope to demonstrate the importance of viewing the film experience as an event. Within the event, the distinction between subject and object is less significant than their mutual interactions. While I pay a great deal of attention to issues of sexuality, gender, and race, my aim is not to evaluate whether certain representations are positive or negative. Instead, I read these representations within the larger fluctuations of the film, its musical, visual, and structural refrains. Between these registers, we can read shifting tensions between movements of openness and differentiation versus the closed meanings of repetitions that ground identity in repressive, binaristic formulations. The circulations of these refrains are highly complex, and their political nuances may elude or exceed the insularity of a textual "decoding."

Within my readings of musical films, then, the notion of artistic intentionality is continually destabilized by the significance of the accidental. Despite the often conservative goals of certain film producers or the slick resolution of the narrative, breaks and stutters on the level of the image and the sound track provide a surplus of meaning that opens the film into new lines of flight. Even in the case of innovative filmmakers such as Godard, Demy, and Tsai— all artists who self-consciously engage with the conventions of the musical genre in their work—I will read certain incongruities and "perversions" of sound and image as amplifications of refrains that exist in less reflective or political works. Indeed, the refrains of works entrenched in established cultural traditions frequently provide the platform for creative innovation, where echoes of established repetitions are introduced into new contexts. Thus, many of the case studies in this book create unexpected groupings, with extreme contrasts between "high" and "low" films (e.g., the pairing of Tsai Ming-liang and Esther Williams). My goal in creating these juxtapositions is to highlight the echoing refrains that exist among seemingly disparate works, refrains that exist on a multitude of registers (e.g., structural, musical, visual, thematic). Each of these case studies, too, will view accidents, rupture, and noise as potentially productive forces that inject difference into even the most staid repetition.

The bond between the works examined in this book, then, is not one of genre, historical period, studio, national cinema, narrative structure, ideological perspective, or even a visual style. What is most interesting to me about these examples is that nearly all resist or exceed precisely those categories so central to contemporary film studies. There are, nevertheless, a number of qualities that these films do share. Most were created outside the Hollywood studio system (in the case of jukebox films and international "art" films) or are marginal examples within the genre (e.g., *Carmen Jones* [Preminger, 1954] and *Neptune's Daughter* [Buzzell, 1949]). In the feature-length works, the intrusion of the musical moment is exceptionally jarring, to a greater degree than is common in most "integrated" Hollywood musicals.[4] Even in the short films, there is a pronounced sense of fragmentation and a lack of cohesion. This lack of a unifying facade (whether intentional or accidental) highlights the tension between forces of difference and repetition; while this tension is certainly not unique to these films, its presence in these works is unusually conspicuous and affecting. Many of these works contain images that raise questions about the politics of representation, particularly in relation to race and gender. Again, this is not a remarkable quality in itself; the existent literature on musical film provides ample evidence that the genre as a whole was fixated on questions of racial and gendered identity. Yet the exceptional disjointedness of the films I examine reveals much about the manner in which the musical moment works to both reinforce and critique those identity positions. Dissonance in the musical moment can serve to interrogate not just particular types of representations but the very operation of cultural systems of representation as a whole. By creating assemblages of images, sounds, and narratives that do not fully mesh, the musical moments collected here create entities that are both fantastic and false—bodies with mismatched voices, impossible visual spaces, and narrative worlds that are pure fabulation. This is perhaps the most significant quality shared by the films I examine: each can be easily "caught in the act of telling tales."[5] My project is to explore the operations and potentialities of these acts of fabulation, with the aim of finding new, dynamic ways to think about questions of repetition and convention in musical cinema. I begin by distinguishing between the musical as a genre and the musical moment as a fluid and malleable expressive form.

## The Musical Moment

Traditionally, music serves as a subordinate element in narrative film, supplementing the image to guide our emotional response to what we see on-screen.

Film music often does not register consciously in the mind of the viewer; it remains as what Claudia Gorbman calls an "unheard melody."[6] Nondiegetic scores typically map themselves onto the rhythm of the image, supporting the flow of narrative action without interrupting it. Film scores exist as fragmented themes that can be woven in and out of the sound track as the image dictates. Michel Chion describes such music as "pit music," functioning much like the invisible accompaniment of an orchestra below a stage.[7] The relations between images and film music of this type are myriad, yet in most commercial cinema, we can speak of an empathy between the two; the music stabilizes the image and secures meaning while remaining as unobtrusive as possible.[8]

There are many instances, however, when this hierarchy is inverted and music serves as the dominant force in the work, creating a musical moment. Certain film scores refuse to remain subservient to the image and achieve a dramatic presence (e.g., Bernard Hermann's scores for Hitchcock's *Vertigo* [1958] and *Psycho* [1960]). Distinct musical themes that indicate a certain character or emotion, too, may begin to signify in more active ways. Walter Murch identifies such themes as partially encoded sounds, sounds that are interpreted in ways similar to language, in opposition to embodied sounds, which are more abstract and directly experienced.[9] Film music that maintains what Michel Chion calls an "anempathetic" relation to the image, being marked by a "conspicuous indifference" to what is happening on-screen, will also draw attention to itself.[10] Such incongruous or inappropriate music (e.g., a frothy pop song that is oblivious to the murder scene it accompanies) foregrounds the work music performs in relation to the image, destabilizing the image and opening it to outside associations. And diegetic music, by nature, will hold a more prominent position in the viewer's consciousness, as its source has a direct place within the narrative. Songs with lyrics, particularly those sung by one of the characters on-screen, focus our attention on the music and disrupt the flow of the narrative, if only because the voice of the singer forecloses the use of dialogue.[11]

The restructuring of the sound track since the 1960s, with the increased reliance on intact popular songs, has dramatically changed the interactions between images and sound in film. Scores compiled primarily from popular music (e.g., *American Graffiti* [Lucas, 1973], *Pretty in Pink* [Hughes, 1986], *Goodfellas* [Scorsese, 1990]) work to signify in entirely different ways than do traditional scores and maintain an active, prominent position in relation to the image.[12] But there is a unique type of musical moment, one that relies on popular music yet is distinct from the compilation score, that is best exemplified by the production numbers in classical Hollywood musicals. The images during these musical interludes are constructed entirely according to the demands of the song. The rhythm of the music prescribes the cinematography and the pacing and timing of edits. The temporal logic of the film shifts, lingering in a suspended present rather than advancing the action directly. Movements within the frame are not oriented toward action but toward visualizing the trajectory of the song; walking becomes dancing, and objects and people become one in a complex compositional choreography. Space, too, is completely reconfigured into a fantastical realm that abandons linear rationality. The types of musical spectacles found in such films are marked by excess, rupture, fluidity, and the dissolution of the space–time continuum that orders the reality of our everyday existence.

In short, the musical moment, as I deploy the term here, occurs when music, typically a popular song, inverts the image–sound hierarchy to occupy a dominant position in a filmic work. The movements of the image, and hence the structuring of space and time, are dictated by song. Musical moments, not surprisingly, are most prevalent within the genre of the musical film, and many of the prototypical characteristics of such moments have evolved from generic conventions. Yet musical moments are rife within a range of media contexts (jazz films, rockumentaries, teen films, biopics, comedies, melodramas, and a plethora of televisual and video formats).[13] Formal tendencies can be traced between the various incarnations of the musical moment. In many feature-length works, the musical moment marks a point of rupture within the larger context of the film. Visually, musical moments tend toward spectacular stagings, fantastical juxtapositions, and movements that would be improbable in a rational world. The musical moment, too, often relies on a set repertoire of scenarios (e.g., underdog kids struggle to put on a show, a lovestruck everyman turns the street into his own stage), formulas (e.g., lovers from opposite sides of the track arrive at compromise through song, the clumsy neophyte learns to sing/dance during the course of a number, the ugly duckling is "made over" via musical montage), and character types (e.g., the starlet, the boy/girl next door, the tap-dancing servant, the vixen, the comic sidekick, the "Latin lover"). The music itself typically adheres to standard pop structures and rhyming schemes; lyrical content is disproportionately geared toward generic romantic scenarios, an important consideration given the cross-marketing of movie sound tracks through radio play and record sales.

In light of the diverse environments in which musical moments thrive and the equally diverse ways in which they are staged, it may prove more productive to define the musical moment not in terms of its formal characteristics but rather in terms of what it *does*—the way that the musical moment works and the functions it performs. Some of these key functions include an inclination toward aesthetic and thematic excessiveness as well as a capacity to interrupt linear flow.[14] Musical moments create realms of auditory and visual experimentation geared toward eliciting pleasurable sensory responses. Much of what the musical moment does, then, is registered within the affective responses of the audience. Musical moments are marked by a tendency to restructure spatiotemporal coordinates, to reconfigure the boundaries and operations of the human body, and to forge new relations between organic and inorganic elements within the frame. At the same time that the musical moment can function as a disruptive force, rending a filmic text open to new types of configurations and external assemblages, it can also work toward more conservative ends. Musical moments can serve to propagate certain types of representational strategies. The repetitions evidenced on a formal register (musical structures, narrative formulas, characterizations) speak to a far-reaching tendency to reproduce, standardize, and codify certain cultural fictions. These fictions, in Western culture, lie at the heart of notions of national, racial, and sexual identity and form the foundation for our understanding of the formation and function of the individual subject as a whole. In effect, the musical moment generates patterns of representational repetition that are, simultaneously and uniquely, open to the interventions of difference. The musical moment is unusual in its capacity to make this tension palpable; it is at once one of the most conservative and the most irreverent filmic phenomena.

## Composition of the Book

In selecting the filmic sequences to be analyzed in this study, my motivation was not to present a catalog of canonical musical moments but to explore these qualities and functions—the things that the musical moment does—from a philosophical perspective. The work that the musical moment performs resonates with certain concepts presented in Deleuze's work, in particular his writings on the refrain, on fabulation, on the processes of deterritorialization and reterritorialization, and on difference and repetition, as engaged with in the arts. By pointing to these resonances, my objective is to shed light on the operations of the musical film in particular and, in a more general sense, on the relevance of Deleuzian philosophy to contemporary work on popular media.

The body of this study consists of four case studies. The first of these studies, chapter 1, examines the anomalous format of the 16-mm-film jukebox, which existed briefly in the United States in two incarnations: Soundies, which were distributed in the 1940s, and Scopitones, in the 1960s. Each format consisted of three-minute musical shorts played in jukeboxes located in bars, hotels, and transit stations across the country. Both were hybrid technologies that in some ways anticipated the advent of the music video. Yet while jukebox films are often dismissed as historical curiosities, I argue that they represent more than just a failed predecessor to the music video. Jukebox films present a valuable opportunity to consider the relationship between image and music in a nonnarrative, thoroughly music-based format. And while jukebox films visualize their music through the most obvious and literal means, resorting to the basest stereotypes at every opportunity, I argue that the awkwardness of the jukebox film can tell us something about the representational logic behind these musical images. The uncomfortable or even failed images of the jukebox film reveal the centrality of anxieties about difference to our system of representation and, more importantly, the potentially open or critical ways music and film articulate these fantasies. Because of the unusual nature of these formats, chapter 1 requires more historical and technological explication than do the other case studies. Yet it also sets in motion many of the philosophical themes rehearsed in the later chapters: the relations between music and the image; the divide between corporeality and the voice; the habitual representations of race, gender, and sexuality in musical images; and the role music plays as a force that ruptures notions of fixed identity.

Chapter 2 turns to Gilles Deleuze and Félix Guattari's concept of the refrain, read through various cinematic versions of the opera *Carmen,* especially Jean-Luc Godard's *Prénom Carmen (First Name Carmen)* (1983) and Otto Preminger's *Carmen Jones.* Deleuze and Guattari's theorization of the refrain, an expressive element that works to mark a particular territory through each articulation, offers a nuanced approach to the musical genre's penchant for repetition and recycling. My project is to trace the permutations of *Carmen's* refrains, looking at their tendencies either to fix meaning (to territorialize a particular understanding of identity) or to use the refrain as a critical tool that destabilizes these associations. Of particular interest to me are Godard's innovative uses of music in *Prénom Carmen;* he reduces Georges Bizet's operatic score to an incidental whistle and replaces this central refrain with the strains of a string quartet rehearsing Beethoven. I also examine the fractured refrains of Carmen Jones and the troubling, phantasmatic bodies created through the film's use of "Black English" and disembodied voices. Preminger and Godard each engage with the structural refrains at the heart of the *Carmen* narrative, unearthing new rhythms and dissonances through the collision of music and body.

Chapter 3 examines the role of history, memory, and fantasy in the musicals of Jacques Demy. Questions of history are difficult to address in a genre often dismissed as superficial, nostalgic, and escapist. It is also true that Demy's films are especially hyperstylized and unabashedly romantic. Yet Demy's body of work as a whole continually deals with history, even if in veiled forms: political and historical situations are woven into utterly fantastical, candy-colored settings, and actual history becomes intertwined with fictional intertextual references, particularly the repetition of characters and themes from Demy's previous films. Drawing on Deleuze and Bergson's writing on memory and perception, I argue that the fantastic, falsifying memory Demy invokes does not obscure history but rather demonstrates the very constructed nature of history and memory as processes. Demy does not achieve this through Brechtian modes of distantiation but by encouraging identification, thus demonstrating the correlations between personal tragedy and the larger world. Music is the force in these films that propels us through this process of remembering, making the transformations that the past has undergone painfully felt. Demy's films are not escapist but present a subtle and compelling commentary on the way history is constructed.

In chapter 4, I address what I have cryptically termed "water-based" musicals. I examine two radically different types of musicals: Esther Williams's synchronized swimming extravaganzas and Tsai Ming-liang's apocalyptic film *The Hole*. Despite the obvious distinctions between these works, I point to several of their correspondences that in many ways encapsulate the larger goals of this project. My focus is the musical's flight into utter abstraction. I search for ways to discuss these abstractions that are attuned to their dynamic and exhilarating transformations of time and space yet do not ignore their often troubling gender politics and their status as commercial products (products often imbued with a decidedly conservative ideological bent).

The "stuttering" flow between narrative and musical number in the Esther Williams film serves to both ground and burst open the temporal and spatial figurations of the film. The artificial revolutions of the dance spectacle themselves vastly complicate traditional understandings of the "real" and further point to the transformative aspects of Deleuze's theory of the virtual and the actual and Deleuze and Bergson's work on the dream-image. I read this openness against tendencies toward closure in the Williams film, a tendency that takes the form of both blatant cross-marketing strategies and the inevitability of a heterosexual romantic finale. Williams's unique corporeal presence complicates readings of the gender politics of the musical spectacle as well as Deleuze and Guattari's concept of "becoming-woman."

Tsai's *The Hole* offers a much bleaker vision. On the eve of the millennium, Taipei is besieged by a virus, "Taiwan Fever," a disease that results in strange, cockroach-like behavior by the afflicted. In an anonymous public-housing complex, several residents remain after that quadrant of the city is quarantined. The most curious aspect of the film is its insertion of music into this bleak environment. The film is punctuated by outrageous musical numbers, using songs by 1950s Mandarin musical star Grace Chang. Tsai makes almost no attempt to integrate songs into the larger narrative and gives us few indications as to how we are to read them. I read popular music, both in *The Hole* and in Williams's work, as a product of capitalist culture that is nevertheless not fully contained by it. The musical spectacle serves as a traitorous by-product of the culture industry, a surplus that bears the scars of its history but nevertheless defies the system that created it. The coupling of disease and music in Tsai's work presents a provocative paradox, which I explore through Foucault and Deleuze's intercessions into a Nietzschean genealogical history.

While the topics of these studies are eclectic, their divergences offer an opportunity to explore multiple facets of the theoretical framework that underpins the project as a whole. My focus is on trends that appear to be recurrent in the history of the musical: images of hybrids, of "in-between" spaces, and of the imperceptible boundaries of transformation. This tendency toward change and indeterminacy forges a structural link between represented bodies and the larger, more open movements of music and image in the films. My study focuses on the complex cycles of repetition and differentiation that drive musical films, positioning film and music not as static texts but as dynamic events. By reading Deleuzian concepts such as the refrain in the context of musical films, my objective is not only to better understand the musical's peculiar construction of difference but also to expand our understanding of the contributions Deleuzian philosophy can make to politically grounded writing on popular cinema.

The remainder of this introduction presents the philosophical concepts that form the foundation for my project. The first section provides a brief overview of previous theoretical approaches to the musical in film studies and outlines my own departure from these models. The following sections outline Deleuze's distinction between the movement-image and the time-image and between pulsed and nonpulsed time. Finally, I present a scene from David Lynch's *Mulholland Drive* (2001) as a means of reading the operations of these concepts as they unfold within the musical moment.

## Genre, Habit, Refrain: Theory and the Musical

The musical's penchant for contradiction has been the subject of much of the critical writing on the format. Indeed, that this contradiction was so deeply embedded in the structural foundation of the musical made it a particularly compelling subject for genre theorists. The late 1970s and early 1980s witnessed a minor surge in interest in the musical in English-language film scholarship. The field of genre studies had been gaining recognition as an analytical tool in film studies, one that might unveil the ideological structures behind the veneer of popular media. Several key volumes published between 1981 and 1987 established the musical as a serious subject of inquiry: *Genre: The Musical,* a collection of essays edited by Rick Altman (1981), Jane Feuer's *The Hollywood Musical* (1982), and Altman's extensive study *The American Film Musical* (1987). While the musical had often been dismissed as superficial and overtly commercial, each of these studies revealed a complicated political dimension to these films.

Rick Altman's *The American Film Musical* not only provides one of the most thorough studies of musical film but also serves as one of the foundational texts of genre theory. The chapters of the book alternate between discussions of the distinct structures of the musical genre and an introduction to the methodology of genre studies itself. Altman finds that the musical is constructed in a manner unlike any other narrative style; rather than tracing the progression of a singular character along a linear trajectory (one driven by narrative causality), the musical develops through a series of parallel oppositions. Altman identifies this as a "dual-focus narrative," one that most commonly takes the form of a clash between the male and female romantic leads.[15] The narrative evolves not through the adventures of a single character but through the initial opposition of two characters and their eventual union via mutual transformation. The dual-focus narrative is thus less reliant on events than on divergent character traits.

The fundamental distinction between the two protagonists is one of gender. This primary difference, however, is always coupled with several secondary dualities. For example, Altman demonstrates that in the 1940 film *New Moon* (Leonard), Jeanette MacDonald and Nelson Eddy are painstakingly characterized as diametrically opposed: MacDonald is aristocratic, wealthy, aloof, and sensitive, while Eddy is uncultured, poor, passionate, and resilient.[16] The entire thrust of the film concerns their inevitable bridging of these differences, a resolution that is achieved largely through song. Music is the force that overcomes difference and signals "romantic triumph over all limitations."[17] What is particularly significant about this formula for Altman is the political weight of the secondary differences that the musical so neatly solves. There are tremendous ideological implications, especially in terms of gender and class, to the oppositions that the musical conquers with romantic songs and triumphant spectacles. Altman isolates several subgenres of the musical (the fairy tale, the show, and the folk musical) and points to the culturally charged ways in which the resolution of difference supports an often conservative ideological agenda. Musicals, for Altman, engage in the creation of myths about the organic and liberatory power of song while paradoxically masking their own artificial means of production: the musical can make the mass commodity appear to be a folk art form.[18] This tendency can contribute to a climate of complacency on the part of real audiences to create their own communal music or initiate actual political change.[19]

Jane Feuer proposes a similar argument in *The Hollywood Musical.* The musical, for Feuer, is marked by a persistently self-reflective nature, featuring songs about singing, shows within shows, recycled material, and a general glorification of the virtues of entertainment. Self-conscious attention to the means of production (views "backstage," scenes of writing and rehearsing, awareness of financial negotiations, the use of direct address that transgresses narrative code) generally serves to demystify the process of creating entertainment. Yet as Feuer demonstrates, the musical utilizes these self-reflective means for a project of remystification.[20] The "work" of rehearsal is never work at all, and music and dance always succeed in solving every real-world problem they encounter. The myth of entertainment that the musical creates becomes an elaborate justification for its own existence and a powerful metaphor for the entertainment industry as a whole.[21]

Richard Dyer's essay "Entertainment and Utopia" further explores the category of entertainment and the musical's relations to its historical, political, and economic conditions. Casting the solutions that musicals offer in more positive terms, he argues that the utopian images of the musical are responses to particular inadequacies in society. Thus, the abundance, energy, transparency, and collectivity of the musical are generated to ameliorate the lack of such qualities in the everyday lives of its audiences.[22] Dyer shares Altman's and Feuer's concerns about the political implications that the musical's solutions offer. Yet Dyer suggests that the oppositions musicals grapple with are not always fully resolved. He makes a further distinction between representational elements in the films ("drawing on the audience's concrete experience of the world") and nonrepresentational (fantastical elements that hint at "how things could be better").[23] The tensions between the musical's contradictory movements proliferate on a number of levels, and while an opposition might be resolved on the register of the narrative, tensions on the level of the nonrepresentational (which Dyer associates with music, movement, and dance) may complicate or contradict those solutions.

Dyer's reading of utopia draws from Ernst Bloch's theory of the anticipatory nature of music. Music, for Bloch, is never a direct reflection of the historical conditions in which it emerges. While music contains representational elements that are bound to its moment of creation, certain aspects of music are "nonsynchronous," out of time with and irreducible to a particular cultural context—"a surplus reaching beyond their mere stationary ideology."[24] This lack of synchronicity does not reflect a universal or timeless status but rather is "illuminated from the direction of the future."[25] This utopian capacity of music is not a model of an ideal state but what Bloch calls a spirit, or, as Dyer describes this capacity, musicals tell us "what utopia would feel like rather than how it would be organized."[26] The open, nonrepresentational, or nonsynchronous aspects of music that Bloch and Dyer point to are necessarily bound to music's more historically grounded and representational tendencies. Yet this anticipatory movement toward the future, the desire for something better, speaks of a powerful creative capacity, a transformative drive toward the not-yet-imagined. "Musicals," Dyer writes, "represent an extraordinary mix of these two modes—the historicity of narrative and the lyricism of numbers. They have not often taken advantage of it, but the point is that they could, and this possibility is always latent in them."[27]

Dyer points to something provocative in this essay that moves beyond structural or textual readings. The distinction he makes between representational and nonrepresentational elements in music is built upon a temporal distinction—a split between linear notions of history that are inclined toward the past and the unpredictable potential of difference that drives toward the future. To suggest that there are certain qualities within popular music and film that exceed and resist the tenets of representation and to further suggest that those indescribable qualities are a powerful force in transforming our future is a compelling proposal. Yet Dyer also suggests, particularly in a later essay on race and the musical, that there is a negative potential associated with the musical's utopian expansiveness—for instance, a wishful occupation of space accessible exclusively to white performers and visualized in a manner that codifies and contains racial difference.[28] The anticipatory nature of the musical moment, as such, must be read against those instances in which such films lapse into the repetition of stultifying (and culturally/historically determined) forms.

Recent criticism of the musical has deepened our understanding of the musical's myriad contradictions through careful analysis of archival production data and more diversified readings of studio subgenres and styles. Sean Griffin, for example, explores the implications of Dyer's work on utopia and race in the musicals of Twentieth Century Fox. He finds that the musical numbers are granted a greater degree of autonomy in the "hodgepodge" vaudeville-revue structure of the Fox musical than they can achieve in the integrated musicals typical of Metro-Goldwyn-Mayer (MGM); the musical moments in these films are less prone to ideological containment and offer greater agency to minority performers.[29] Despite the musical's somewhat dubious reputation as a populist, commercial product, there is ample evidence that the genre has consistently provided a forum for nonconformist perspectives. Matthew Tinkcom and Steven Cohan, in this vein, have presented groundbreaking studies of the musical in relation to camp. In *Working like a Homosexual: Camp, Capital, and Cinema,* Tinkcom excavates the fraught conditions under which queer artisans, particularly those working in the Arthur Freed unit under Vincent Minnelli, were able to insert camp aesthetics into films that could "pass" as heterosexual products while remaining "readable" to queer audiences. Camp, here, emerges "through the ruptures and fluctuations of monetary and cultural value."[30] Cohan argues that the MGM house style as a whole is marked by incongruity, defined as "frivolous, escapist entertainment for a mainstream audience" while at the same time being indelibly linked to "a viewing position located on the margins of dominant culture."[31] For Cohan, these contradictory positions in fact complement one another; at the time of the initial production of these films, this dualism helped to secure the popularity of the cycle with a wide audience and has remained core to the reception of the MGM musical throughout its history even as cultural understandings of genre and camp have continued to evolve.

Cohan's readings of specific musical sequences are particularly refreshing, as he guides us through the incongruous pleasures of performances by Judy Garland, Esther Williams, Gene Kelly, and Lucille Ball and the spectacular stagings of MGM's aggregate (versus integrated) numbers. Like Dyer, Cohan is concerned not just with the structure and syntax of the musical but also with the way in which musicals *feel,* their affective power. To critically engage with these ineffable and excessive qualities of the musical is to address an aspect of the genre that structural analyses tend to sidestep—namely, what is it that happens, exactly, within the musical moment? Reading the musical through the lens of camp, Cohan argues, allows us to understand the musical number historically, in terms of the camp codes that were built into these sequences, and in terms of the meanings they take on for audiences in new cultural and historical contexts, as those codes are rewritten.

My approach to the musical moment is indebted to the work cited previously, but it also departs from it in significant ways. The tension between repetition and difference that I draw on is in many ways related to the ideological conservatism Feuer and Altman highlight and to the anticipatory and resistant potentials outlined by Dyer, Tinkcom, and Cohan. Yet my analysis of this dynamic involves very different objectives and uses a distinct methodology. Generic and structural approaches to the musical focus a great deal of attention on the relationship between the narrative and the musical number, on the lyrical content, and on the representations contained within the image, but the music itself remains elusive. Studies focusing on the specific "codes" written into the musical (the codified ways in which race, or gender, or class are figured) tell us a great deal about how these categories are represented within various texts but tend to reduce the films to static, dissected texts; that which might exceed these codes (affect, performativity, musicality) tends also to exceed the language of analysis. While my discussion of the musical moment intersects at points with readings of the musical as camp, my focus more broadly considers the operations of difference on the heterogeneous, affective, and performative elements that surface within the musical moment (elements that include but are not limited to camp).

Deleuzian philosophy offers avenues of rethinking musical moments in film in dynamic ways, not in isolation but in the complex and embodied ways in which they are produced, perceived, and "read." By approaching the musical moment in terms of its temporality and in terms of the rhythms and variances that manifest themselves on a variety of sonic, visual, and structural registers, my objective is to bring into focus those nonrepresentational aspects of the musical film that so frequently escape analysis. While my study includes close attention to individual musical moments, I present them not as texts to be "decoded" but as dynamic events, distinct temporal occurrences that are always open to the outside. Many of the repetitions I locate within the musical moment coincide with the ideological meanings Feuer and Altman have brought to light. Rather than describing these repetitions as generic characteristics or codes, however, I describe them, following Deleuze and Hume, as "habits" or "customs."[32]

*Habitus,* as the concept is used by Hume and Deleuze, differs in marked ways from the notion of a generic convention. Both habit and the generic convention imply a type of repetition. But the most significant distinction has to do with the situating of habit not as a static type of representation within a text but as a process of contraction that takes place within the mind. Deleuze writes:

> *Repetition changes nothing in the object repeated, but does change something in the mind which contemplates it.* Hume's famous thesis takes us to the heart of a problem: since it implies, in principle, a perfect independence on the part of each presentation, how can repetition change something in the case of the repeated

element? . . . Hume takes as an example the repetition of cases of the type AB, AB, AB, A. . . . Each case or objective sequence AB is independent of the others. The repetition (although we cannot yet properly speak of repetition) changes nothing in the object of the state of affairs AB. On the other hand, a change is produced in the mind which contemplates a difference, something new *in* the mind. Whenever A appears, I expect the appearance of B. . . . Does not the paradox of repetition lie in the fact that one can speak of repetition only by virtue of the change or difference that it introduces into the mind which contemplates it? By virtue of a difference that the mind *draws from* repetition?[33]

A habit, for Hume, is a means of anticipating a future action based on one's experience. The accumulated repetition of similar scenarios perceived in the past is contracted by the mind, establishing an internal pattern by which expectations are formed. Certainly work on conventions within genre studies suggests a similar dynamic: the repetition of generic codes leads to the expectation of certain structures and character types. Yet Deleuze is suggesting a much more foundational and transformative process, one that is connected to the most basic operations of perception and cognition. Habit here is not the mere repetition of a code but the introduction of *difference*, of something new, within the mind that is impacted by the perception and anticipation of a pattern.

Chapter 1 explores this notion of habitus in relation to the representational strategies within the jukebox film, concentrating on this notion of the difference that arises from the contemplation of a perceived repetition and the manner in which habit relates to questions of temporality and to the creation of "fictions of the imagination."[34] One of my key interests in this concept is to complicate the manner in which we contend with stereotypical, stilted, or "bad" film. By locating meaning not within the text but as something that is generated through an engagement with it, we can find, even within politically compromised works, an unanticipated impact. The ability of a film to introduce rifts, differences, and rhythms might not be fully apparent when one's analysis is limited to a reading of narrative or structure; a film's disruptive potential might, too, be indirectly proportional to the types of representations it contains.

The philosophical concepts deployed in later chapters work to extend, and at times to challenge, structural and generic approaches to the musical moment. Chapter 2, for example, takes up the concept of the refrain to consider the involutions of difference and repetition that occur on the various representational registers within individual films and between textual articulations. Whereas previous critiques of the musical have targeted the manner in which it masks historical reality, I take up the notion of fabulation, in chapter 3, to explore the ways in which the musical's cultural fictions can multiply and destabilize the past. Chapter 4, in turn, uses Siegfried Kracauer's description of the historical image to deepen our understanding of the musical moment as a commoditized spectacle. I concentrate on the ways in which this image can be mobilized to create new corporeal assemblages and to engage in genealogical excavations of history.

Gilles Deleuze's writings on difference, repetition, and temporality suggest a means of approaching the tension in musical film between, to use Dyer's terminology, the representational and the nonrepresentational. The difficulty with semiotic or structuralist approaches to film and music lies with their methodology, which fragments and freezes mobile media into isolable blocks. An inherent abstraction takes place in such a move, the imposition of an external model that minimizes those aspects of the song or the film it is unable to account for. In the sections that follow, I outline Deleuze's departure from such models. I begin with his work on cinema in relation to a Bergsonian understanding of time and movement. I then turn to Deleuze and Guattari's writing on music and temporality. Throughout each discussion, and throughout the remainder of this book, the contradictory movements of film and music, working at once to ground and to escape from representational meaning, remain at the center of my inquiry.

## Images of Thought and Acts of Creation

Gilles Deleuze, in his books on film, *Cinema 1: The Movement-Image* and *Cinema 2: The Time-Image,* proposes a thoroughly unique approach to film theory. Drawing on his own philosophy of repetition and difference and on the work of Henri Bergson, the *Cinema* books extend these theories to foreground those aspects that are most essential to the medium: that film unfolds in time and is composed of ever-differentiating planes of movement. Deleuze's writings as a whole resonate with correspondences among concepts of transformation, difference, and the forces of impersonal time. Bergson's work is consistent with the thrust of this project, so Deleuze's exploration of Bergson in this context seems unquestionably valid. In addressing the cinema, however, Deleuze transposes these theories, which are inherently bound up in the shifting and unique movements of life, and uses them to discuss the mechanized and standardized movements of film, a means of reproducing or representing that life.

How are we to account for Deleuze's or Bergson's theories of temporality, both based in philosophies of life, creation, and difference, when confronted with an aesthetic object such as film: a fixed, repeatable representation? Exploring the larger processes that drive Deleuze's work as a whole, we are faced with more fundamental questions: Why can or should we use Deleuze to think about film? What potential does Deleuzian theory offer to those who work on film, and what implications will his work have for the field of film theory? To begin mapping these implications, I first examine what might appear to be a contradiction in the *Cinema* books. Deleuze calls on Bergson to address film, while Bergson himself used the medium as a model for the forces of rationality that immobilize and fragment time. Yet there is no contradiction between Deleuze's and Bergson's approaches when we view film not as a model for perception or as a reflected image of reality but as a unique image with its own duration. What this seeming conflict points to is at the heart of the problem of representation (as a concept and in practice). At stake are not only all theories that address the arts but larger questions regarding the nature of the real. The key to unraveling this problem lies in the complex understanding of time that Bergson proposes. By using this theory to reevaluate cinema, Deleuze does not misconstrue the mechanisms of film. Instead, following Bergson, Deleuze further expands our understanding of where the real lies, reinterpreting the way in which we understand the temporal nature of film. The result is a fundamental destabilization of the very idea of a representation, displacing notions of signification and association in favor of acts of creation and images of thought.

The greatest achievement of the *Cinema* books is that they suggest a means of looking at film that explodes static views of the work that the work of art does. Rather than "representing" something, film, for Deleuze, has the potential to create its own fluid movements and temporalities. These movements, while related to formal elements of rhythm and duration within the film itself, cannot be reduced to specific techniques or concrete images. Similarly, the temporality that Deleuze locates within the cinema cannot be pinned to a specific type of shot nor a particular moment in the shooting, editing, projection, or reception of a film. By refusing to thus situate his theory, Deleuze completely sidesteps psychoanalytic and semiological film theories that would locate the "meaning" of film beneath a surface level of signs. The ramifications of Deleuze's project far exceed the scope of this project. My goal, nevertheless, is to map several of its threads. The first is an interrogation of what varied meanings the term *representation* might have for Bergson or Deleuze with regard to cinema. The second involves the relations between film and the realm that can be designated as the "real." Finally, the overarching question that motivates me is whether it is possible to maintain a commitment to the "art of living" that Bergson—and Deleuze—so convincingly promote while doing work on the "objects" of visual culture.

The *Cinema* books map a rift in filmmaking that can be roughly situated at the end of World War II. This split cannot be reduced to a historical shift but exists instead in differing configurations of movement and time. The movement-image, according to Deleuze, is exemplified by classical Hollywood cinema. Time proceeds only as dictated by action (the action of narrative, of cause and effect, of rationality). For Deleuze, temporality in the movement-image is governed by the "sensory-motor schema."[35] All movements are determined by linear causality, and the characters are bent toward actions that respond to the situations of the present. Even when temporal continuity is momentarily disrupted (e.g., in a flashback), these moments are reintegrated into the prescribed evolution of past, present, and future. The movement-image is structured not only by narrative but also by rationality: closed framings, reasonable progressions, and continuous juxtapositions.

The time-image, however, breaks itself from sensory-motor links. The emphasis shifts from the logical progression of images to the experience of the image in itself. What we find here are pure optical and sound situations (opsigns and sonsigns), unfettered by narrative progression, and empty, disconnected any-space-whatevers. This move from "acting" to "perceiving" carries over to the characters in the film, who cease to be "agents" and become, instead, "seers." Although Deleuze is hesitant to identify any single film that embodies the time-image, moments in films by Pasolini, Ozu, and Godard, for example, gesture toward that ideal: moments of rupture, hesitation, irrational cutting, or prolonged duration. Movement that is aberrant (i.e., not rational or action oriented) can be seen, according to Deleuze, to be caused by time itself. Built through irrational movements and opsigns and sonsigns, the time-image thus exists not as a chronology but as a series of juxtaposed "presents." What is achieved is exceedingly rare: a direct image of time.[36]

Deleuze's reading of Bergson does away with many of the basic assumptions of film theory (the separation of subject and object, the primacy of the apparatus, the psychological nature of perception). But to designate images as time based or movement based runs the risk of remaining merely descriptive if one does not fully grasp that the distinction between the two is a question of neither form nor content. Bergson's writing resists being reduced to a structural model; the experience of life, he claims, exceeds the comprehension of the intellect. And the integrated relationship between subject and object, matter and memory, that Bergson proposes results in a shift in emphasis from the aesthetic object to the act of creation. Indeed, Bergson's contribution to thought rests not in a new analysis of art but in rethinking the practice of "the art of living."[37]

To understand the consequences of this shift for film theory, one must first turn to the distinction that Bergson draws between the methodologies of the intellect and intuition. The intellect, Bergson argues, is always bent on action. It is the component of consciousness that allows a being to comprehend its environment and survive within it. While its mode of perception is essential to life, however, the intellect does not have a privileged access to reality. Bergson writes:

> If the intellect were meant for pure theorizing, it would take its place within movement, for movement is reality itself, and immobility is always only apparent or relative. But the intellect is meant for something altogether different. Unless it does violence to itself, it takes the opposite course; it always starts from immobility, as if this were the ultimate reality: when it tries to form an idea of movement, it does so by constructing movement out of immobilities put together. . . . *Of immobility alone does the intellect form a clear idea.*[38]

The intellect, in order to perceive and act upon reality, must thus reduce it to a series of frozen moments. Unlike the direct, reflective mode of what Bergson calls intuition, the intellect works scientifically. It extracts objects from motion in order to evaluate the action that it might perform upon them, restoring an abstract *idea* of motion upon them after the fact, like lines drawn between points on a graph.

Intuition, by contrast, is the mode through which one gains access to the undifferentiated flow of life, the real. All matter, for Bergson, exists as images defined by the range of their possible actions (real or virtual) upon other images. The human subject is an image/object like any other, with the distinction that, as a living being, it has the potential both to generate its own actions and to function as a perceptive center, organizing itself in relation to other images. While part of this organization involves the mechanisms of the intellect, there is a component that is opposed to spatialization and is inclined instead toward the temporal. Within each "living center" exists a potential delay between the moment of perception and the moment of action. The greater this delay or "zone of indeterminacy" becomes, the greater access the subject will have to an alternative axis of movement: that of intuition.

Bergson's intuition, unlike the colloquial use of the term, involves a precise methodology. Rather than immobilizing and distilling from matter that which can be acted upon, intuition delves simultaneously inward to the depths of the self and outward, beyond the self, to grasp objects in their entirety, as they exist in duration. Duration here refers not to "time," which for Bergson is a concept already fractured into spatial components (minutes, seconds, years, etc.). Instead, each image contains its own unique duration, its own capacity for change. Intuition is a mode of unmediated access to the play of forces that comprise existence. Unlike the intellect, which is oriented toward the interest that a being has in the objects on which it can act, intuition is driven by the inward motion of instinct, a form of sympathy "that has become disinterested, self-conscious, capable of reflecting upon its object and of enlarging it indefinitely."[39] As Deleuze writes about the temporal nature of intuition, "Intuition is not duration itself. Intuition is rather the movement by which we emerge from our own duration, by which we make use of our own duration to affirm and immediately to recognize the existence of other durations, above or below us."[40]

Cinema, for Bergson, or rather the cinematic apparatus, corresponds directly to the function of the intellect. He describes the phenomenon of film as a series of immobile snapshots of reality. The camera isolates fragments of reality, erasing the nuances of transformation occurring between frames. In order to achieve movement, the film must be unwound through the projector, thus restoring the illusion of continuous motion. But the motion we perceive is not the unique movement inherent to the object filmed. The camera/projector apparatus extracts from reality an "impersonal movement," a movement that can be generalized and regulated at a precise duration, a calculable frame rate. "Such is the contrivance of the cinematograph," Bergson writes, "and such is also that of our knowledge."[41]

The first pages of *Cinema 1: The Movement-Image* address Bergson's theory of "the cinematographic illusion." Deleuze suggests that Bergson makes an oversight in locating cinema and natural perception along the same continuum. While the mechanisms of film might mask themselves as those of perception, Deleuze argues that in actuality the projector "corrects" the illusion from the outset through its regulated reanimation of the image: "Cinema does not give us an image to which movement is added, it immediately gives us a movement-image. It does give us a section, but a section which is mobile, not an immobile section + abstract movement."[42] He further asserts that the apparatus of the camera possesses temporal capabilities that complicate and supersede those of the projector. The artificiality of cinema, because of its mobility and freedom from fixed points of perception, is thus fundamentally different from natural perception. Cinema, for Deleuze, does not repeat the illusion of reanimation that Bergson attributes to it, and by thus recognizing the qualitative difference between cinematic and natural perception, Bergson's concept of the movement-image might have implications for the cinema that Bergson himself could not perceive at the time.

Deleuze potentially misrepresents the breadth of his theory in this attempt to recuperate the cinematic apparatus.[43] If one considers film to be an attempt to reproduce physical reality, there is no doubt that the image on the screen cannot encompass the complex existence of the matter before the lens of the camera. Clearly, Deleuze is not asserting such a simplistic understanding of the function of cinema. At the same time, to argue that the mechanisms of film apparatus somehow ameliorate the visual "illusions" that the film audience necessarily experiences is to leave such an assumption unchallenged. This is not a criticism that I would levy against the *Cinema* books as a whole. Indeed, Deleuze deftly avoids easy associations between physical "images" and Bergson's more complex use of the term, let alone any confusion between notions of "the real" and the objects that the camera represents. While I have reservations about Deleuze's argument in this instance, the goal of his investigation is, in fact, consistent with Bergson's larger project. The apparent discrepancy between Bergson's and Deleuze's approaches to film is a reflection of a fundamental shift in their understandings of the function of cinema. I see this shift between the way in which Bergson discusses film (as a metaphoric model for a mode of thought) and the way in which Deleuze uses Bergson to discuss film (where film is no longer a "model" but contains its own potential image of thought) as an entryway for exploring the question of representation that lies at the heart of the *Cinema* books.

When Bergson compares cinema to the processes of the intellect, he describes it as a model of representation. Just as the intellect selects from the swirling movements of surrounding matter only those images upon which the body can act, the cinematic apparatus immobilizes instances, slicing them from the undifferentiated flow of life and reanimating them through the uniformity of the machine. Bergson's discussion of the cinematic apparatus perfectly describes his theory of the intellect (one might even pursue another line of inquiry: how do technological developments enable or influence the evolution of concepts?). But the analogy he makes is not sufficient for describing (or dismissing) the cinematic experience as a whole.

The mechanism of thought that functions "cinematically" creates a "theoretical illusion" for Bergson, obscuring our perception of "the true evolution, the radical becoming."[44] But one would be mistaken to deduce from this that the "reality" that the "cinematographical mechanism of thought" prevents access to would in fact be representable given a more fluid apparatus or model. Or further, that Bergson's critique of a modality of thought can be interpreted as or extended to a critique of the medium. What his cinematographical model does provide is a powerful critique of the very mechanisms of representation. Representation operates through immobilization, spatialization. The representation becomes a "sign" through which we interpret the always-implied referent. It asserts correspondences, analogies, and associations among elements at the expense of their differences, their dynamisms, their movements and changes.

The problem of representation is one that extends almost limitlessly, a question that permeates nearly all aspects of human existence: perception, language, and thought. How is it possible to move beyond the realm of representation? And if it is indeed a mechanism that can be overcome, what alternative methodologies might be left in its wake?

Deleuze and Guattari, in their discussion of the rhizome, distinguish between a map and a tracing. The trace is described in terms strikingly similar to Bergson's model of cinematographic thought: the trace is "like a photograph or X ray that begins by selecting or isolating, by artificial means such as colorations or other restrictive procedures, what it intends to reproduce."[45] The strength of the map, by contrast, is that it never operates by means of resemblance. While a map functions always in relation to something beyond itself, it engages in those relations as a toolbox, a set of potentialities that are never predetermined and that can in turn effect changes upon the images and objects they come up against:

> What distinguishes the map from the tracing is that it is entirely oriented toward an experimentation in contact with the real. The map does not reproduce an unconscious closed in upon itself; it constructs the unconscious. . . . The map is open and connectable in all of its dimensions; it is detachable, reversible, susceptible to constant modification. . . . A map has multiple entryways, as opposed to the tracing, which always comes back "to the same."[46]

The function of the map described here suggests a vehicle for thinking outside representation, a modality not dissimilar to that of Bergson's intuition. Like the flow of images that Bergson designates as the real, the map interacts with configurations of elements that defy binaristic classification (subject/object, spectator/text, etc.). With reference to the rhizomatic potential of literature, Deleuze and Guattari write:

> There is no longer a tripartite division between a field of reality (the world) and a field of representation (the book) and a field of subjectivity (the author). Rather, an assemblage establishes connections between certain multiplicities drawn from each of these orders, so that a book has no sequel nor the world as its object nor one or several authors as its subject. . . . The book as assemblage with the outside, against the book as image of the world.[47]

The assemblages that film forms with its outside will necessarily differ from those formed in literature or the other arts. Nevertheless, Deleuze and Guattari's formulation bears weight on my discussion here. An artistic medium cannot be generalized as having "productive" or "regressive" relationships with the real. Yet individual expressions, in a range of media, can perform in ways that are rhizomatic/crystalline or tracelike, depending on their particular relation to the outside and the direction of their movements.

As such, I agree with Deleuze that it is inaccurate to describe cinema on the basis of a model of perception. At the same time, both cinematic and perceptive modalities exist in relation to a "real" that is, for Bergson (and Deleuze), more complex than has been indicated thus far. In *Matter and Memory*, Bergson proposes a definition of matter as an "image" that falls somewhere between our colloquial understandings of objects and representations.[48] For Bergson, the brain does not produce a representation of what it perceives. Perception is the mutual influence of images upon one another, of which the brain is only another image—it does not "produce" anything but filters impulses into actions or nonactions. The implications for film are twofold. By addressing the perceiving subject as one image among the world of images, Bergson steps outside models that locate perception and memory within the mind of the subject. I further suggest, following Deleuze, that Bergson's theory of matter allows us to see film not as a fixed representation, a concrete image of a "real" object, but as an image in its own right, with its own duration and axes of movement. What we might call the film image thus occurs in the gap between subject and object, through the collision of affective images.

Deleuze's formulation of the film image as a mobile assemblage (sometimes a frame, sometimes a shot, a sound, or the film as a whole) lends itself to this reading, refusing to reduce the physical image on the screen to a mere reproduction of an assumed real object it represents. Such a formulation similarly reevaluates the relationship between the concrete optical and sonic images that compose the film. Rather than conceiving of each component as a concrete building block, it allows for shifting and multiple conglomerations of elements that are themselves dynamic and mobile. A film cannot be distilled to an analyzable structure that originates from outside itself. Instead, each film image is contingent, particular, and evolving.

The potential affective force of film is not that it more closely resembles the objects that it represents (having a more direct relationship to those objects via the photographic method than more abstract systems of representation such as language or painting). Rather, this potential lies in film's ability to key into durations that would defy the limitations of the intellect, working not toward action but toward the zone of indeterminacy that lies between perception and action. Bergson writes:

Pure duration is the form which the succession of our conscious states assumes when our ego lets itself *live,* when it refrains from separating its present state from its former states. . . . In recalling these states, it does not set them alongside its actual state as one point alongside another, but it organizes them with itself *[avec lui],* as it happens when we recall the notes of a tune, melting, so to speak into one another.[49]

But film images, while possessing individual durations, cannot engage in the active process of recollection that Bergson describes. Indeed, while my investigation of film has been driven by Bergson's theory of intuition, one could not claim that film functions intuitively. The cinematic experience, for Deleuze, is not a pure state of reflection. One cannot "think inside" film; film must be conceived of as a problem that arises from outside. Meaning, as such, cannot be conceptualized as signification nor as something garnered through a direct synthesis or sympathetic penetration of the object. Deleuze posits instead a theory of expression, filmic images that are temporal and dynamic. It is the image that is encountered directly, presenting a complex provocation to thought.

I see this provocation as the true potential of film. The act of creation, for Bergson, is a solution to a challenge from the outside, from life. The question of cinema is not a question of representing movement but of provoking new movements and new images of thought. The forces of creation and invention are tapped into when perception, rather than isolating an image for the purposes of action, orients itself toward memory, the virtual potential of the past. "When perception is attentive," Dorothea Olkowski writes, "every perception becomes an act of creation in which the perception opens as many circuits as there are memory images attracted by this new perception, making of every perception a qualitative multiplicity."[50] The act of creation occurs with the introduction of the new. In the case of the body, the new exists as these perceptions, affections, and thoughts, that which the body creates from the impulses and images it perceives.

"Style in philosophy," Deleuze writes, "strains toward three different poles: concepts, or new ways of thinking; percepts, or new ways of seeing and hearing; and affects, or new ways of feeling. They're the philosophical trinity, philosophy as opera: you need all three to *get things moving.*"[51] Cinema contains the potential to transect all three poles. While its relation to percepts and affects has been touched on in terms of the act of perception, the concept draws cinema toward a new type of image, the image of thought.

D. N. Rodowick notes that the "image of thought" is not a representational image (i.e., the concept is not contained within a concrete, physical image). Rather, the image of thought is a movement, a process of continual differentiation. While this movement, in terms of film, takes its roots in what Deleuze calls the movement-image, Rodowick notes that an image of thought, for Deleuze, becomes an active force only when it takes a step further: "But in order to claim for philosophy what is its activity by right, the philosopher must invoke the more fundamental 'movement' of the impersonal form of time and eternal recurrence."[52] This is what leads to the distinction between the movement-image and the time-image: a qualitative difference whereby what is seen and what is conveyed becomes less significant than what is not revealed, what is unknown.

> Only the movement-image pretends that thought can be presented directly in or by the image. Alternatively, time always divides thought from the signs that express or represent it. Through the force of the eternal return, time affirms a specific power, or rather "impower" of thought: "we are not yet thinking."[53]

It is this third axis of movement, toward the concept or the image of thought, that allows film the potential to "get things moving." It never progresses by means of representation, a tracing, but always through the crystal, the rhizome, and the unforeseeable foldings of creation. "There's a hidden image of thought that, as it unfolds, branches out, and mutates, inspires a need to keep on creating new concepts, not through any external determinism but through a becoming that carries the problems themselves along with it."[54] Born from the unpredictable collision of forces that coalesce in the act of creation, the image of thought bears the motion of the question that has been reformulated, carrying it not toward solution but opening it further into new, ever-differentiating questions.

Deleuze's assertions in the *Cinema* books can be read as a call to action on two fronts. The distinctions he draws between movement-images and time-images challenge artists to create works that transcend the representational, that explore the interstices between memory and perception, that approach what we might call a pure image of time, an image of thought. The tools he provides for conceiving of film beyond the confines of representation pose a further challenge to those who think and write about (or through) film. The provocation, then, for both the filmmaker and the film theorist, is one posed by philosophy. The challenge is to see film not as a means of representation but as an assemblage of images in flux with the world of images, to see the history of film and the history of philosophy as convergent. The art of living remains the becoming of true creation, but the image of thought introduces the stutters and hesitations that give us access to this movement. "It's the image of thought that guides the creation of concepts. It cries out, so to speak, whereas concepts are like songs."[55] Bergson writes of the creative capacity in art, "When music cries, it is humanity, it is the whole of nature which cries with it. Truly speaking, it does not introduce these feelings in us; it introduces us rather into them, like the passers-by that might be nudged in a dance."[56]

## Pulsed and Nonpulsed Time

Both Bergson and Deleuze draw on musical terminology when describing the nature of the creative arts, suggesting that we understand creation not as a phenomenon that originates within an individual subject but as a force that overwhelms individuals, sweeping them into the larger movements of the world. The language we commonly use to discuss music lends itself to this kind of imagery. Music is one of the more abstract and least directly representational of the arts, and it has become commonplace to describe the aesthetic experience of music as one of immersion. The modus operandi of the musical film appears to be the visualization of this phenomenon—to embody the feeling of being carried away by the musical force that is bigger than any individual being, to be introduced into its flows.

Yet one must be cautious about such romantic visions of the work that music performs. Music clearly does possess many representational qualities—certain keys are associated with different emotions; certain rhythms, melodic structures, or instruments are used to invoke a culture, time period, or character type. Popular music in particular remains firmly grounded within specific cultural and historical contexts. The lyrics of pop songs convey messages as directly as any linguistic sign and moreover are bound by the stricture of predictable meters and rhyming strategies. The structures of the kinds of songs typically used in musicals are highly formulaic, their verse-verse-chorus-verse progressions echoing the overplayed sentiments of the lyrics in their comforting familiarity. As critics such as Feuer and Altman have aptly demonstrated, the musical's claims of liberation and release often mask cookie-cutter templates and conservative political agendas that are anything but free. The musical's songs of love give voice to the desire for something more, yet the glimmer of hope they offer may serve to placate listeners into accepting the conditions from which they yearn to escape.

Deleuze's writing on music distinguishes between creative movements of differentiation and repetitions that affirm the self-identity of the same. One might read the highly predictable and regulated songs of the musical, as such, in opposition to truly creative musical works. The distinction Deleuze draws, however, is not a simple clash between mass-produced musical commodities and avant-garde compositions. As with his discussion of the cinema, Deleuze draws on a wide spectrum of musical styles and examples in his writing, including popular and folk music and even bird songs. And too, as with his thinking about film, the central question to be asked of any musical work is the manner in which it contends with time.

For Deleuze, one can identify two opposing poles of musical temporality against which individual works will align themselves to varying degrees. The first consists of a metered or "pulsed" understanding of time. Here time is fragmented into predetermined blocks of equivalent length—measures—that provide a uniform, linear means of calculating musical movement. We might link this measured formulation of time with the rationale of the sensory-motor schema and the logic of the intellect. Music is frozen into compartmentalized snapshots such that we might grasp its complex evolutions. Yet the regulated duration of each measure is an artificial imposition of an abstract temporality that is not specific to the highly differential durations of individual musical compositions. This imposition is analogous to a chronological model of time and history, where time is broken down into measurable blocks of minutes, days, and years that can be reconstructed according to a linear trajectory. Each block or point follows the next in a calculable, unidirectional manner.

Pulsed time in music provides a hidden (inaudible) structure upon which the composition is built. Deleuze and Guattari describe this type of organizing structure as a plane of transcendence. The guiding principle of an entity is not perceptible in itself, yet it can be inferred by analyzing the structure of that entity. In the case of music, the guiding principle would be a measure or pulse that gives rise to the sounds that we hear.[57] The pulse acts as a kind of seed from which form and structure emerge. This plane of transcendence operates according to a particular type of temporality: *Chronos,* or "the time of measure that situates things and persons, develops a form, and determines a subject."[58] *Chronos* and the plane of transcendence can be associated with any type of creative work (painting, literature, music, film, philosophy), yet this terminology can perhaps be most easily understood through musical examples. The vast majority of Western music is founded on measured or pulsed time. The temporality of the meter, imperceptible in itself, provides the regulatory structure on which the composition becomes audible. Music on this plane works to represent through analogy, metaphor, and metonym; it distills ideas, emotions, people, and places, translating them into expressions via measured time.

At the same time, the nature of pulsed time cannot be reduced to a regular beat. Deleuze speaks extensively of "irregular" pulsed time as well, musical works that are composed of irregular beats yet nevertheless retain a pulse that is imbedded in strategies of repetition and self-identity. While pulsed time is aligned with *Chronos,* our notion of the pulse can be extended not only to the meter of the measure but also to the pulse that is part of the drive to represent. In each case, we can speak of the imposition of equivalencies that minimize individual differences to emphasize resemblance. Pulsed time for Deleuze thus occurs whenever an expressive element is used to represent, to define, or to create a subject—all actions Deleuze and Guattari associate with movements of territorialization. "Every time that there is a marking of a territoriality," according to Deleuze, "there will be a pulsation of time."[59]

There is another plane, however, that does not operate according to this temporal modality. Deleuze and Guattari identify this as a plane of consistency. Consistency here indicates not stasis but certain qualities shared by particular elements—the resonances among them. It contains no innate structure or form and instead remains highly attuned to the variable durations of diverse elements. Rather than leading teleologically toward an organizing framework, the plane of consistency is "an *involution,* in which form is constantly being dissolved, freeing times and speeds."[60] Whereas the plane of transcendence involves representation, extracting certain qualities and recasting them within a preexisting form (it sounds *like* a bird, it looks *like* a girl), the plane of consistency enters into each element in its own specificity. "The plane of consistency is the abolition of all metaphor," Deleuze and Guattari write.[61] Rather than representing a thing or a concept, the plane of consistency examines the temporal relations (the speeds and slownesses) that comprise each element as well as the temporal differentials between each other element.

Rather than sounding *like* a bird, then, the plane of consistency explores the unique relations that are birdness and uses these relations as the basis for a creative intervention. Thus, the composer Olivier Messiaen in his *Catalogue d'oiseaux (Catalog of Birds)* piano series (1958) explores in great detail the specific intervals of individual birdcalls. He does not transcribe each call verbatim but brings that melody into dialogue with any number of new, denaturalized elements (e.g., the specific tonalities and temporalities of the piano), transforming the call and placing it within a new network of temporal relations.[62] Likewise, in the film *The Birds* (Hitchcock, 1963), Deleuze and Guattari note, "when Hitchcock does birds, he does not reproduce bird calls, he produces an electronic sound like a field of intensities or a wave of vibrations, a continuous variation, like a terrible threat welling up inside us."[63] The issue is not fidelity, reproduction, or imitation. Indeed, it may be significant to note that both Hitchcock and Messiaen used technological interventions—synthesizers—to rip the birdcall from its naturalized setting and to cast it into a new sonorous environment.[64] The refrain of the bird, which had functioned in nature to mark the bird's individual territory, is now *deterritorialized* within the composition, launching into a new line of flight.[65] The plane of consistency consists of discovering the intensities, speeds, and delays of the entity being studied and then opening those movements into new, unpredictable assemblages with other mobile elements. Thus, the interval of the birdcall becomes the springboard from which the act of creation arises.

Within the plane of consistency, time is not spatialized into predetermined measures; "rather it is a question of a freeing of time, Aeon, a nonpulsed time for a floating music."[66] Deleuze and Guattari draw here on the writing of the avant-garde composer Pierre Boulez and his distinction between pulsed (striated) and nonpulsed (smooth) time. Nonpulsed time works in direct opposition to *Chronos* and can be associated instead with *Aeon,* "the time of the pure event or of becoming, which articulates relative speeds and slownesses independently of the chronometric or chronological values that time assumes in the other modes."[67] Whereas in pulsed or striated time the measures are counted out, Boulez argues, "in smooth time, time is filled without counting."[68] Smooth or nonpulsed time is "unhinged" or "floating," not fixed by predetermined coordinates. Duration here is built on the highly specific and transitional temporality of the elements that comprise a *haecceity,* the "thisness" of a particular here and now. The relation of intensities that provides the basis for the plane of consistency is built on the "molecular" interaction of various elements in a haecceity. These interactions take place through transformation according to a temporality that is unbound by abstract, pulsed measures. According to Deleuze, "a non-pulsed time thus puts us in the presence of a multiplicity of durations, heterochronous, qualitative, non-coincident, non-communicating: one does not march in time *[en mesure]* any more than one swims or flies in time *[en mesure].*"[69]

The artists Deleuze and Guattari discuss in terms of the plane of consistency share a highly modernist, avant-garde sensibility: Boulez, Messiaen, Paul Klee, John Cage, and Jean-Luc Godard. Each of these artists makes a clear break with structures of causality, chronology, and representation that typically dominate the media in which they work. Yet Deleuze does not denigrate pulsed time as an outmoded practice that should be discarded in favor of exclusively nonpulsed temporalities. Neither of these temporalities exists in a pure form, and indeed, most works will fall somewhere between the two extremes, containing simultaneous pulsed and nonpulsed elements. Nonpulsed time, in fact, can only arise from within the pulsed; its existence is contingent on the initial territorial refrain that it uses as the basis for its new line of flight.

This point is central to an understanding of Deleuze's larger project. Many of his more radical formulations (the body without organs, the line of flight, nonpulsed time) have been dismissed as unachievable, ungrounded, or even undesirable propositions. Feminist theorists have presented cogent critiques of the political damage concepts such as the body without organs or becoming-woman might wreak on the cause of those who have been denied legitimate subjecthood.[70] Yet the radical nature of Deleuze's theory is proportional to the entrenchment of the system it resists. His proposals are unachievable in an actual sense, yet they provide salient tools for chipping holes in the structures that bind and repress. Deleuze thus speaks of nonpulsed time as something that we can experience only from our necessarily grounded positions within pulsed time:

> It goes without saying that one never finds oneself facing anything but mixtures. I don't believe that anyone whatsoever could live in a non-pulsed time, for the simple reason that he would literally die there. Likewise, when we spoke at length of the body without organs, and the necessity of making ourselves one, I never thought that one could live without the organism. Likewise no question of living without relying on and being territorialized on a pulsed time, which permits us the minimum development of forms of which we have need, the minimal allocations of subjects that we are, because subjectivation, organism, pulsation of time, these are the conditions of living. If one leaps over that, it's what we call a suicide.[71]

Nonpulsed time is not an ideal state we can ever, or should ever, hope to enter into. Yet the movement toward nonpulsed time provides a powerful instrument of change, a means of destabilizing and rupturing restrictive structures, even if such interventions are transitory.

Nonpulsed time, as such, does not occur exclusively within the realm of the avant-garde. There are instances wherein what may appear to be utterly measured may move in the direction of the nonpulsed. Deleuze says of the opera, for instance, "We can consider certain motifs in opera in association with a character, but Boulez has shown clearly how motifs in Wagner are not associated solely with an external character but were transformed, had an autonomous life in a floating non-pulsed time in which they themselves became internal characters."[72] The creative force of nonpulsed time can be found not only in atonal and electronic music but within the more traditional work as well. Deleuze was a tremendous fan of the chanteuse Edith Piaf, for "she has this way of singing off-key and then constantly catching the false note and making it right."[73] Piaf's distinct style marks a kind of innovation, the introduction of something new from within the popular. Deleuze says that the role of nonpulsed time comes down to "wresting something" from the territorializing forces of time, of structure, and of "the formation of subjects."[74] Nonpulsed time cannot exist without the pulsed, but it emerges as a force of resistance. From inside the strictures of the pulsed time, sonorous elements began to bifurcate and transform, creating new relations and temporalities that destabilize representation, identity, and structure. Deleuze calls this "the birth of a material free of the form."[75]

## Affect and Fabulation in the Musical Moment

The musical genre is deeply rooted in the machinations of performance, affect, and emotion. Its intense reflexivity, as Feuer has demonstrated, results in a near-obsessive fascination with examining its own performative operations. Within the musical, love and emotion are privileged topics—if not the sole thematic focus. The act of performing serves as a demonstration of the impact that affect has on the human body and, moving through its viscera via sound, wider social spaces. Yet the emotional outpourings of the classical musical are often experienced by contemporary audiences as cloying or saccharine. Parodies of the musical present it as the epitome of disingenuousness. Its unrelenting advocacy for performative expression ("Gotta sing! Gotta dance!") and its formulaic musings on love may be felt as forced or superficial. The musical might reflect on performance and affect, but its own performative mode appears to be one of simulation.

This observation clearly dovetails with readings of the camp codes embedded within the genre. Theories of camp would suggest that the explicit falsity of the musical lies at the heart of its creative and resistant potential. The affective spectacle of the musical is often ironic and can contain a political edge, utilizing the obvious fabrication of a scenario as a critical weapon. In turn, fans of the musical, particularly those attuned to the operations of camp, might experience a genuine affective pleasure arising precisely from the genre's contradictory gestures. Without diminishing the clear presence and significance of the aesthetics of camp within the musical, I suggest that the concept of fabulation provides a means of expanding our understanding of the operations of these contradictions.[76] Fabulation, for Bergson, is a kind of mythmaking, born out of affective experience (most dramatically in response to trauma or a shock) that seeks to ameliorate that encounter with the limits of reason through a creative representation. For Deleuze, fabulation can take on a political dimension, when creative representations begin to speak in a "minor" tongue, to point to the potential for new collective assemblages and unimagined territories. Camp, I argue, is but one of numerous strategies of fabulation at work within the musical.

A musical moment from David Lynch's *Mulholland Drive* (2001) may concretize this dynamic between affect and fabulation and the relation between these processes and cinematic temporality. In a film steeped in incongruities, the performance that takes place inside the Club Silencio is remarkably surreal and hermetic.[77] Much like a production number (or a dream), its spatial and temporal coordinates are distinct from the surrounding narrative. In this scene, the protagonists Betty and the amnesiac Rita, on a quest to unlock the secret of Rita's past, follow a series of clues to the Club Silencio. As they enter the darkened theater, a bearded man on stage intones:

> No hay banda. There is no band. . . . This is all a tape recording. No hay banda, and yet, we hear a band. If we want to hear a clarinet, listen.

The strains of a warbling clarinet waft from the stage, though none is visible. The man, whose manner is reminiscent of a magician, names a series of instruments, each in turn becoming audible, before summoning a trumpet player from behind the curtain, a muted horn pressed to his lips. The trumpet player begins to play, then suddenly stops, lifting his arms and instrument into the air as the sound continues, uninterrupted. The magician continues his performance, "It's all recorded. No hay banda. It's all a tape. It's all an illusion." He gestures dramatically toward the corners of the stage, from which various sounds emerge as if by command, his own voice swelling and diminishing in relation to his distance from a microphone at the center of the stage. Throughout, the scene cuts to medium reaction shots of Betty and Rita seated in the audience, clinging to each other in fear. "Listen," the magician hisses, throwing his arms up to the crashing sound of thunder and flashing lights. His glowering, intense gaze is intercut with shots of Betty, who, transfixed, begins to convulse uncontrollably. The magician smiles and disappears in a puff of smoke, and the stage is bathed in a shimmering blue light.

The blue light fades, and a master of ceremonies steps from behind the curtain, introducing, in Spanish, the next act, "La Llorona de Los Angeles, Rebekah Del Río." Del Río approaches the microphone and begins to sing an a cappella, Spanish-language version of Roy Orbison's "Crying."

Despite the extended introduction stressing the illusory connection between image and sound within Club Silencio, Del Río's performance is felt as intensely embodied. The resonations of her voice and breath flesh out the space of the theater. The camera, which held back at a distance during the previous performance, now moves in close. We see the pores and sweat on Del Río's heavily made-up face, a jeweled artificial tear painted on her cheek. Betty and Rita appear in extreme close-ups now, too, their cheeks wet with real tears. Orbison's song is rendered unfamiliar through the Spanish translation, the lack of instrumentation, and Del Río's passionate phrasing. The exchange of close-ups continues as Del Río's voice crescendos, until there is a sudden cut to a medium shot of her standing on stage. Her lips have stopped moving, and she sways briefly before collapsing on the floor. Two men enter and carry her limp body off stage, while her voice carries on, unaffected.

This scene, which occurs at a pivotal turning point in the film, exists as an interlude, a moment of suspended temporality within the labyrinthine plot. While *Mulholland Drive* as a whole interrogates the cultural and psychic

Rebekah Del Río in *Mulholland Drive* (Lynch, 2001).

Laura Elena Harring and Naomi Watts in *Mulholland Drive*.

construction that is Hollywood, this scene in particular reenacts the apparatus of cinematic spectatorship. The explicit focus is on the fabricated marriage of sound and body and on the impact of this fabrication on the bodies that perform and perceive it. The performers here are experienced as "live," but they remain divorced from the prerecorded sound track. The gestures of the bodies on stage, in conforming to the sound, create a fiction of synthesis. Beyond the miming of the performers, there is much about the staging that is coded as "fake." Del Río's sparkling red and yellow eye shadow is thickly applied, and her lipstick is penciled beyond her natural lip line. The performative nature of the female protagonists' behavior has also been well established at this point in the narrative. Betty's small-town naivety and pluck border on the parodic. Rita's entire identity is a performance, and in this scene, her platinum wig functions as a simulated double for Betty's blonde bob. Regardless, the conjoining of image and sound is experienced by the spectators depicted on-screen in an intensely affective, visceral manner, even when the nature of the illusion is made explicit. The actual spectators of *Mulholland Drive* experience this contradiction doubly; we, too, become mesmerized by Del Río and are shocked when she collapses. And Betty's and Rita's responses, at least for this viewer, felt affectingly genuine despite the lack of narrative justification for such a heightened outpouring. Del Río's spangled tear and the tears of Betty and Rita form a circuit of exchange that extends to the viewer, particularly when we see the convulsions of affect coursing through both sets of bodies.

*Mulholland Drive* is woven from a thick web of intertextual references that shift and metamorphose within the convoluted narrative. In this manner, they perform a refrainlike function in the film, transforming meaning and introducing difference with each repetition. Many of these refrains coincide in the Club Silencio scene. We encounter echoes of Lynch's previous films (in particular, Isabella Rossellini's night club act and Dean Stockwell's lip-synching performance in *Blue Velvet*, 1986) and to outside texts (such as Jacques Rivette's *Celine et Julie vont en bateau [Celine and Julie Go Boating]*, 1974). Roy Orbison becomes a refrain, referring back to Stockwell's simulated rendering of "In Dreams," yet reembodied without accompaniment in a different tongue and voice. References to the musical genre as a whole punctuate the film, most dramatically by the actress Ann Miller, who, transmogrified by time, appears as two separate characters within the film. Betty herself comes to Hollywood after winning a jitterbug competition, and we see (as Feuer might note, impossibly polished) auditions for 1960s-styled musical numbers as they are being filmed. The musical, or more specifically, the process of playback that provides the technological basis for the musical moment, serves within *Mulholland Drive* as the embodiment of Hollywood's illusory nature.

Playback is an unnatural process through which the image (including both the movements of the actors and the staging of the scene) is created in tempo with a prerecorded sound track. The musical audition scenes in *Mulholland Drive* further emphasize the fabricated nature of the image–sound link; here we see the actors lip-synching to a sound track that is doubly framed within the set of a sound recording booth filmed on the set of the fictional film studio. The power of Lynch's project in this film, however, is not one of unmasking an ideological illusion. What is most affecting in this film is the force of the impact it creates, one that immerses the audience within its dreamlike world while simultaneously reinforcing its own status as a falsifying fiction. The representational elements within the Club Silencio scene in particular (the familiar tune, the lyrics, the link between image and sound) have been wrested from their habitual structures of meaning. The audience experiences that rupture intellectually and affectively. This positioning of the spectator as at once inside and outside the filmic experience is one of the most powerful things that the musical moment does. Lynch's musical moment here amplifies, and indeed comments on, the operations of the musical moment in cinema as a whole. As the narrative of his film demonstrates, and as I hope to illuminate in the course of the chapters that follow, the creative fictions written within the musical moment tap into larger cultural narratives and processes of subjectification that are contingent, multiple, and highly adaptive.

In short, my project in this book is to explore the contradictory functions of the musical moment by examining the myriad tensions they contain—between pulsed and nonpulsed time, between the movement-image and the time-image, and between repetition and difference in general. In doing so, I have drawn on examples of musical works that exhibit what Deleuze might call a resistant style,[78] an expressive modality, much like Piaf's blue notes, that actively denaturalizes and destabilizes the framework of the popular from within. Thus, the accident or the stutter attains a privileged stature within my analysis as an inadvertent point of resistance. And this excess is perhaps most visible in musical films that leak beyond the boundaries of an established form. The mistimed step, the disembodied voice, the grotesque or perverse visualization— these moments serve to rupture the measure, to introduce new intensities, to give birth to new temporal spaces, and to generate new thoughts.

Yet the process of differentiation cannot remain accidental if it is to actualize change. Rupture or discontinuity only becomes significant when it results in an act of creation, when it unleashes a new line of flight away from the strata of the same. Innovative style is a transversal that resists unification; it refuses to submit diversity to abstract frames of measure. It also teases out the subtle resonances that exist between diverse elements—it vocalizes the connections between the individual and the world by traversing and permeating the boundaries between them.[79] Thus, we might read the distinctive styles of filmmakers like Jean-Luc Godard, Jacques Demy, Tsai Ming-liang, or David Lynch as actively forging such a transversal through their unconventional use of image and sound. I would also offer that even the accidental rupture provides the opportunity for a different kind of transversal—a potential waiting to be actualized. It becomes a provocation for a new style of thinking through film and music, for thinking differently. The musical film may remain rooted in the striated layers of representative, measured time. But by allowing ourselves to be introduced into the flows of difference to which it aspires, we may wrest something from its repetitions that is entirely unexpected.

*One*

# Illustrating Music: The Impossible Embodiments of the Jukebox Film

> There is no homogeneity of body and voice, none in any case that the cinema can show in a way that is real. . . . There is only a *yearning* . . . for unity, and the cinema can show this yearning. It's even one of the things cinema is best at telling us about.
>
> —MICHEL CHION, *The Voice in Cinema*

Michel Chion, writing on the distinction between film and television, argues that "the difference . . . lies not so much in the visual specificity of their images, as in the different roles of sound in each."[1] Referring to television as "illustrated radio," Chion describes the medium as driven by sound, speech, and music. The image in television and video serves to supplement the sound, which bears the primary burden of conveying meaning. The examples Chion draws on (televised sporting events, video art, and the music video) all share this quality; the sound track tells us what is happening, while the images are added on. The specific nature of this addition is of course vastly different, ranging from the illustrative images cut into a newscaster's report to the "visual fluttering" of a music video or video game.[2] Yet whether these images are synchronous, explanatory, harmonious, or discordant, each must move through sound in order to be understood, a movement that inverts the cinematic image–sound hierarchy.

What is perhaps most provocative about Chion's analysis is the implication that the technological medium alone does not determine what constitutes the televisual. Instead, transformations in audiovisual regimes can be mapped through shifting relations among images, sounds, and their temporal and spatial affectivity. These knotted evolutions are sparked on multiple fronts and invariably involve overlapping technologies, texts, and ideas. To understand the emergence of a new regime would require mapping the configurations of music and image that compose its modality as they occur in other technological contexts. Devices such as the cinematic jukebox offer glimpses of music–image combinations that, although markedly different from either the feature-length musical film or the music video, reveal much about the underlying logic of the representational strategies of each.

The cinematic jukebox's two most successful manifestations surfaced several decades apart: the Panoram Soundie in the 1940s and the Scopitone in the 1960s. Soundies and Scopitones were short-format musical films viewed in jukeboxes outfitted with 16 mm projectors and ground-glass screens. Located in bars, hotels, clubs, and bus stations, these hybrid devices occupied a curious cultural and aesthetic position. This position had as much to do with the peculiarity of the films' visualizations as it did with the unusual format; the images that accompanied each song were crafted with an excessive literalness that was distinct from other contemporaneous musical films, often resulting in stilted and disquieting combinations. Although these experiments were relatively short-lived (and financially unsuccessful), they nevertheless indicated the potential for a new kind of image, one that was distinct from feature-length works and that seemed to be driven by a purely musical logic.

Cinematic jukeboxes generated limited press during their lifetime, and the coverage that does exist focuses almost exclusively on the question of novelty, a trend that has remained intact in contemporary scholarly work. Largely critically ignored, Soundies and Scopitones are only occasionally cited as records of rare performances or as failed precursors to the music video, fleeting anomalies not substantial enough to maintain more than a passing interest.[3] Hovering outside the realms of film and television, featuring material that is often obscure and unsophisticated, jukebox films might be easily dismissed as historical curiosities. Yet I argue that jukebox films provide a significant field for research into the relations between popular music and image precisely because of their anomalous nature. Ungainly and disjointed, jukebox films nevertheless maintain a deeply affecting presence. Their impact, in fact, seems to emanate directly from those moments of stuttering. Although the woodenness of many of these productions might thwart the intentions of their creators, the films' awkward gestures highlight the mechanisms by which they operate—structures that would be much less obvious yet no less prevalent in more sophisticated works.

My interest in cinematic jukeboxes centers on several key issues. The first is the unique experience of viewing jukebox films. As a format founded on sound, musical shorts may have more in common with other aurally based media than with more traditional filmic or televisual works. The jukebox as an apparatus underscores the links between the jukebox film and the record album—Soundies and Scopitones are, in effect, illustrated songs following paths of distribution and consumption similar to those of recorded music. These material circulations greatly influenced the films' visual construction, as did the location, size, and operation of the jukebox.

Second, in focusing on the relations between popular music and image, jukebox films provide a particularly salient example because they are entirely music based. Much of the literature on film music looks either at music's role as a supplement to the image or, in the case of musicals, at the interactions between musical numbers and narrative. Similarly, although music video scholarship has paid critical attention to the enmeshed interests of the video and recording industries, closer examinations of music video texts often disproportionately center on their imagery or lyrics.[4] Freestanding musical shorts, because they contain no overarching narrative framework, allow us to more fully explore the function of music in its own right. The jukebox film must be considered as part of a regime in which the preexisting song takes precedence over the image.

Finally, Soundies' and Scopitones' circuits of movement are incredibly complex, profuse, and at times contradictory. These flows include not only the films' material circulations (in terms of both distribution and presentation) but also the reproduction of familiar songs and the recycling of culturally coded images and modes of representation—all factors contributing to the mobile ways in which the films construct meaning. The seemingly obvious or literal nature of the images chosen to accompany songs becomes complicated when one considers the functions jukebox films performed and the snared collisions between their various aesthetic and social elements. Soundies and Scopitones are therefore best understood not as individual, fixed texts but through an examination of the larger tensions between these shifting elements. Even the most cliché-ridden musical short can tell us vital information about its aspirations (however unsuccessfully it meets them), goals that are invariably more complex than the film's means of expression.

My project in this chapter is to explore the peculiar modality of the jukebox film and the representational strategies that emerge from within its musical moments. My primary focus is on the tension between the habitual, stereotypical illustrations employed by these films and their affective excesses, those elements that seem to move beyond the representational. Within the jukebox film, and indeed within the musical moment as a whole, there is a curious interdependence between habit, or cliché, and a heterogeneous residue—a difference that is borne out of the films' repetitive format. While the jukebox film illustrates the musical performance in a literal and representational manner, its signs do not remain fixed. In many instances, they begin to function as semi-autonomous visual and sonorous situations, freed, to varying degrees, from their intended meanings. Much of this excess may be accidental, emerging from the compromised conditions under which these films were produced. The affective impact of the films, nevertheless, is palpable and continuous with the operations of the musical moment in general.

Jody Berland suggests that an understanding of the music video must entail "a retrospective summary of the economic, iconographic, and structural issues relevant to the continuous integration of pop music with the powerful visual media." These interlaced interests work through audiovisual technologies to create new spaces, conceptions of community, and sets of practices. The most significant issue, she writes, is

> the technological mediation of sound in relation to that of images, and the need to understand such mediation as a productive process that constitutes or changes our relations to each other in spatial and temporal as well as symbolic terms.[5]

Although music television's apparatus is different from that of the cinematic jukebox, the process Berland points to highlights the degree to which all audiovisual technologies are multifaceted, interdependent, and nested within larger cultural modes of seeing, hearing, and communicating. This framework guides my approach to cinematic jukeboxes, providing a means of understanding these devices' cultural positions and the modes of viewing and listening they might have engendered. Given the limited scope of this chapter, however, and the dearth of available data regarding the production, distribution, and reception of Scopitones and Soundies, I am less interested here in the commercial and economic development of these mediums. Instead, I focus on the representational methods employed by these films, examining their music–image combinations and the responses they attempt to produce. There are, of course, vast differences between Soundies and Scopitones: their precise format, their countries of origin (Scopitones were invented in France, Soundies in the United States), their aesthetics, and their historical occurrence. The particularities of each technology thus provide the foundation for my inquiry.

## The Soundie

In September 1940, the Mills Novelty Company premiered its Panoram "movie machine" in Hollywood: a large cabinet with a screen on which patrons could watch three-minute musical films, one number for every ten cents deposited.[6] Soundies, as these films came to be known, were distributed to Panoram juke-boxes in bars, restaurants, transit stations, and hotels throughout the United

Panoram Jukebox publicity photo, *Look Magazine*, November 19, 1940.

States. One of several coin-operated image and sound devices being developed in the early 1940s, the Panoram's success, while limited, far exceeded that of its competitors.[7] The Soundies catalog featured a range of musical styles: big band swing, country-and-western and "hillbilly" acts, romantic ballads, and "exotic" Hawaiian and Latin numbers. Perhaps most significantly, a large number of African American artists and jazz orchestras created Soundies at a time when the circulation of these performances on film was exceedingly rare. The distribution of film reels for the Panoram was exclusive to the Soundies Distributing Corporation of America, which released nearly two thousand Soundies during the company's seven years of operation.

Yet even early press lauding the Panoram as the next sure thing expressed some reservations about the quality of the product. "If early 'soundies' are on the monotonous side," *Look* magazine commented, "they will probably get by on their novelty."[8] Indeed, novelty and topicality were the primary operatives of the Soundie, with vaudeville-style acts, burlesque numbers such as Sally Rand's "The Bubble Dance," a flurry of World War II–related numbers, and comedy titles such as "Who Threw the Turtle in Mrs. Murphy's Girdle?" Certainly, the fusion of image and popular music was not what made the Soundie new. Musical features dominated the box office in the 1940s, and there was a tradition of musical shorts dating back at least to the Vitaphone. The visual aesthetics of the films were also far from innovative. Limited by extremely small budgets and resistance from both the film and recording industries, the producers of Soundies created shorts that were often formulaic, stilted, and riddled with clichés. Despite attempts to engage viewers with comedic acts and even sexually suggestive material, the Soundies Distributing Corporation was never able to build or sustain a consistent audience.

The novelty of the Soundies appears to be tied to the unusual format of the medium: the integration of moving images with musical jukeboxes, the location of the machines in nontheatrical public spaces, the reliance on exclusively musical subject matter, and the visual documentation of artists outside the Hollywood studio system. These material conditions resulted in image–sound combinations that did, in fact, differ significantly from more traditional musical films. Soundies were never intended to be miniature musicals. Experienced by audiences of the 1940s as a phenomenon that closely echoed that of popular recorded music, the Soundie required a new kind of image, one not dictated by narrative but by the affectivity of song. Unlike feature-length musical films, Soundies contain no surrounding narrative. The visual structure of the jukebox film is set by the music, and the emotions expressed are native to the song alone; even in those Soundies with a rough story line, one cannot truly speak of character development. Although some shorts might mimic the tropes of Hollywood production numbers, they share little else in common. The development of the Soundies' display and distribution system was influenced by a combination of technical, economic, and social concerns. Unlike traditional jukeboxes, the design of the Panoram did not allow listeners to choose individual songs. The cabinet contained a 16 mm projector holding an eight-hundred-foot loop of film. The film was projected onto a mirror, which in turn reflected the image onto an eighteen- by twenty-two-inch ground-glass screen.[9] Because the loop was continuous, patrons could only watch and listen to whichever song was next on the reel. Producers were therefore anxious to include a range of musical genres to attract as many customers as possible. Each week, the Soundies Distributing Corporation provided Panoram owners with a new reel of films. According to Soundies expert Mark Cantor, these eight-song preassembled reels adhered to a loose formula that included a variety of set genres. It became common practice, for example, to include an African American number in the eighth position on the reel. Although the Soundies catalog offered the option of customized reels, the company provided a "general outline of what a reel should look like (one vocalist, one novelty number, one ethnic number, one dance number, etc.). Renters certainly could, however, choose to tailor their reels according to more specific demographic tastes. That shorts by African American artists were listed in a separate "Negro" section suggests that racial divisions might have affected the distribution of these Soundies, although little data regarding actual distribution patterns has survived.[10]

Many Soundies were set in barrooms and addressed their audiences in ways that suggested a continuity between the diegetic space and the space of the viewer—with an invitation to sing along or even to make a request.[11] Others relied on the premise of a nightclub performance or the barest sketch of a narrative based on the song's lyrics. The stars of Soundies shorts covered a broad spectrum, from well-known artists such as Louis Armstrong and Hoagy Carmichael to unknowns who went on to greater fame: Gale Storm, Cyd Charisse, Nat "King" Cole, and Liberace. The location of the Panoram machines seems to have had some bearing on the selection of images: many, like Spike Jones's "Clink! Clink! Another Drink," featured drinking as an explicit theme. Soundies also contained an inordinate amount of "cheesecake"—nearly every number, regardless of genre or lyrical content, included a parade of pretty girls (often the same six pretty girls) in revealing outfits vaguely related to the song's theme.

Soundies, by definition, take music as their primary element. The sound was recorded prior to filming, and the performers would lip-synch to the song

Spike Jones and His City Slickers, "Clink! Clink! Another Drink!" (1942).

as it was played back. As a result, the music does not become folded into the visual narrative that it accompanies, but rather, the visuals are conceived of as a complement to the preexisting sound. This hierarchy becomes painfully obvious the more Soundies one views. Filmed at breakneck speed and on a shoestring budget, most performances were starkly set and costumed, and it was not uncommon for the performers to occasionally stumble out of synch.

In many ways, the Soundie can be likened to the record album. The two industries were closely linked, and their products moved along similar paths of distribution and consumption. Critical to an understanding of both the cinematic jukebox film and the musical jukebox is the experience of time that each evokes. Popular recorded music has a unique and multifaceted temporality. The record is portable, reproducible, and can be played repeatedly at will. Yet pressed into its grooves is the indexical mark of the voice, the strains of the instruments, an indelible reference to a particular instant. Murmurs of that irretrievable past reemerge, anachronistically, in the present of each listening. In addition to its temporal manipulations, the recorded popular song unleashes new configurations of space. There is a continual pull between proximity and distance, the closeness of the recorded performance belying, or at times highlighting, the remoteness of its point of origin. These temporal and spatial relations become even more involved when music is paired with the filmed image. Film is similarly imprinted with the mark of the past and is experienced in the ephemeral, temporal, and repeatable duration of the projection. Both mediums bear a distinct emotive force that circulates beyond the moments they capture.

Like the record player or sound-only jukebox, the Panoram affords the viewer a strange amalgam of intimacy and longing in a public setting. The prurient nature of some of the images might lend an intimate tone, but the size of the screen would as well, since it required that viewers stand in close proximity to see the image. The familiarity of many of the artists and tunes could only heighten the sensation of nearness, as would the individual control over repeatability that the jukebox provided (though one would have to spend eight dimes and a good portion of time waiting for the desired number to work its way around the reel). The limitations of recording and playback technology, however, reassert the remoteness of the originary performance. The affectivity of the Soundie seems to arise from this incongruity, the continued rehearsal of an instant that can never be fully grasped.

The images of the Soundie, even at their most uninventive, appear tailored toward this somewhat conflicted viewing experience. Despite the range of musical genres and shooting styles embodied by the Soundie, several common tensions persist. One of the most obvious exists between the prerecorded sound track and attempts to mime visually a live rendition. Soundies commonly act as a document of a singular performance, especially in the case of well-known, more expensive performers such as Cab Calloway, Duke Ellington, and Stan Kenton. The scenarios for these Soundies are extremely simple and straightforward. Positioned on decorative stages before audiences in a club, the musicians are the primary focus of the camera. More often than not, these films contain no narrative elements and are accentuated only by occasional shots of dancing couples or chorines. In these performance-based Soundies, one is aware of the artists in an intimate, bodily sense. Removed from the inaccessible sheen of the glitzy, big-budget numbers found in the typical feature-length musical, these performances seem more spontaneous and sincere. Since many of these musicians had not been filmed previously, the impact of such Soundies, displayed in a small format and controlled by the viewer, cannot be overestimated. Yet, at the same time, the clumsiness of the production, the clear distance between the poorly synched and separately recorded tracks, opens a fissure that makes the viewer's distance from the performance painfully felt. Moreover, these glitches throw into question the authenticity of that performance itself; faced with the evidence of its existence, the event remains uncannily detached.

A second tension emerges between the nonrepresentational status of music and fumbling attempts to represent it quite literally. Soundies functioned not only as documents but also as enhanced visual illustrations. This role is most evident in comedy numbers or lower-budget filler numbers, which impart a cute visual twist on what would otherwise be an uneventful rendition. Whereas more established or dynamic musicians were able to hold the viewer's attention within the simplest of scenarios, lesser-known performers needed additional visual emphasis. Stock musicians and comedic vaudeville acts were employed to fill out the shooting schedule during extended periods of dispute between Soundies producers and musicians' unions.[12] Many of these songs relied on humorous lyrical content or generic themes (wartime propaganda, traditional Irish songs, etc.) rather than on inherent musical interest. The directors faced the challenge of translating these often mediocre numbers into a visual format as quickly and inexpensively as possible.

The solutions to this challenge range from the mundane to the utterly bizarre. The images in these films frequently correspond directly to the lyrics. In "The Wise Old Owl," Sylvia Froos's straight rendition of the swing ballad is punctuated by the hoots of a stuffed owl jerking back and forth on a branch over her head. Comedy numbers usually consist of rough narrative reenactments. Cindy Walker's "Seven Beers with the Wrong Man" depicts Walker in an Old West–style jail cell, intercutting slapstick scenes of her seduction. Soundies that fall within distinct musical subgenres employ the most obvious locations and tropes as a backdrop. Countless country-western shorts, for instance, take place in barnyard settings. Other Soundies use the visual component of the medium as fodder for one-liners. "The Biggest Aspidastra in the World" depicts singers with the Johnny Mercer Orchestra lauding the features of their aspidistra plant. As they emphasize the first syllable of the word, however, the camera pans to a row of girls with watering cans, who bend over to reveal their ruffled panties. Such scenarios encapsulate the dissonant humor of the Soundie, which results from the desire to interpret the song absolutely literally, excessively so. The image becomes a comic, or perhaps even a monstrous, illustration of the lyric.

## Habits, Clichés, and Phantasms

Habit, as described by David Hume, plays a critical role in our acquisition of knowledge and in mediating our relationship with the outside world. On the one hand, habits produce beliefs that arise from the realm of experience. Through the course of one's interactions with the material world, the mind begins to perceive patterns, resemblances, and repetitions. These resemblances are contracted within the mind in order to form a belief, a set of principles that might explain these patterns, and a set of expectations regarding the unfolding of future events. On the other hand, habits are fundamentally distinct from experience; there is an interface between the two, but they are not identical. The formation of beliefs is based on certain "fictions of the imagination" whereby discrepancies in continuity or temporal occurrence are minimized in favor of an illusion of principled coherence and unity.[13] Indeed, there is a degree to which habit is subject to the whims of fancy. As Deleuze notes, "By itself, habit can feign or invoke a false experience, and bring about belief through 'a repetition' which 'is not deriv'd from experience.'"[14] In other words, repetitions of all sorts may be taken up by the imagination, resulting in the generation of false beliefs.

For Hume, these fictions of the imagination provide the foundation for stereotype and prejudice. Although the general rules that form the basis of prejudice might contradict empirical observation ("an *Irishman* cannot have wit, and a *Frenchman* cannot have solidity"), these erroneous beliefs are nevertheless based on habit: "When we have been accustom'd to see one object united to another, our imagination passes from the first to the second, by a natural transition, which precedes reflection, and which cannot be prevented by it."[15] Here we see the connection between habit and the realm of representation.

Perceived repetitions of representational elements form associations that provide the basis for social and political beliefs. Yet this is a foundational principle, extending beyond representation into the most basic operations of perception and causality. This may help to explain the intractability of cultural associations that defy "sense and reason."[16]

Hume paints the fictional dimension of habit in both positive and negative lights. Habit extends imagination, resulting at times in the generation of false beliefs. Yet habit has a corrective function in the realm of judgment, one that has the ability to disprove illegitimate fictions, realigning understanding with experience. In *Difference and Repetition,* Deleuze offers an even more productive reading of habit's propensity toward creative falsification. The perception of repetition is a multidimensional process, one that involves the introduction of something new, a difference. On the most foundational level (the level of a "passive synthesis," or a contraction of time), that difference is the very idea of a repetition imagined by the mind that perceives. This habitus is "hallucinatory," but it is the force that binds together the subject; the subject "produces itself or 'draws itself' from what it contemplates."[17] Habits are thus inherently transformative and bound to the social. Their generative function provides the basis for more active temporal syntheses (memory and the time of the event and of eternal return), each of which are further marked by a certain fictitiousness. While the difference introduced by habit remains more grounded and is more easily recuperated, there is a potential generated precisely through its illusions, one that allows for, ultimately, creative thought and processes of becoming.

I suggest that the musical moment employs certain habitual means of representation that produce, in turn, transformative fictions and hallucinations. The unity of sound and body that occurs in the musical moment is phantasmatic, a fiction of the imagination that does not exist. These fictions were not necessarily created with artistic intentionality. It is far more likely, in fact, that they draw upon clichés reflexively, with the objective of repeating and reinforcing familiar associations. Yet a stuttering occurs here, the introduction of a difference that ruptures the chain of associations. Rather than correcting this error and presenting a "true" image of the unified self, the rupture cannot be papered over—the fiction of an originary, "real" unity has already been revealed. What we experience, in many musical moments, and in the images of the jukebox film in particular, is a simulacrum. When the false nature of that phantasm is allowed to come to light, the models upon which it is based, those habitual means of representation, are exposed as fictional clichés. The cinematic image here leaks beyond the boundaries of its habitual framework. We encounter a challenge to the representational chain, an affective excess that makes the stereotype resonate differently. The cliché, in the musical moment, can become a springboard for new associations, associations forged through an encounter with outside meanings.

## Affective Assemblages and Paper Dolls

In his writings on film and sound, Chion develops the idea of "added value" to describe "the expressive and informative value with which a sound enriches a given image so as to create the definite impression . . . that this information or expression 'naturally' comes from what is seen, and is already contained in the image itself."[18] Although the concept of added value is useful in exploring the function of music in narrative film, it is a relation that does not exist in musically based visual formats. Discussing the music video, Chion writes:

> This is yet another way in which the music video leads us back to the silent cinema—seemingly a paradox, since we're talking about a form constructed on music. But it is precisely insofar as music does form its basis, and none of the narration is propelled by *dialogue,* that the music video's image is fully liberated from the linearity normally imposed by sound.[19]

Charges of musical cliché are levied against narrative film when sound and image exist in a direct and obvious relation to each other. Abstraction and autonomy are cited as the best means of complicating these relations. Yet as both Chion and Claudia Gorbman suggest, in musically based works, all visual movements are in a sense abstractions in that they are dictated by the logic and temporality of music rather than narrative. The elements within the film frame, set in motion by the music, become mobile, freed, at least to a certain degree, from the burdens of signification, motivation, and logical development.[20]

The musical logic Chion and Gorbman point to, I argue, dictates the Soundie's visual construction. Instead of reading Soundies as linear constructions, it may be more productive to view them as constellations of images. Soundies' images in fact obtain their emotive affectivity through the tensions between their irrational and anachronistic juxtapositions. The images, melodies, and ideas that constitute meaning within Soundies circulate in ways that are always fluid and multifaceted. To phrase this slightly differently, one might argue that the habitual, representational links between expressive elements (lyrics, image, body, music, voice, and sound) are loosened within the space of the musical moment. While clearly still bound by certain associations, they are nevertheless able to reverberate semiautonomously and to forge new, nonrepresentational links. For example, sung words might begin to function sonically rather than linguistically, or bodily gestures might coincide with the music in unanticipated ways. Each element within the Soundie works as part of a mobile assemblage, but the overall effect is rarely one of harmonious synthesis. Instead, each component (the culturally charged scenario, the poorly timed performance, the familiar tune) seems to reverberate disparately, leaving the impression of discordant refrains that are always somehow out of time.

Although the producers of Soundies might have designed imagery in a literal and linear manner, the overall effect of the Soundie's sonic and visual couplings is a viewing and listening experience that is hardly straightforward. Indeed, it is the very failure of the Soundie to recreate an integrated, convincing illustration of a performance that exposes the conflicts at the core of that project. Moreover, the often politically troubling imagery of the Soundie, which seems to stoop to the most obvious and stereotypical portrayals of gender, race, and ethnicity at every opportunity, points to the prevalence of such representations within the twentieth-century cultural imagination. The glaringness of such depictions, surely amplified by historical distance, suggests the possibility that these perspectives are more subtly embedded in the songs themselves. The uncomfortable melding of abstract and representational elements in the Soundie opens the musical image to multiple, critical interpretations, readings that perhaps would be foreclosed by more slickly produced or narrative-based works.

The Mills Brothers' Soundie for their hit "Paper Doll," for example, opens with the brothers seated in a garden set. Three of the brothers have smiling women seated on their knees, while the brother singing lead cuts out a picture of Dorothy Dandridge with a pair of scissors. He sings of a paper doll "to call his own," wishing for her affections rather than "a fickle-minded, real live girl." As he places the cutout paper Dandridge on the ground, she dissolves into a live image and begins to dance energetically in a short, frilled dress. The brothers look down as they sing over her miniature, ghostly figure superimposed before them.

"Paper Doll" is composed of two distinct sections. In the first half, the camera's attention is divided between documenting the singers' performance and enacting the song's lyrics. Although adequate attention is paid to the real "dolls" adorning the brothers' laps and the cutting of the photograph, the center of action is each singer's face: the "column of air" leaving the mouth that constitutes, for Chion, the visual essence of the vocal performance.[21] Both the imagery and the musical rhythm shift dramatically, however, when Dorothy Dandridge's paper cutout comes to life. The focus, too, shifts from an enhanced documentation of the Mills Brothers' performance to a surreal visualization

The Mills Brothers and Dorothy Dandridge in "Paper Doll" (1942).

removed from the actions of the singers. The relationship between image and sound at this point is significantly transformed. Our perspective on the singers is now the back of their heads looming over Dandridge, an uninviting composition lacking a clear visual reference to the sound source.[22] Dandridge's spastic movements have little relation to what is happening musically, or perhaps they only seem out of time because her tapping feet are silent. In combination with her girlish frock, Dandridge's choreography seems to reflect less the delicate steps of a breathing paper doll and more the gesticulations of an invention gone awry.

To say that Dandridge appears as a projection of the Mills Brothers' fantasy of femininity is nearly beside the point. Although such a reading would correctly highlight the problematic, sexist premise of the song and film, it leaves unexamined the uneasy excessiveness of Dandridge's pasted-on figure, a presence that resists any obvious critique. The image is in fact so literal that it exceeds or even defies the meaning of the original lyric. Dandridge's disquieting presence, however spectral, makes the desire for "the truest doll in all this world" too palpable, too real. And this, to me, is where the discomfort lies. The stolid framework of the scenario gives rise to an image that is surprising and unsettling, for it confronts us with an impossible embodiment. What we see laid bare is the very structure of the fantasy.

To reframe this in relation to the question of habit, we might say that "Paper Doll" invokes a series of visual, linguistic, and musical clichés, each based on the repetition of familiar cultural associations. A fiction is generated—a fiction regarding the unity of body and sound and the simultaneity of image and music. An additional fiction is created regarding the expression of masculine, heterosexual desire via cinematic and musical narration, as well as a fiction regarding the mutability of the female subject. A fiction of intimacy is written here, too, as the song, the camerawork, and the technological apparatus work to position the viewer as the singular recipient of the message. But something goes wrong. The clichés are so overwrought and so strangely rendered that the invisible, automatic associations between their elements is exposed. The signs cease to function as transparent representations and begin to resonate expressively, *as* sounds and images rather than bearers of meaning. The habitual code is loosened—the links depicted here no longer feel natural or familiar. And a distance is struck between the viewer and the space of the film as the appeal for emotional entry is thwarted.

Deleuze might describe this as an expressive system that has become "overstrained."[23] When an isolated disturbance occurs within a homogenous language system, the result is a variation in that individual speech act. "But if the system appears to be in perpetual disequilibrium, if the system bifurcates—and has terms each one of which traverses a zone of continuous variation—language itself will begin to vibrate and to stutter."[24] What we witness in such cases, in other words, is not an individual stammering but a systemic one. While Deleuze associates these systemic disruptions with the interventions of a creative artist, that he describes the impact of this action as a *stutter,* an involuntary or a mechanical failure, suggests that we might locate similar glitches and failures within expressive systems that are accidentally pushed beyond their limits. In each instance, there is a representational breakdown and the generation of a heterogeneous, affective surplus.

Music, as a nonrepresentational medium, is itself visually unrepresentable. Chion compares attempts to film an instrumental performance with pornography's attempt to capture the sexual act: no matter where you train the camera, what you are looking for always seems to be elsewhere.[25] Soundies do not succeed in this impossible task. Yet where these representations falter, a different framework becomes apparent, one that imbues these images with their haunting affectivity. This is where the primacy of music, and a musical logic, is essential. What would otherwise remain a stereotypical or prosaic image becomes abstracted, exaggerated, and immoderate. That which is threatening need not be resolved or punished as it often is in narrative forms. Within Soundies there is room for irrationality, transformation, eruption—even a joy in difference. Surely the threat of the irrational never exceeds its containment within the song, but its mere existence hints at a nascent potential.

## Overlapping Technologies

The Soundies Distributing Corporation ceased the distribution of films in 1947. Conflicts with musicians' unions, competition with other entertainment industries, and the pressures of wartime manufacturing plagued the enterprise throughout its lifetime. The shorts enjoyed a comparatively long run on the home movie market, however, as the films were purchased by several corporations (namely, Castle and Official) and spliced onto "thematic" reels for mail-order distribution.[26] Several new series of musical films emerged shortly after the Soundies, including Snader Telescriptions and Studio Telescriptions, musical shorts produced exclusively for television in the early 1950s. Many telescriptions filmed and recorded sound simultaneously in simple studio settings, resulting in significant shifts in tone and address. The telescription market proved to be limited, however, becoming outmoded after only a few years of production. *Bandstand,* the Philadelphia television program that evolved into *American Bandstand,* was introduced as a telescription-deejay show in 1952.

Audiences disliked the format, however, and it was quickly reformulated into a performance showcase with a teen studio audience.[27]

Given the anomalous nature of Soundies technologies, it is interesting to consider the ways in which its habitual mode of address intersected with competing media technologies. Television was beginning to assert its presence during the Panoram's brief lifetime, yet the transition between the cinematic jukebox and television was not entirely straightforward. Jukebox technology, in fact, may have influenced early perceptions of television's position within public spaces. Although much attention has been paid to the cultural impact of television in the home, Anna McCarthy points to the integral role television plays in nondomestic environs. In her study of television in 1940s taverns, McCarthy discusses the early use of coin-operated devices to regulate relations among spectators, customers, and the television monitor. In an attempt to maintain beverage sales and dissuade those seeking a free show, television juke-boxes were marketed to bar owners, providing an allotment of viewing time for each coin deposited.[28] The Panoram and television were each seen as a challenge to the social atmosphere of the bar and to preexisting forms of entertainment. When placed in taverns or clubs, both formats faced regulation and fierce opposition from theater owners and other media interests.[29] It is clear that each technology occupied a contested and often undefined space within the shifting terrains of the entertainment industry and the public sphere.

There are crucial differences, however, between the manipulations of space and time produced by the film jukebox and early television. The use of a coin-operated interface represented an ill-fated attempt to harness television's continuity and immediacy, arguably the most characteristic aspects of the medium. The film jukebox, however, is structured around the fixed musical moment, the encapsulated time frame of each three-minute song. Soundies, for example, began and ended with titles and credits or visual devices such as opening and closing curtains. The coin-operated interface of the film jukebox also lent intimacy and control to the viewer rather than an unwelcome intrusion. The brevity of each song, coupled with the cost of feeding the machine, prevented the film jukebox from providing the kind of ambient presence McCarthy argues television provides.

The transition between the Panoram Soundie and television is thus extraordinarily tangled. Like television, the Panoram was a sound-based format and had closer ties to the radio and music industries than to the film industry. Yet the Panoram offered an affective experience markedly distinct from that of television, even in instances where the placement and operation of the device was relatively similar. Soundies set a precedent that clearly influenced later televisual manifestations, yet at the same time, they were incapable of capitalizing on the simultaneity of the video medium. The tensions between these two formats had much to do with their status as emergent technologies in the 1940s. In the 1960s, however, when a second incarnation of the cinematic jukebox was released, television held a more established position within the public and private spheres. Popular music, too, underwent significant transformations in terms of marketing, audience, and style. The Scopitone jukebox thus differed from the Panoram in terms of format, aesthetics, and social function. Once again, however, this second incarnation of the jukebox film demonstrated a marked dependency on habit and cliché in its visual presentation.

## The Scopitone

In her essay "Notes on Camp," Susan Sontag places Scopitone films third in her list of "random examples of items which are part of the canon of Camp." Though she does not describe Scopitones in detail, they seem to epitomize her definition of "pure" or "naïve Camp"; Scopitones do not intend to be funny, yet humor emerges precisely from their excessive ingenuousness.[30] Released in the early 1960s, Scopitone jukeboxes offered a selection of hip-shimmying bubblegum pop. Shot with very small budgets, Scopitone films featured a catalog of performers and songs that, even at the time, were decidedly square. Given the complex evolution of the term, however, I hesitate to identify Scopitones as "camp." Many critics have thoroughly countered Sontag's assertion that "the Camp sensibility is disengaged, depoliticized—or at least apolitical" through theorizations of the practices of performance and political critique associated with camp.[31] Given camp's centrality to queer theory and culture, it seems inappropriate to apply the term to cultural artifacts that lack a critical rhetorical stance, let alone any shreds of self-awareness or irony.

Yet, at the same time, the multifaceted nature of the term "camp" may suggest a useful means of approaching Scopitones. Despite the debates that surround camp and the somewhat related categories of kitsch and cheese (also common descriptors for Scopitones), each term is interchangeably applied to objects, events, and strategies of interpretation.[32] Meaning, this slippage implies, resides neither with the object nor with the subject who perceives it but in the collapsed space of their interaction. Labeling Scopitones campy or cheesy may reveal little about these films in themselves, yet it is critical to understand that these texts are inseparable from the act of reading them. Responses to anomalous material such as jukebox films are almost entirely determined by one's cultural and historical position. This is perhaps the most prominent tension

JOIN THE GROWING NUMBER OF COIN MACHINE DISTRIBUTORS WHO ARE REALIZING THRU TREMENDOUS PROFITS THAT...

# $copitone

IS THE STARS MOST FREQUENT ADDRESS

## TOP AMERICAN AND INTERNATIONAL STARS

Featuring DEBBIE REYNOLDS, BARBARA McNAIR, JAMES DARREN, VIC DAMONE, JOI LANSING, JANUARY JONES and many other national and international artists, all in dazzling productions in full-color, full-sound.

*NOW See and Hear Your Favorite Stars on*

## $copitone's

*Carousel of Stars!*

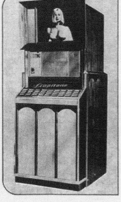

**THE RECOGNIZED WORLD LEADER IN THE FIELD OF COIN-OPERATED AUDIO-VISUAL ENTERTAINMENT**

In night clubs, lounges and hotels throughout the country, hundreds of American-made Scopitones already on location are established profit-makers for their operators. Thousands of Scopitones have been proven in operation throughout the world for many years. The first and finest coin-operated audio-visual entertainment medium, Scopitone is available for immediate delivery with a library of over 300 film titles including a vast selection of dazzling American hit productions.

Scopitone now has world-wide distribution for this unit (except France).

Canadian Distributor: Gerard THIBAULT, Scopitone Canada, Inc., 355 Rue St. Paul, Quebec 2, Canada.

For information, write or call National Sales Manager

## $copitone

(Division of Tel-A-Sign, Inc.)
3401 West 47th Street, Chicago, Illinois 60632
(312) FR 6-8800

Scopitone promotional brochure, 1966. Courtesy of Bob Orlowsky and the Scopitone archive. http://www.scopitonearchive.com.

contained within the reading of kitsch, camp, or cheese: the temporal and spatial distance of the audience from the artifact's place of origin.[33]

Sontag does in fact see this temporal displacement as essential to a camp sensibility. "The process of aging or deterioration," she writes,

> provides the necessary detachment—or arouses the necessary sympathy. . . . Time contracts the sphere of banality. (Banality is, strictly speaking, always a category of the contemporary.) What was banal can, with the passage of time, become fantastic. . . . Thus, things are campy, not when they become old—but when we become less involved in them, and can enjoy, instead of be frustrated by, the failure of the attempt.[34]

It is somewhat curious, then, that Scopitone films should take such a prominent position in Sontag's camp catalog in 1964, the year they were first released in the United States. Perhaps this can be attributed to a geographic displacement. Scopitones were a French invention, and though many shorts were produced in the United States, the earliest titles were predominantly European. The production standards for French Scopitones were generally low, and they frequently depicted artists unknown to North American viewers singing popular English-language songs in French.[35] There are other ways in which Scopitones distanced themselves from certain audiences. Even English-language Scopitones favored older, established performers singing bouncy pop standards over more youth-oriented rock groups. The most immediately obvious feature of Scopitones is their shameless, clumsy reliance on sexploitative visual material, regardless of the subject matter or tempo of the song. It would be difficult to argue that even a viewer in 1965 could watch a Scopitone such as Jody Miller's "The Race Is On," which depicts four female dancers in bikinis and feathered tails prancing like horses around a race track, without experiencing some form of disconnection. Once again, we witness the cliché run amok. Yet there was an earnestness to the habitual expressions of the Soundie that is missing in the Scopitone. Here we experience less the yearning for unity rendered via cliché than the flagrant celebration of the cliché *as* a cliché, repeated compulsively in all its Technicolor glory.

Indeed, Scopitones represent a departure from Soundies in a number of ways. Scopitone jukeboxes were selectable, presenting viewers with a choice of up to thirty-six separate titles. The visual composition of Scopitones is completely dissimilar to earlier jukebox films; they were shot on color stock and filmed either on location or on highly stylized sets. Scopitone films contained a magnetic sound track, which provided a vast improvement on the quality of the Panoram's optical sound track. The subjects of Scopitones were more

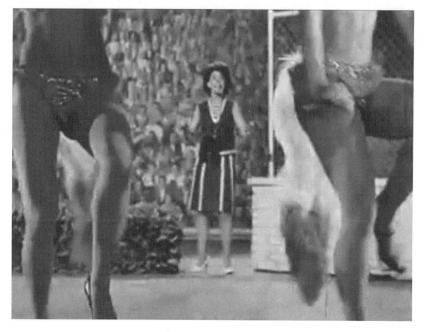

Jody Miller in "The Race Is On."

stylistically limited than the subjects of Soundies, mainly consisting of upbeat standards. As in Soundies, in Scopitones the preexisting, prerecorded song dictates the structure of its visualization. And here again there is a marked disjunction between the sound and its image, a stuttering that feels at once intimate and remote. The Scopitone's disorienting effect is distinct from that of the Soundie, however. Certainly, both formats suffer from low production values and from an overreliance on habitual visualizations, two factors that contribute to the failed synthesis of the tracks and the unsuccessful engagement of the viewer. But whereas the distancing tension between image and music in the Soundie has much to do with the novelty of the format, the primary tension in the Scopitone seems to lie elsewhere. Instead, the disconnection between sound and image may arise from the Scopitone's idiosyncratic attempts to be both an innovative and a staid form of entertainment. The contradictory nature of the Scopitone is linked to this pull between the new and the outmoded and the various pleasures and discomforts to which it gives rise.

Unlike Soundies, Scopitones emerged at a moment when the televisual apparatus had achieved a highly developed state. There is even evidence to suggest that Scopitone technology was envisioned as a competitor to television. In a release promoting the Scopitone's potential for "'theme' and 'mood' advertising," *Billboard* predicts "it is replacing television sets in some cafes and bars, and if the insertion of advertising is successful it promises to replace TV altogether because of its revenue-generating advantage."[36]

Yet the Scopitone jukebox did not follow through on this threat and in fact enjoyed only a limited presence in the United States. In many ways, this failure was caused by the lack of integration of the recording and jukebox film industries—a shortcoming that music video producers were careful to avoid. Whereas music videos were considered one of the most potent tools for advertising popular music in the height of the MTV era, the music industry in the 1960s viewed jukebox films as ineffective at best and a liability at worst. Reporting on the lack of British-produced Scopitones circulating in the United Kingdom, *Billboard* attributed the problem to the uncooperative nature of the British record industry. "Record firms generally feel that the cinema juke box is a good medium for standards, but they have reservations about the use of the unit for current hit material."[37] Although French "diskeries" allowed for the simultaneous production and release of Scopitones and record singles, the U.S. and British industries did not follow suit. Caught somewhere between television, the recording industries, and the coin-operated jukebox distribution networks, the Scopitone represented a failed synthesis of interests.

The Scopitone jukebox was developed in France from surplus military equipment in the late 1950s. The first model was released in 1960 by the Compagnie d'Applications Méchaniques à l'Electronique au Cinéma et à l'Atomistique (CAMECA) to be distributed throughout Europe.[38] The Scopitone machine featured a complex loading mechanism: up to thirty-six films were held on a rotating drum that could play and rewind each individual selection. In 1963, the Scopitone was brought to test markets in the United States, and in 1964, Scopitone, Inc., a subsidiary of the Chicago Tel-A-Sign manufacturing company, introduced an updated model of the jukebox for nationwide distribution.

Initially, U.S. Scopitone machines were stocked with French and European titles licensed from CAMECA. The French Scopitones were shot on extremely low budgets, often outdoors, using available light and Eastman Color stock. French-produced Scopitones featured performers such as Françoise Hardy, Vince Taylor, Serge Gainsbourg, and Brigitte Bardot, and lesser-known artists such as Les Surfs, Aimable et Zappy Max, and Les Soeurs Kessler.[39] These performers had limited appeal outside France, however, and by late 1964, Harman-ee Productions (a branch of the Hollywood company Harman Enterprises, owned by Debbie Reynolds and Irving Briskin) was enlisted as the principal producer of Scopitone films in the United States. The production values were significantly increased for these shorts. Shot in Technicolor, the U.S. films were vibrant and less susceptible to fading. They also made greater use of sets, props, and scenarios loosely inspired by song lyrics. The catalog of U.S. Scopitones was far smaller than that of the French; artists included Debbie Reynolds, Nancy Sinatra, Neil Sedaka, Lou Rawls, Della Reese, January Jones, and the Hondells.

The industry response to Scopitones, as to Soundies, often contained thinly veiled skepticism. A *Billboard* article titled "Cinema Juke Box: Just a Novelty?" reports decidedly mixed predictions from coin-operated industry representatives.[40] In an explicit attempt not to challenge the domain of the music-only jukebox, Scopitone avoided appeals to the burgeoning youth market. *Billboard* assesses Harman-ee's strategy:

> Programming is based on the theory that the machines will be placed in adult locations and that grown-ups want to hear familiar artists singing familiar songs.
>
> If Scopitone becomes established in teen-age locations, the programming will have to be supplemented with films made by some of the newer pop artists. In that case, the film producer would have to gamble. The current material is primarily library stuff. It's not calculated to die quickly. And as making a film entails a lot more expense than cutting a single, it is unlikely that the emphasis will shift too much from bread-and-butter artists to new chart entries.[41]

Many of the problems cited in trade publications seem to anticipate the successful strategies of the music video industry: close ties between the video and recording industries; the cooperation of artist trade unions; and shared systems of marketing, research, and distribution. One anonymous industry executive "noted for progressive business practices" stated that "after close acquaintance with the music-film trend he has become convinced that the audio-visual concept is here to stay—but not in its present form."[42]

## Habitual Excesses and Social Assemblages

Scopitones represent more, however, than just a failure on the road to the music video. Like Soundies, they draw on jukebox-specific manipulations of space and time, modes of address, and visual and sonic relations. After viewing any number of Scopitones, one quickly surmises that their primary objective is to display as much scantily clad female flesh as possible. Certainly Soundies had relied on similar appeals to audiences, but shifts in musical style and thresholds of permissiveness rendered the Scopitones far more explicit. Shooting styles were also greatly transformed by the 1960s; mobile cameras, zooms, extreme close-ups, and fast edits allowed for the inclusion of more gratuitous footage.

The use of such material in Scopitones is frequently incongruous. There is no question that the preponderance of bikinis and up-the-skirt camera angles is blatantly sexist and exploitative. Yet the producers miscalculate the timing and impact of this imagery on every level, nearly to the point of desexualization. It is impossible to measure, of course, the degree to which this retrospective response is a result of historical distance. One can nevertheless with some certainty point to empirical elements in the films that demonstrate attempts to incorporate disparate interests. Many of the vocalists selected to appeal to the adult market were middle-aged themselves. Singers like Kay Starr appeared in modest attire yet were always surrounded by a chorus of Scopitone "beauties."[43] In "Wheel of Fortune," Starr sings on a casino-styled set, begging the wheels of fate to grant her love. The lilting tempo of the song, however, is undermined by the undulations of young dancers in spangled showgirl skivvies; attempting to match their gyrations to the song's slow rhythm, their legs visibly shake as they spin on roulette tables. It is in fact quite typical for the movements of Scopitone dancers to exist completely outside the temporality of the song. The frenetic bouncing of the bikini-clad women in most films suggests that, for the producers, eroticism is equated with jumping up and down as quickly as possible while completely ignoring the accompanying music. This results in many baffling juxtapositions, such as in Brook Benton's "Mother Nature, Father Time." While Benton soulfully coos his warning, "If Mother Nature don't stop you, Father Time sure will," his image is intercut with that of a nearly naked woman in a bonnet and a bearded man in a loincloth flailing against each other.

Other unbalanced combinations are surely amplified through hindsight yet nevertheless seem hopelessly mismatched. Lesley Gore, who was later to become a celebrated lesbian icon, gives an incredible performance in "Wonder Boy," asking the bookish male object of her affections, "If you're so smart, how come you don't know I adore you?" This viewer found it simultaneously delightful and tragic (perhaps truly campy?) to watch Gore moon over the oblivious boy while a bevy of girls in miniskirts and well-exposed white panties do the twist behind her. Line Renaud, in "Le Hully Gully," sings while strolling around a swimming pool, seemingly unaware of homoeroticism generated by her male back-up dancers, clad in tiny, tight swimsuit briefs, who kick and dive in line formation. Not all Scopitones' visual contradictions are so pleasant. Dick and Dee Dee's "Where Have All the Good Times Gone?" features the couple wandering around a semideserted amusement park. Given the haphazard

Brook Benton sings "Mother Nature, Father Time."

Benton's performance is intercut with images of "Mother Nature" and "Father Time" gyrating to the music.

nature of this scenario, it seems likely that most of the visual compositions were created on the spot with little planning or foresight. The bizarre and disturbing decision to include a woman dancing in front of a rifle in a target shooting game, then, registers as a needless shock, casting a violent, misogynist pallor over the entire film.

Like the Soundies, Scopitones demonstrate a staunch reliance on the literal. Joi Lansing's "Web of Love" is exemplary in this regard. The song's sequences escalate in their preposterous illustration of the lyrics. Lansing compares love to a witch doctor while sitting in a frothy cauldron surrounded by unconvincing "natives"; when she describes herself as a bird in a cage, she stands in a birdcage, flapping feathered arms across her cleavage. The next verse calls love "a big black cobra," at which point a man clad in a patterned body suit attempts to slither across Lansing's lap. Although Lansing's body remains well exposed throughout, the ridiculousness of these images, clearly comic yet not fully ironic or self-conscious, drastically undermines the potential eroticism of the scene.

The question of habit, here, is a complex one. Scopitones don't merely exceed representation, they revel in it. While direct lyrical interpretation might be a habitual practice, the manner in which the Scopitone does so tips beyond custom into absurdity. And the gratuitousness of the Scopitone's representation of femininity is particularly, compulsively banal. There is something bordering on the pornographic in the way in which gender is figured and the way in which all representation in the Scopitone eventually returns to this "home ground," the ur-image, the crotch shot. It is not surprising to learn that film jukeboxes were later recycled to show pornographic films in peep arcades—both formats share very similar modes of address and figure their audiences in very similar positions of immersion and complicit exposure.[44] A further structural resonance exists between the pornographic film and the Scopitone—they are like infinitely repeating jokes that always end with the same punch line. What feels pornographic here, however, is not the exposure of the interiors of the body but the exposure of the tenaciousness of these representational clichés.

I am reminded here of Steven Shaviro's description of the feelings of embarrassment and abjection generated by the comedy of Jerry Lewis. "It becomes more and more apparent," Shaviro writes, "that the subjectivity of Lewis's personas is crudely stereotypical, entirely composed of affects derived from the social realm."[45] Rather than presenting an individualized portrait of "wounded interiority," "the social field of American late capitalism is directly invested by the disintegrative movements of Lewis's physical comedy."[46] Scopitones perform a similar function. Contemporary nods to the Scopitone, as it is referenced in indie rock music videos or featured in screenings at record fairs, treat

Joi Lansing in "Web of Love."

the format with a knowing, ironic gloss.[47] Yet nostalgia and irony act as pro-
phylactics against embarrassment. The viewer is "called out" by the Scopitone
in ways that are difficult to articulate but that involve a particular kind of affective exposure. At the time of their release, the viewer would be interpellated
by the technological interface, particularly when the private selection of a track
was rendered publicly visible. Even in contemporary viewing scenarios, this
calling out extends beyond the individual to engage in a systemic stutter. As
Shaviro notes of Lewis, the Scopitone's affective impact "seems oddly based
on an exaggerated respect for social values and norms, rather than a gleeful
defiance of them."[48] Scopitones do not subvert misogynistic representations,
they *pervert* them through their "excess of zeal." As Deleuze writes about the
masochist, "By scrupulously applying the law we are able to demonstrate its
absurdity and provoke the very disorder that it is intended to prevent or to
conjure."[49] As with Jerry Lewis, the producers of Scopitones most likely did

Joi Lansing captured by the "witch doctor" in "Web of Love."

not approach their projects with a self-conscious will to disrupt systems of power. Nevertheless, the persistent and gratuitous manner in which they reproduce habitual associations denaturalizes and renders visible those social links. That this perversion takes place within the space of the musical moment heightens the capacity for compulsive repetition beyond the framework of narrative recuperation. I also argue that the very specific operations of sound at work in the musical moment heighten the ambiguous positioning of the viewer caught up in this peculiar mode of address.

## Proximity, Distance, and Sound

If the film experience is to be considered an event, the temporal and historical conditions of each encounter will clearly impact the kinds of affective and social assemblages that experience can forge. It is important, in this light, to consider the film jukebox's unusual mode of exhibition. Scopitones did not possess the spontaneity of televised performance programs such as *Shindig,* *Hullabaloo,* and *American Bandstand* (although there is a great deal of similarity between the imagery used in Scopitones and in the prerecorded musical performances sometimes aired on these shows), nor were they remotely similar to feature-length rock-and-roll films. While not exactly a fusion of either of these formats, the Scopitone fell somewhere between them, creating an entirely distinct, more intimate mode of address. Unlike either the television music show or the rock film, the images of the Scopitone figure the individual viewer solidly within the space of the song—not as an anonymous audience member but through the personalized nature of the images and projection apparatus. Scopitone users selected tracks individually and had to stand near the machine to enjoy their purchase. The cinematography imagines a singular viewer as well, since performers always address the camera directly (not to mention the direct address of the up-the-skirt shot). While this experience takes place, paradoxically, in a public space, the individualized fantasy that the Scopitone encourages seems not unlike that of the music video. Although vastly different in their imageries and market appeals, both the Scopitone and the music video position the viewer as the sole recipient of the performance.

Steve Wurtzler characterizes various sound "events" according to a spatial/temporal schema of absence and presence, simultaneity and anteriority.[50] Recorded events, through their spatial and temporal remove, are thus experienced differently than live performances. Yet as Wurtzler is quick to point out, there are numerous events that confuse and collapse these binaries: telephone conversations, live television and radio broadcasts, and lip synching. Moreover, the discursive address of a particular medium may further obscure distinctions between the original and the represented. Television in particular constructs itself according to the parameters of the simultaneous such that even prerecorded material may be experienced as somehow live.[51]

Scopitones do not purport to be live, but they do position themselves at the interstices of the temporal and spatial axes Wurtzler identifies. In this way, the address of the Scopitone correlates to that of the music video. Scopitones and music videos both strive to overcome the repeatability of the reproduction and the public format of the presentation to elicit an intimate and direct connection. The proximity of the microphone to the performer during sound recording works to generate what Rick Altman calls a "for-me-ness" quality, whereby the sound remains direct, close, and at a consistent volume even when the images show the sound source at a distance. The effect is that the sound has been created specifically for the listener, "lending a discursive 'feel' to images that seem to deny discursivity."[52] Whereas in film this recording practice is often used to increase the legibility of dialogue (although it is by no means limited to this purpose), in the freestanding musical short, the consistency and closeness of the music ensure a personal connection with the viewer. At the same time, the stability of the music allows the image to veer into fragmentation and irrationality. As Berland observes about the contemporary music video, "However bizarre or disruptive videos appear, they never challenge or emancipate themselves from their musical foundation, without which their charismatic indulgences would never reach our eyes."[53] Thus, while the images of the Scopitone visualize the music with little spatial or temporal consistency, the music itself works to collapse the distance between listener and event. The Scopitone's visualizations are neither as free nor as seamless as the music video, yet they do rely on this same commingling of abstraction and intimacy. Rather than flights into utter irrationality, however, the misguided contradictions contained within the Scopitone expose the viewer's conflicted position. The seduction of the personalized appeal is undermined by the failure of its realization, forcing each component (image, music, film, viewer, viewing environment) into an uneasy confrontation.

## Impossible Embodiments

One cannot trace a simple historical trajectory between the various filmic and televisual technologies I have touched on here. Nevertheless, critical connections exist between each of these formats in terms of their illustration of popular music. The discomfort elicited by Soundies and Scopitones seems to emerge from their spatial and temporal dislocations. Yet these disorienting qualities point to the very thing that the films seek to accomplish—to achieve presence. With the ubiquity and simultaneity of television and video, the music video does this work in radically different, more effective ways. This shift represents more than an advancement in sophistication, however; it is the evolution of a mode of listening, seeing, and communicating that developed with and through earlier technologies.

The impossibility of embodiment and presence lies at the heart of the work jukebox films perform. As the chapters that follow argue, this is a tension core to the musical moment as a whole. The moments at which the union between sound and image is proved false is the point at which these films, intentionally or not, are the most affecting. The impossibility of the combination, however, extends beyond the rift between body and voice. The social and political implications of each embodiment are also hyperexaggerated, depicting a confluence of elements that feels decidedly false. Jukebox films reflexively, perversely illuminate the associations that "sense and reason" would prefer to leave buried. These habitual representations demand critique, but I argue that at the same time they contain a highly productive tension. The labor of their aspirations is palpable, and their stutterings, even when funny or endearing, are overwhelmingly uncanny. The viewer here is caught up in the films' contradictory modes, hyperconscious of the formal intent yet overwhelmed by an affective surfeit that resonates on an individualized, corporeal level. The failures of these performances, and our fragmented involvement with them, expose a rift in our system of representation. Within the jukebox film, the proliferation of such phantasms may be accidental. But their affective impact, their exuberant, multivalent dissonances, often overpower the simpler, metered melodies these films purport to sing.

# Two

# Dissonant Refrains:
# *Carmen* on Film

Les tringles des sistres tintaient
avec un éclat métallique,
et sur cette étrange musique
les zingarellas se levaient.
Tambours de basque allaient leur train,
et les guitares forcenées
grinçaient sous des mains obstinées,
même chanson, même refrain.

The rods of the sistrums were jingling
with a metallic burst of sound,
and on the strains of this strange music
the gypsy women rose to their feet.
Tambourines kept the rhythm,
and the frenzied guitars
ground away under persistent hands,
the same song, the same refrain.

—GEORGES BIZET, "Chanson Bohème," *Carmen*
(libretto by Henri Meilhac and Ludovic Halévy)

In *A Thousand Plateaus: Capitalism and Schizophrenia,* Gilles Deleuze and Félix Guattari introduce the notion of the ritornello, or the refrain. Using an amalgam of musical, scientific, and philosophical terminology, they expand the definition of the refrain from its colloquial usage to encompass a highly complex phenomenon. On the most basic level, refrains are fragments of sounds, colors, gestures, or other expressive elements that circulate and repeat through individual articulations. These circulations contain temporal facets, marking with each variation a certain duration; yet they also have an involved relationship to space. The refrain becomes a means of *territorialization,* an utterance that delineates a particular territory through its echoes. A bird's song, for example, is a refrain that marks its domain.[1] Refrains can act to constitute a territory across physical distances: a child hums a familiar tune to comfort herself when far from home; folk songs have ties to nations, but they can also create mobile territories of people bound by the refrain that they share (*A Thousand Plateaus,* 311, 347). Refrains may play more specialized functions, defining spaces, actions, and roles. A song shared between lovers marks their bond. Songs sung by workers solidify their labor through a refrain of solidarity. A lullaby becomes a refrain that encloses mother and child in a shared space of safety and love; it marks the territory, Deleuze and Guattari write, of "the child's slumber" (327).

This theorization of the refrain suggests a provocative approach to the question of music and film, in particular the musical genre's penchant for repetition and recycling. Tracing the larger movements of popular music as it is interpreted cinematically opens into even wider refrainlike functions as songs traverse between media and sites of iteration, taking on new associations with each shift. This chapter uses Deleuze and Guattari's refrain as a point of departure for the exploration of one exceptionally complicated series of musical "remakes": adaptations of *Carmen* on film. The refrain as well as Deleuze's broader work on repetition and difference offer a new perspective on the circulations of melody, voice, narrative, and myth that have rendered the tale a rich subject for continued reinterpretation. Unspooled by Prosper Mérimée's novella and further amplified by Georges Bizet's opera, the story of *Carmen* is one of the most familiar and frequently referenced in Western culture. Filmmakers in particular have been drawn to the tale of the seductive Gypsy murdered by her spurned lover, creating at least 110 versions of *Carmen* as of 2005.[2] Tracing *Carmen*'s cinematic refrains becomes an arduous task in the context of this long tradition of reworking. While the strains of Bizet's opera may be the most prominent and identifiable reiterations, one might also point to the recurrences of characters and plot as well as the story's thematic refrains: the exoticism of the Spanish setting; the Gypsy as racialized Other; undercurrents of class, labor, and community; the sexual assertiveness of Carmen; and the seeming inevitability of her death.

The *Carmen* narrative first appeared in 1845, when Prosper Mérimée published the first three chapters of the tale in the travel journal *Revue des Deux Mondes*. As Peter Robinson notes, contemporary readers could have easily failed to identify the story as a work of fiction because its format carefully mimics the tropes of the travel memoir.[3] *Carmen* is framed as the account of an archaeologist who, while doing research in Spain, encounters a mysterious yet compelling outlaw, Don José. Don José's story, which the narrator recounts for the reader, comprises the majority of the text, relayed through this double mediation as the tale unfolds through a series of temporal shifts. Carmen, a powerfully sensual and headstrong Gypsy, has seduced Don José, led him to kill his lieutenant in a fit of jealousy, and persuaded him to abandon his post in the Spanish Army to join her band of Gypsy smugglers. Chapter 3 ends with the narrator visiting Don José before his execution—Don José having been sentenced to death for murdering Carmen after she leaves him for a toreador. A somewhat puzzling fourth chapter was added to the text in 1847, consisting of the narrator's disparaging commentary on the history and culture of the Gypsies.

Georges Bizet's opéra comique version of *Carmen* premiered in 1874 and was a critical and commercial failure in France before his death the following year. Contemporary critics derided the fusion of musical styles at work in the piece: "Spanish," or somehow imagined Orientalist flourishes, popular cabaret music, and the controversial influence of the Wagnerian style.[4] The opéra comique genre itself was composed of conflicting elements, consisting of a mixture of spoken and sung dialogue and more populist subject matter than traditional operas. Composed initially in conjunction with the librettists Ludovic Halévy and Henri Meilhac, the opera *Carmen* makes several significant deviations from the novella. Most important, it removes the figure of the archaeologist and his framework entirely. A female character, Micaëla, Don José's virginal fiancée, is further added as a foil to Carmen. As Susan McClary demonstrates, though the framework of narration is removed from the opera, Bizet composed the work with an equally complex combination of musical styles that reflected a musical commentary on the narrative. Built from a spectrum of high and low references and musical figurations of racial and sexual difference, the opera's score creates an embedded reflection on these characterizations. The opera was much more positively received abroad after Bizet's death in 1875 (reformed in a more traditional recitative version by Ernest Guiraud), its popularity flourishing as its initial dissonances lessened through historical distance.[5]

Echoing outward from these seminal texts, the varied refrains of *Carmen* each reverberate in a fraught and contentious relationship to space. The "exotic" Spanish landscape and the nomadic territory of the Gypsy to which Mérimée and Bizet refer are, as many critics have discussed, more accurately located within the space of the French nineteenth-century imaginary. Carmen's character herself functions as the space on which fantasies of femininity are embodied and rewritten. As these refrains circulate, adapting and evolving to each new setting and retelling, the spaces that they carve out also begin to shift.

Carlos Saura's 1983 film, for instance, maps the descent of a Spanish choreographer whose flamenco version of *Carmen* parallels his real-life obsession with the female lead.[6] MTV's *Carmen: A Hip Hopera* (Townsend, 2001) stars Beyoncé Knowles, Mekhi Phifer, and Mos Def in an urban-contemporary version of the opera in which an aspiring actress defiles a Philadelphia cop, drags him to Los Angeles, and falls in with a top-40 rapper. Mark Dornford-May's *U-Carmen e-Khayelitsha (U-Carmen)* (2005) is set outside of Cape Town, South Africa, and translates Bizet's libretto into Xhosa. It is this process of metamorphosis that makes the repetitions of *Carmen* so fascinating and tangled. How, specifically, do the meanings of *Carmen*'s refrains transform with each retelling? Might a radical restructuring of the story result in the marking out of new territories? Or does the core of the refrain persist, its symbolic and semiotic space remaining ever present within each strain?

What follows is an attempt to map several of the refrains that emerge in *Carmen*'s various embodiments as they open and reverberate from two film versions that dramatically depart from their origins. I first turn to Jean-Luc Godard's 1983 film *Prénom Carmen* and the role music plays in unleashing a myriad of refrains and assemblages. A second section looks at the function of the refrain in the film version of *Carmen Jones* (Preminger, 1954), which transforms Bizet's opera into an all-black musical (using Oscar Hammerstein's "Black English" lyrics) set in the United States in the 1940s. Although far more unified in structure and far less politically progressive, *Carmen Jones* nevertheless engages with refrains in a manner that is intrinsically bound to that of *Prénom Carmen* and to the refrains of *Carmen* in general. I identify several tensions generated by the refrains operating within these works. In each there is a movement between the familiar ground of "home" and the juxtaposition of elements that break new, expressive ground. Each also uses devices that serve to frame the narrative, destabilizing, and at times commenting upon, their own strategies of representation. Finally, the audiences encountering these films are forced to oscillate between positions of pleasurable immersion and formal self-awareness. This last tension is particularly manifest within the films' musical moments; *Prénom Carmen* might be read as an expansion and amplification of the visual-sonic dissonances that *Carmen Jones* set into motion.

## Refrains of Absence and Difference: *Prénom Carmen*

*Prénom Carmen* is, on the surface, one of the least faithful contemporary adaptations of the original tale. Godard quite self-consciously creates a pastiche of elements borrowed from Mérimée, Bizet, and the history of *Carmen*'s various interpretations. The setting for the film is decidedly modern and designed to invite a direct critique of the gender politics of *Carmen*'s originary versions. The title character is a radical leftist terrorist, a politically driven woman whose goals presumably transcend her personal interests. The characterizations in the film as a whole are stylized and two-dimensional. Drawn with deliberate exaggeration, the collisions and interactions between the key players become, at times, outright farcical. While exaggeration and theatricality are central to the operatic form, *Prénom Carmen* seems to focus its attention on the surface of these representational practices, utilizing them to create a new, emotionally convincing account of the *Carmen* story. The structure of *Prénom Carmen,* as is to be expected in a Godard film, becomes a central component in constructing the meaning and subject of the work. Narrative action is continually interrupted by long, extradiegetic shots of the ocean and sequences in which a string quartet rehearses Beethoven. These musical interludes can perhaps be seen as Godard's most irreverent move: Beethoven's quartets, along with a pop song by Tom Waits, come to replace Bizet's music altogether, reducing the latter to an occasional whistle heard on the lips of a passerby.

These factors render *Prénom Carmen* a peculiar subject for a study of the construction of meaning in the larger history of *Carmen* on film. How can questions regarding *Carmen*'s refrains be addressed by a film that intentionally ignores *Carmen*'s primary musical text, its most familiar and predominant chorus? My reasons for taking this approach are threefold. First, Godard's conscious manipulation of the elements of the *Carmen* oeuvre indicates his awareness of their refrainlike function: meaning circulates through snatches of melody, stereotypical characterizations, and operatic dramatizations.[7] The excessive proliferation of these elements in the film makes their significance all the more apparent. Second, the intrusive structure of *Prénom Carmen* highlights the significance of form, both as a meaning-constituting element and as a refrain that is in itself central to the *Carmen* story. Finally, Godard's curious use of music works to foreground the larger function of music within the history of *Carmen*. Music lies at the heart of one of the key Carmenic refrains reverberating throughout *Prénom Carmen:* namely, the complex, often ambiguous representational framework the story relies on and its relationship to the question of difference. Despite Godard's unusual scoring techniques in this film, music and sound provide the very basis for this framework.

The self-conscious intertextuality of *Prénom Carmen*'s larger structure is echoed in the film's narrative. Like many relatively contemporary interpretations of *Carmen* (especially the film versions by Saura, Rosi, and Brook, also released in 1983 and 1984), Godard's engages in a critical reappraisal of both Mérimée's novella and Bizet's opera. Transposed to modern-day France, Carmen is now Carmen X, part of a group of leftist terrorists. Her uncle, Jeannot God-ard, played by Godard himself, is a senile and, in Carmen's words, washed-up filmmaker. She convinces her uncle to help her friends shoot a documentary film, although she later reveals that the film is merely a ruse (capitalizing on the latest video craze) for her gang to kidnap a wealthy businessman.

First, the gang holds up a bank. It is unclear whether the robbery is under-taken in order to fund the film project or the group's larger political goals, goals that are never even vaguely intimated during the course of the film. Joseph is the rather naïve and overenthusiastic guard at the bank who, after a cartoonish shoot-out scene, ends up rolling about on the floor of the bank with Carmen in a passionate embrace. Their affair flourishes when they escape to Uncle Jeannot's beach house. Yet the relationship begins to unravel when they rejoin the gang in Paris, particularly when the well-educated and somewhat elitist leader, Jacques, refuses to allow Joseph to participate. Joseph's anger and alienation build as Carmen herself begins to reject him. His desperation cul-minates in a confrontation with Carmen during the filming/kidnapping attempt in a hotel lobby. It is unclear, in the end, whether Joseph shoots Carmen, she

Maruschka Detmers as Carmen X in *Prénom Carmen* (Godard, 1983).

shoots herself, or in fact if she has been shot at all. She is alive, slumped on the floor, in the last frames of the film, which closes on an almost redemptive note: "What is it called," Carmen asks, "when everything's been lost, but it's daybreak and yet we're still breathing?" A bellboy, attempting to aid her, answers, "It is called sunrise."

These narrative scenes are only one of several major refrains that compose *Prénom Carmen,* each weaving in and out of the other with a slow, deliberate rhythm. Long shots of the ocean and the sounds of crashing waves and sea- gulls punctuate the film, accompanying each other at times or appearing sep- arately, paired with other images or sounds. The narrative action frequently and abruptly cuts to scenes of the string quartet. The musicians pause to argue about technique and rehearse troublesome passages over and over. These inter- jections have a shifting relationship to the plot. They initially, and primarily, appear to be extradiegetic, yet they emerge as intertwined with the various layers of the narrative as the film progresses. The shots of the sea become a refrain for Joseph and Carmen's love after their stay at the beach house—they serve as a reference point, or a return to the safety of that earlier time and place. The viola player in the quartet, Claire, appears in later scenes as Joseph's previous love interest, a somewhat displaced refrain for Bizet's Micaëla char- acter. The scenes with the string quartet perform a shifting, rhythmic function, providing another expressive thread that is woven into the primary narrative itself when the group is hired by the filmmaker/terrorists, providing diegetic accompaniment for the film's climax.

It is critical to note that while these various refrains do in fact prove to be interrelated, the end result is not one of synthesis or integration. Just as soon as one element joins another in a moment of harmonious collaboration, they are interrupted, separating into free-floating sonic and visual elements. Image and sound are continually mismatched: the sounds of the sea in certain scenes overlap shots of characters speaking, at times replacing the audio of their dia- logue entirely. The music played by the quartet, too, accompanies many scenes nondiegetically, serving in some instances to support the action, in others halt- ing abruptly midscene, leaving in its place extended stretches of pure silence.

Structurally, this eccentric combination of image and sound foregrounds the conventions, the arbitrary nature, of their coupling. The characters fre- quently refer to sound. Uncle Jeannot tells Carmen, "We should close our eyes, not open them," as he shows her his new "camera," a portable stereo, which he holds to his ear. Joseph, at one point later in the film, refuses to accept Carmen's rejection, protesting, "That's not you speaking: the sound of the sea was missing."

Godard as Uncle Jeannot, demonstrating his new "camera" in *Prénom Carmen*.

It might thus seem as though the core refrains of *Carmen* have been thoroughly dissipated by Godard's radical dismantling of the story and opera and his utilization of both as the fodder for a more generalized meditation on the nature of sound and image in film. *Prénom Carmen's* unconventional format, however, despite its deviations from Mérimée and Bizet, may engage with *Carmen's* refrainlike mechanisms more directly than more faithful cinematic versions. The concept of the refrain is not limited to the echoes of concrete sounds and images. Beyond the more ephemeral repetitions of narratives, characterizations, and themes, refrains might be more deeply embedded within particular representational strategies. Indeed, the absence of *Carmen's* most familiar and central elements highlights their dynamic and shifting role in *Carmen's* various manifestations. As Phil Powrie notes, *Prénom Carmen's* "significant intertexts . . . conjure up a distant, indeed absent narrative, so that *Prénom Carmen* comes into being only as a palimpsestic gesture which structures the original Carmen narrative as loss."[8] The Carmen narrative, as well as Bizet's music, become a missing refrain that haunts *Prénom Carmen,* a refrain that nevertheless works to define the space of the film through absence.

Moreover, the fragmentary and stuttering quality of the film's multiple registers and references results in a work whose meaning is created through the mobile collisions and recombinations of its various disparate refrains. Although *Prénom Carmen* thus distinguishes itself from more unified renditions of the narrative, it draws attention to the operations of these circulating elements within the *Carmen* oeuvre as a whole.

## Territory and Refrain

It is critical to note that the refrain, as Deleuze and Guattari describe it, is not merely the repetition of certain expressive elements. Repetition is certainly a foundational component of the refrain, but this repetition occurs in relation to wider processes of territorialization. The notion of rhythm is key here, particularly as rhythm operates between various milieus, or "coded blocks of space-time."[9] "There is rhythm," Deleuze and Guattari write, "whenever there is a transcoded passage from one milieu to another, a communication of milieus, coordination between heterogeneous space-times" (*A Thousand Plateaus,* 313). This rhythm is not a literal beating-out of metered time nor the repetition of identical elements. Whereas meter, a coded unit of measure, remains grounded in "a noncommunicating milieu," rhythm is "critical," "it changes direction," operating in the spaces of transition between milieus, bringing different milieus into dialogue with one another (313). Rhythm, in other words, is not the repetition of the same but the production of difference. "A milieu does in fact exist by virtue of a periodic repetition," Deleuze and Guattari explain, "but one whose only effect is to produce a difference by which the milieu passes into another milieu. It is the difference that is rhythmic, not the repetition, which nevertheless produces it: productive repetition has nothing to do with reproductive meter" (314). Periodic repetition thus creates milieus, coding space and time into cohesive blocks, but rhythm is the force that forges connections between divergent milieus.

The act of territorialization, then, arises from the movements of milieus and rhythms, when milieus and rhythms "cease to be functional" and begin to "become expressive" (315). Territories are formed when the codes that have certain functional qualities within one milieu are transcoded—decontextualized, or deterritorialized, in effect—such that they take on new qualitative or expressive qualities, qualities that allow them to mark out new ground. Thus, "the refrain is rhythm and melody that have become territorialized because they have become expressive—and have become expressive because they are territorializing" (317). Deleuze and Guattari draw on the natural world to illustrate this point: the vibrantly colored genitalia of certain primates, for example, take on an expressive function when they are displayed to lay claim to a certain turf (315). Here the functional purpose of the sex organ is transcoded, taking on an expressive role in its engagement with external elements (encounters with individuals from other species or social groups). There is a rhythm to this act—not a literal rhythm, in terms of the beating out of a pattern, but the introduction of expressive difference as a means of negotiating the coincidence of distinct milieus (the space-time of the individual and the space-time of the environment).

This discussion of the refrainlike function of monkey genitalia may seem an odd digression, but the point Deleuze and Guattari make here is key to my discussion of *Carmen.* The frequent references Deleuze and Guattari make to the animal world make it clear that the refrain is not a literal reiteration of a musical motif. The refrain is an act of expression, any act of expression, that creates rhythm and difference between milieus. Music is refrainlike, and many refrains may function with a certain musicality, but that is because they are expressive in nature, they introduce a certain openness and play in their circulations. Thus, the marking out of a territory is not a repressive establishment of a code, a repetition of the same; it is the forging of assemblages between heterogeneous milieus. Within the territory, however, expressive qualities may begin to shift, evolving into stylistic motifs and counterpoints with a certain degree of autonomy, "budding, producing" (325). No longer a placard merely staking out the boundaries of the territory (like the dog that marks his space or the primate who flashes his sign), these autonomous refrains develop their own internal relations, expressive styles further detached from their significatory functions (319). These refrains can, in turn, undergo a process of becoming and deterritorialization. A refrain thus transformed can harness its expressive force to open territories to the outside, branching into new relations and assemblages.[10]

To speak of a refrain in the context of film versions of *Carmen,* then, is not simply a matter of identifying recurring motifs. A refrain in film is an expressive element (in my interpretation, aesthetic, structural, or thematic) that serves to mark out a territory but may, at the same time, resonate in ways that expand or challenge the parameters of that territory, or may even dismantle and take flight from those territorial boundaries. Linda Hutcheon describes cultural and artistic adaptations using both anthropological and biological terminology, models that intersect with Deleuze and Guattari's philosophical project in interesting ways. She speaks of adaptation in one sense as a form of "indigenization," an "intercultural encounter" through which narratives are "nomads" that travel between cultural locales, transmogrifying on the basis of the conditions within these shifting territories, often forming new, hybrid forms of expression.[11] Hutcheon also evokes theories of biological adaptation to speak of processes of "cultural selection," which, like the forces of natural selection, allow for propagation through a complex dynamic "both conservative and dynamic . . . stabilizing and mutating," always in relation to the shifting demands of the external environment (167). The expressive elements within *Carmen*'s various iterations might be similarly read as forces that migrate between shifting territories, occupying varying positions in relation to the codes and demands they encounter, operating at times to reinforce and at others to resist and transform.

Viewing Godard's work through the lens of the refrain offers a new means of reading his expressive strategies. We see in *Prénom Carmen* the collision between distinct territorialized components, brought into a new symphonic assemblage. The intercutting of the string quartet's rehearsals is consistent with Godard's larger body of work in which he repeatedly highlights the means of production and the materiality of film. The bank robbery sequence is exemplary in this regard. The scene opens with Joseph pacing before the bank's entryway, his rifle slung over his shoulder. Beethoven's opus 74 accompanies the scene nondiegetically, until the image abruptly cuts to the Prat Quartet rehearsing the piece.[12] The players break off as one of them remarks that the tone must "be more mysterious," "it develops and then it becomes more tragic." The camera remains trained on the quartet for well over a minute as they begin the passage again, before cutting back to Joseph comically and aggressively hustling pedestrians away from the bank. As the terrorists burst through the door, tackling Joseph, the music periodically pauses and resumes in varying intervals. Joseph chases the gang in a hail of bullets while several of the customers huddle in fear on the floor and others go about their business, oblivious to the chaos. The scene then cuts back to the quartet, with one player insisting, "It must be more violent." They repeat several bars twice, with increasing "violence," and the scene stays with the players for several minutes until they once again break off. "Act, don't ask," Claire intones, and the image returns to Joseph, stumbling over furniture and fallen customers as he searches for the gang within the hallways of the bank. The music has stopped, yet Claire's monologue continues over the image, which cuts back to her several times as she discusses the concept of destiny. Throughout the remainder of the scene, the strains of the music momentarily resume and halt, in varying relationships of contrast and empathy with the image. Joseph engages in an exchange of gunfire with the gang before encountering Carmen X on a staircase. Realizing that both are out of ammunition, they wrestle on the floor for several seconds before fervently groping one another. "Let's get out of here," Carmen says as

Counterpoint between the bank robbery and the musical rehearsal in *Prénom Carmen*.

a female custodian calmly mops up a puddle of blood behind them and shots are fired in the background.

The disruptive cutting in this scene, the comedic theatricality, and the multiple references to the process of production are typical of the film as a whole as well as of Godard's directorial style. More than Brechtian methods of distantiation, however, the self-referential qualities in *Prénom Carmen* transcode and deterritorialize the structural refrains core to the *Carmen* story. Delving into *Carmen's* history, one might locate certain framing devices that recur throughout its multiple incarnations. Mérimée's novella, as mentioned previously, is narrated by a French archaeologist who recounts and critiques Don José's story, adding a lengthy commentary on the Gypsy language and culture. Although Bizet's opera does away with this narrative framework, his musical interpretation of the story adds what we might similarly call a self-reflective metacommentary. In Bizet's initial opéra comique version of *Carmen,* the distancing effect of the collision between speaking and singing draws attention to the work's formal constructs. *Prénom Carmen* repeatedly searches for "the moment that comes before naming," a stage prior to language and the symbolic order.[13] Yet the film pursues this moment through an overwhelming collage of musical and textual references. This self-conscious interrogation of the processes of symbolization and representation echoes those framing strategies in Mérimée and Bizet at the same time that it pushes the project to a new threshold. Evlyn Gould argues:

> Though Godard's film does not use Bizet's score, its unique counterposing of dramatic dialogue and quartets complements the diegetic splicing of shots of ocean waves into the action of the narrative and can only be explained by its renewal, for the modern spectator, of the formal effects of Bizet's original comicopera form. But this form is itself a renewal of Mérimée's fundamentally formal antagonisms cast in what Wayne Koestenbaum has called opera's "queer marriage" of music and words.[14]

For Gould, the thread between the three works is the active role these frameworks force the reader/listener/viewer to engage in, "an oscillating position between identification and resistance."[15] The overt structure of *Prénom Carmen,* while seemingly an utter departure from *Carmen's* foundational texts, in fact reflects the formal core of those works at the same time that it asks its audience to reflect on that tangled web of associations.

## Rhythm and Difference

We might say, then, that Godard has ignored certain of *Carmen's* more immediate and territorializing refrains in favor of those structural refrains that serve a deterritorializing function, creating, in the process, rhythms and counterpoints that destabilize the narrative's established codes. One of the codes that Godard and Anne-Marie Miéville's adaptation challenges most directly has to do with the representation of gender and sexuality.[16] This shift in focus from Mérimée's and Bizet's texts has serious implications in the context of *Carmen's* narrative. Both Carmen X and Joseph are Caucasians, a move that displaces the racial tensions so central to the opera and novella. Although the orientalism of the Spanish setting and the conflicts among the Gypsy workers, the Spanish officers, and the French narrators are removed from *Prénom Carmen,* some of the signifiers of Otherness persist, if in somewhat veiled forms. Maruschka Detmers, the Dutch actress who plays Carmen, has dark features deemed exotic enough to land her roles as diverse as a Hungarian-Jewish freedom fighter in *Hanna's War* (Golan, 1988) and a Cuban American in *The Mambo Kings* (Glimcher, 1992). In *Prénom Carmen,* Detmers is not racially coded in this way, yet her character does stand in stark visual contrast to the fairer Claire, whose conservative clothing and closed body language further differentiate her from the assertive, frequently unclothed Carmen X. Rather than exploring

*Carmen*'s troubling racial politics, this move could be read as leaving those prejudices intact and projecting them onto an equally troubling portrayal of female sexuality. Conversely, one might question whether relocating Carmen to a French setting has a productive potential. While in this instance it obscures the issues of racism and nationalism key to the original story, it does return *Carmen* to the French culture that spawned it, the culture that the story and music, in fact, had far more to do with than the phantom of Spain that they imagine. David Wills makes a compelling argument in this vein, linking the proliferation of *Carmen* films in 1983 and 1984 and the economic and national identity crises occurring within the European community.[17]

Issues of class are raised as well in *Prénom Carmen,* and though they may override race as a subject of inquiry, they do so in ways that provocatively play with *Carmen*'s original hierarchies.[18] Joseph is alienated from the gang because he is from the working class, lacking the education and familiarity with Marxist theory that the terrorists share. His ostracism might be an indictment of the gang's hypocrisy; they openly dismiss the less-privileged Joseph, while the goals of their activities remain entirely ambiguous. Godard is engaging with a thematic refrain that emerges in many of *Carmen*'s manifestations: Don José's position as perpetual outsider, Carmen's centrality to the community of Gypsy outlaws, and the political nature of her defiant sexuality. We see echoes here of both the novella and the opera, where Don José is coerced into joining a smuggling operation that he does not understand. Nevertheless, he is forced to maintain a passive role in their crimes, standing by mutely while Carmen uses her sexuality to secure safe passage of the outlaws and their goods.

Carmen X's ambiguous political position in *Prénom Carmen* appears to be a reworking of Carmen's longstanding role as a figure of resistance. Filmmakers such as Francesco Rosi have foregrounded Carmen's galvanizing role in her community, flaunting her refusal to abide by the rules of an occupying force. In the scene where she is interrogated and arrested after a fight with a fellow factory worker, Carmen (Julia Migenes-Johnson) refuses to respond to the Spanish soldiers who question her. "Cut me, burn me, I'll tell you nothing," she sings, deflecting each question with a "tra la la la."[19] While Bizet wrote this adversarial stance into the opera itself, Rosi figures it as political rather than merely sexual. Throughout the film, Carmen is framed firmly within the collective of the workers, whom Rosi depicts at great lengths in extended group shots as well as close-ups of individuals at work and in their impoverished camp. Here, Carmen appears within a semicircle of fellow female workers, all similarly dressed with their fists on their hips. The sexuality Rosi's Carmen throws in the face of the disdainful soldiers is not meant to seduce but to undermine and mock.

Godard, too, makes the political nature of Carmen's resistance explicit. Yet whereas Carmen's role as representative of the ethnic Gypsy community is fairly well established in the story's earlier incarnations, in *Prénom Carmen,* Carmen X is the central figure for a political group whose mission is contradictory and comically obscure. Joseph, in this context, seems to be the blameless victim of misguided radicals. Carmen X repeatedly calls Joseph "Joe," which he adamantly resists, enacting a tension that is at once a manifestation of Carmen X's sometimes cruel and patronizing attitude toward Joseph and a direct reference to Preminger's *Carmen Jones.*[20] Rather than identifying with Carmen's brave resistance as a political act, the viewer is led to sympathize with Joseph much as earlier audiences might have lamented Don José's fate at the hands of the treacherous band of Gypsies.

But perhaps we are not meant to read Carmen X's defiance in the context of a concrete social community. Carmen X does emerge as a figure of admirable strength, yet her resistance manifests itself most forcefully within the registers of representation, gender, and difference. While issues of race and ethnicity are not explicitly addressed in the film, Godard and Miéville's interrogation of gender is substantial. Carmen X is a mesmerizing and complex character who rarely falls into the role of the fickle-hearted seductress. Although Carmen X's fate in the film is ambiguous, her dialogue and narration throughout provide a direct commentary on the dichotomy of fate/freedom central to the *Carmen* story as a whole.[21] The virgin/vamp duality established in Bizet's opera is further displaced, for despite the visual contrast initially established between the two characters, Carmen X and Claire are almost never presented as rivals. Unlike Carmen and Micaëla, they take the form of parallel voices existing on predominantly distinct narrative registers. Both speak at length, in monologues, about the tension between fate and improvisation, one of the key conflicts that drives the film. In articulating this shared quandary, Claire has more in common with the historian's role in Mérimée's novella than she does with Micaëla; she provides a narrator's commentary on the action that is unfolding.[22] Masculinity, too, is destabilized. Phil Powrie, for example, points to the ways in which Joseph's character operates in a position of ambiguous gender identification, in effect recasting the myth of the femme fatale into one of male desire and masochism.[23]

Rather than exploring these representations in further detail, I put these observations aside to locate the problem of gender difference addressed by the film within the larger economy of difference it interrogates. Within *Prénom Carmen,* the emphasis on difference and the other is realized most clearly in the conflict established between music and image.[24] Sound, that which film traditionally renders subservient to the image, is brought to the forefront in a direct challenge of this hierarchy. Music is not a metaphor for femininity, and femininity does not signify music in any direct way. But each does function as a repeating *refrain* of difference, the unfixed domain of the Other. I argue that this is in fact the refrain most central to the *Carmen* myth: that of difference in the realm of representation.

The question of repetition and difference lies at the heart of Deleuze and Guattari's interest in the refrain, and their examination of the concept centers on the degree to which individual refrains either minimize difference or allow it to flourish unresolved. Looking in this way at the specific function that a repetition performs, they isolate several distinct ways in which the refrain can relate to space. It can, as in the examples of the refrains that work as placards (the primate's genitals, the musical motif that signals the entrance of a character) act to territorialize, inscribe, or fix. Carmen's "Habañera," for example, as McClary has demonstrated, constitutes an incredibly complex ground, one that includes Cuban-style cabaret; bourgeois nineteenth-century notions of the exotic, feminized, hip-swaggering "chromatic excesses"; and the ambiguous space between communal performance and personal expression.[25] With each rearticulation of this refrain, in various venues and mediums, this same ground, more often than not, is reembodied.

Yet there is a certain creative potential that can take hold of the refrain and make it a deterritorializing force. A refrain may be highly determined and grounded, but it will also "bring 'play' to what it composes," opening up into new configurations that transect the space of which it sings (*A Thousand Plateaus*, 336). Many versions of *Carmen* thus utilize the "Habañera" to critically renegotiate questions of community, nationality, gender, and race. Sound and music especially, for Deleuze and Guattari, are able to move between divergent spaces and to elicit affective responses. On the one hand, this accounts for music's tendency toward emotional manipulation (348). On the other, sonorous elements have a greater potential to free themselves from repressive frameworks, to carry us elsewhere. Carried along by the expressive power of the refrain, music can break preexisting configurations open and create, out of that raw material, new ways of seeing, hearing, and thinking.

This notion of a creative play that utilizes the rhythmic power of the refrain to open up new layers of affect and expression reveals much about the way *Prénom Carmen* figures itself in relation to the larger *Carmen* myth. The multiple registers in the film, its polyvocality and abundant intertextual references confront the audience with the raw elements of the *Carmen* laid bare, resonating autonomously from their earlier, functional status. More than a deconstruction, the intense dialogue between refrains found in *Prénom Carmen* can be read as improvised variations that destabilize the link between quotation and source.

The *Carmen* story is founded on a self-conscious interest in representation and difference, from Mérimée's complex narrative framing strategy to Bizet's dramatic collision of musical styles and spoken dialogue. I identify the strains of this kind of framework within *Prénom Carmen* as a structural refrain, one that is manifested most dramatically on a sonic register. The territory these refrains circumscribe is that of representation itself, the representation of difference. David Wills makes this argument when he writes that the music in *Prénom Carmen* becomes "that through which the economy of representation is both articulated and disrupted, inasmuch as it provides a difference against which the visual can define itself while at the same time participating with the visual in the same field of possible representations."[26] Sound and music, which are used in formally similar ways in the film, become a refrain not only for the kind of representational frameworks found in Bizet and Mérimée but also for that which is continually elided, dominated, and contained through the process of representation.[27]

This, I argue, is the primary motivation for Godard's use of Beethoven's quartets as opposed to Bizet's opera. Unlike the dramatic form of the opera, which utilizes highly coded signifiers for gender and race, the quartets cannot be definitively linked to particular characters or traits.[28] This is not to say, of course, that Beethoven's music, in its nonnarrative and nontheatrical form, is free from political implications. It is to say, however, that the *use* of Beethoven in *Prénom Carmen* functions entirely differently from the use of Bizet's opera. Music in *Prénom Carmen* does not signify directly but points instead to the very *weight* of signification music is forced to bear in film.

What becomes provocative about the repetition of refrains in this instance is the manner in which each element has become dislocated from any direct representational relationship. Unlike simpler refrain functions, such as the bird song, here the refrain functions as a floating element that frees itself (to varying degrees) from its traditional, fixed associations and begins to form new meanings and associations as it adheres to and interacts with other elements and refrains. The distinction to be made here is that the refrain does not serve as a simple placard for a particular territory. Instead, it becomes part of a process of transformation and transcoding. Again, this is not to say that these elements become dehistoricized or depoliticized, utterly removed from their original contexts. Their emotive impact arises from the foundation of those rich historical associations. Yet each reiteration of the refrain works to decode and decontextualize established meanings and modes of representation. The originary meanings do not disappear, but through the variations of each recurrence, they become open to interrogation and heighten the potential for new associations, combinations, and meanings.

Godard's use of Beethoven's work is particularly significant in this regard.[29] The reception and categorization of Beethoven has been the subject of fierce debate and has undergone significant historical shifts. Beethoven's late string quartets, Godard's primary source in this film, were regarded by many of Beethoven's contemporaries as dissonant and fragmentary deviations from his earlier work, and he received a great deal of criticism for abandoning the classical tenets of unity and reason. He was later embraced as the creative progenitor of the Romantic movement, his late string quartets being viewed as intensely private works that experimented with form and expression in radical new ways. Musicologists of the early twentieth century, however, went to great lengths to disavow Beethoven's romanticism, rooting his work in the eighteenth-century tradition by pointing to the influences of Haydn and Mozart and to the persistence of classical forms such as the sonata.[30] More recently, theorists have addressed both tendencies within Beethoven from a variety of interdisciplinary perspectives. Feminist musicologists have elaborated on the violent movements of his compositions and the associations they have accrued in their cultural recyclings.[31] The late string quartets have also been read through the lenses of semiotics and postmodernism.[32]

The circulations of both Beethoven's music and the commentary it has generated are salient here in two key ways. First, within Beethoven's later compositions, there is a formal tension between fragmentary, deconstructing references and a movement toward reunification. Second, that Beethoven's work has served as a perpetual site of contention and critical reevaluation foregrounds the roles of interpretation and reading as central processes in the experience of works of art. Responses to Beethoven's work, through their interrogation of Beethoven's influences and his dissonant, expressive tendencies, throw into question conceptions of originality and creativity in the artistic process. In essence, these debates engage with what we might call the refrain, the resurfacing of themes and influences, the modes of reception they demand from their audiences, their deviations and flights into new territories, or conversely, their synthesis and ultimate return to the same ground.

The history of the reception and recycling of Beethoven might thus be read as partially analogous to that of *Carmen*. A particularly rich point of correlation might be drawn between the complex relations among dramatic, literary, and musical texts found within both Beethoven and *Carmen*. Leon Botstein argues that shifts in the reception of music in nineteenth-century Vienna led audiences to become increasingly reliant on secondary texts and guidebooks in their listening practices. The former "impenetrability" of Beethoven's late quartets gave way to their rediscovery, when they "assumed special stature as secret, opaque, and visionary objects requiring special extramusical commentary."[33] He further locates the late quartets within nineteenth-century dramatic traditions, hypothesizing that they may "have been impelled explicitly by so-called extramusical narrative impulses."[34] Christopher Reynolds similarly discusses the nineteenth-century practice of providing textual accompaniment to a musical work, verbal visualizations that were provided either by the composer or an outside interpreter. While textual annotations of music had fallen out of favor by the twentieth century, contemporary filmic interpretations of Beethoven have reinvigorated, for Reynolds, "a metaphorical way of hearing related to that which flourished in the nineteenth century":

> Indeed film, with its operalike dependence on music to convey, create, or comment on aspects of the drama, is the most active heir to a metaphorical mode of expression and hearing that once linked composition and criticism. . . . Whether for Berlioz and Wagner or Kubrick and Godard, artistic reuse of canonical works takes part in defining the reception of those works, no less than more obvious forms of criticism.[35]

The tension between text and music, composition and criticism, that Botstein and Reynolds locate within the late quartets resonates equally well with Mérimée's novella, Bizet's opéra comique, and Godard's film. Each of these tensions I would identify as having a refrainlike function. Most significant is the tension within the refrain between the mobile expression unleashed by each articulation and the grounded cultural spaces to which each chorus refers. Echoing Reynolds, I further argue that the recycling of refrains works not only to transform that space but also, potentially, to critically interrogate it. While each of the works discussed here might engage with this collage of contradiction differently, with different degrees of resolution, it is difficult to deny that each demands a new mode of seeing and listening.

Schubert's criticism of Beethoven in a diary entry could easily be read as a contemporary response to Godard; he derides the "eccentricity which joins and confuses the tragic with the comic, the agreeable with the repulsive, heroism with howlings and the holiest with harlequinades, without distinction."[36] Each permutation of *Carmen* might likewise evoke such dissonant collisions, and *Prénom Carmen* seems particularly attuned to the implications of these juxtapositions, utilizing them in ways that draw attention to their representational strategies. Its jarring structure might not free itself entirely from the ground that Carmen sings, yet its active engagement with the viewer throughout these various oscillations carries each refrain beyond the realm of mere repetition. "To improvise," Deleuze and Guattari write, "is to join with the World, or meld with it" (*A Thousand Plateaus,* 311).

## Sutured Bodies and Metered Rhythms: *Carmen Jones*

To return to the questions posed in the introduction of this chapter, it seems that the refrain does contain a productive potential to open into new territories. Yet as Deleuze himself remarks, this potential is rarely actualized. If it is far more common for cinematic refrains to become reterritorialized or codified, how might this theory be of use when dealing with works that are less self-conscious than *Prénom Carmen?* And how are we to understand the relationship between works that creatively resituate refrains and those that remain stereotypical or grounded? Are there ways in which even those refrains that circulate within fixed territories might be read in more complex or nuanced terms?

Otto Preminger's *Carmen Jones* provides a stark contrast to *Prénom Carmen.* After exploring the critical rhythms created by Godard's film, one might find *Carmen Jones* a curiously conservative example. Yet there are a number of links that suggest a deeper connection between the two works, the most obvious being Godard's well-documented admiration of Preminger. Godard has cited *Carmen Jones* as the inspiration for Miéville and himself when writing *Prénom Carmen,* and the film is loaded with quotations and scenarios culled from Preminger's adaptation.[37] Throughout his career as a critic and filmmaker, Godard has expressed his affinity for Preminger, so this connection is, on the one hand, not entirely surprising. On the other hand, given *Carmen Jones's* significance as a pop opera starring an all–African American cast, that Godard's improvisation on the film should sidestep questions of race and ethnicity is somewhat perplexing. And given Godard and Miéville's shared radical politics, their unqualified embrace of *Carmen Jones,* a work that has been critiqued for its problematic representations of race, is also puzzling.[38]

My objective is to explore the operation of various refrains within *Carmen Jones* and their resonances with *Prénom Carmen* and the *Carmen* oeuvre as a whole. The racial politics of *Carmen Jones,* particularly when viewed with historical hindsight, are deeply flawed and have been the subject of criticism both at the time of the film's release and in subsequent scholarship. While acknowledging the centrality of these politics to the entire project of the film, I would like to also consider the ways in which the refrain might complicate our understanding of *Carmen Jones* and its peculiar affectivity. This is not to excuse the film from political culpability; I argue that *Carmen Jones*'s refrains bring it into direct dialogue with *Carmen*'s long and troubled political history. Nevertheless, it is to suggest that *Carmen Jones* presents an atypical manifestation of these refrains and that its representational strategies are more complex than they might initially appear. Indeed, the unusual staging of the film highlights questions of identity, embodiment, and the limitations of signification; these are the questions, I argue, that provide the most direct link between Preminger's and Godard's cinematic projects and to *Carmen*'s foundational refrains.

Although the film version of *Carmen Jones* has typically been studied outside of Preminger's larger filmography—it is most often critiqued in terms of its representation of race or as an example of a *Carmen* remake—the operations of the film takes on new significance when read in the context of Preminger's style. This film shares with many of his other works a strange melding of realism and theatricality, a controversial social history, and a mobile visual perspective that masks more than it reveals. Otto Preminger is an enigmatic filmmaker whose reputation has been historically unstable. He was praised by critics at *Cahiers du Cinéma* in the 1950s and 1960s and was subsequently taken up as a key example of an American auteur. Yet Preminger's films encompass a diverse range of styles and subject matter, making it difficult to distill a clear directorial consistency in his work. Even Andrew Sarris has remarked on the lack of thematic cohesiveness in Preminger's work; Sarris cites as a connecting thread instead a certain "coldness" in Preminger's tone, his use of a seemingly objective point of view, and his resistance to montage.[39]

This sense of a tonal objectivity has in some ways inhibited critical scholarship on Preminger. John Orr notes that the pioneering qualities within Preminger's films (particularly his challenges to the Production Code) are muted by his "style of invisible narration, which downplays its innovating force at the edge of classicism."[40] Preminger's narrative transparency manifests itself in the fluid and seemingly objective movements of his camera, which glides throughout the various spaces of the diegesis, creating an unbroken sense of continuity. The disembodied omniscience of this roving eye, which skims the surfaces of the mise-en-scène, may contribute to the perception of Preminger as aloof. Jacques Rivette, in his review of *Angel Face* (1952), isolates a critical dimension of this technique:

> If half the action remains a mystery, it is rather that the solution offered by the logic of the narrative has no correspondence with the emotions aroused: an interest outside that of the plot continually rivets our attention on the gestures

of characters whose images at the same time prove to us the lack of any real depth. Yet it is depth they aspire to, depth of the most artificial kind, since it does not come from the suspect, questionably subtlety of human beings, but from art itself, from the use of every means that the cinema offers the filmmaker.[41]

This tension is foundational to Preminger's style. His films are crafted with a penetrating attention to narrative space, moving effortlessly from interior to exterior. Yet depth, here, is an artifice. Within Preminger's work, the logic of the narrative space is often overpowered by the excesses of gesture, performance, and surface-level expressions of the cinematic form.

I suggest that this tendency in Preminger's style taps into one of *Carmen*'s key refrains—a self-conscious commentary on acts of narration and on the interconnections of body, space, and identity. Preminger's floating perspective engages with the refrainlike function of cinematic strategies of representation and in doing so presents a veiled commentary on claims to depth, and to truth, made by many culturally sanctioned modes of discourse (*Anatomy of a Murder* [1959] is exemplary in this regard). The penetration of space enacted by his mise-en-scène creates a communication between milieu, blocks of space and time, that are usually separated. Read in this context, certain images in *Carmen Jones* that, in isolation, appear painfully stilted or off-key might be the result of a collapsing of disparate discourses and representational spaces. And those elements in the film that register as discordant or false—in particular, the unharmonious clash of voice, music, body, and staging—might serve to both echo and amplify similar discordant themes in the larger history of the *Carmen* tale.

This is not to say that *Carmen Jones* is a wholly self-conscious, critical text or that Preminger was masking purely progressive views within the guise of stereotypes. Despite his progressive political intentions, Preminger's perspective was clearly limited, and the film is rife with racist characterizations. My second key assertion regarding *Carmen Jones* is that a great deal of tension exists in the film that exceeds directorial intentionality. Some of this tension may be accidental or the manifestation of historical and political tensions within the film's images. A tension is present here, too, between the objectives and styles of the various participants involved in the film's creation. The performances of the actors on-screen and of the vocalists off-screen, for instance, are viscerally at odds with the authorial voices of the script and of the staging. What we find in *Carmen Jones* is an irresolvable collision of artistic and cultural refrains. This disharmony places the viewer on unstable ground, shifting between identification and resistance—the experience is contradictory, disturbing, and deeply affecting.

## The Adaptations of *Carmen Jones*

Oscar Hammerstein II's *Carmen Jones* premiered on the stage in 1943. Hammerstein's book brings *Carmen* to an all-black air force base in the rural southern United States, translating Bizet's lyrics into a particular version of colloquial "Black English" that primarily takes the form of a preponderance of "des," "dises," and "dats." The role of Don José is rewritten as Joe (played in Preminger's 1954 film version by Harry Belafonte), a private who is training to become a pilot. Joe is engaged to Cindy Lou (Olga James), a sweet and naïve girl from his small hometown who, as Joe sings, talks "jus' like my maw." Carmen Jones (Dorothy Dandridge), a worker at the base's parachute factory, is a hotheaded temptress prone to superstitions and wild behavior who quickly sets her sights on Joe. Joe arrests her after a fight with a coworker, yet she deftly seduces him on the way to the civilian jail and runs away while he sleeps. Joe is imprisoned for failing to obey orders and, after his release, beats his commanding officer unconscious in a fight over Carmen at a juke joint. To avoid punishment, he and Carmen flee to Chicago along with several of Carmen's friends (Pearl Bailey and Diahann Carroll) and the wealthy prizefighter Husky Miller (Joe Adams), who has designs on Carmen. Joe is forced to remain hidden in a squalid one-room apartment and soon becomes jealous of Carmen's movements around town. Carmen, in turn, feeling suffocated by her relationship with Joe, is also contending with the pursuits of Miller and the pleas of her friends to give in to his advances, their only insurance for remaining on Miller's bankroll. After having her violent death predicted in a card reading, Carmen submits to Miller, seeing this as her last hope for freedom and escape. Joe hunts her down in a backroom at the arena where Miller is boxing and strangles her when she refuses to return to him.

The racial politics of this project are troubling to say the least. Although Hammerstein, and later Preminger, purported to create a thoroughly contemporary American version of *Carmen,* they did so by appealing to stereotypical associations of African Americans with violence, naïveté, sexuality, physicality, and "natural" affinities for rhythm and music. Hammerstein's lyrics are particularly off-putting and mesh rather unconvincingly with Bizet's score, which is left primarily intact, if segmented and reordered. Carmen's signature "Habañera," for instance, becomes "Dat's Love," with lines such as "Love ain't nobody's angel chile" and "If I love you, dat's de end of you." By recasting the work with an entirely black cast, *Carmen Jones* finds itself in a predicament similar to that of *Prénom Carmen,* having vacated the narrative of the internal racial conflicts it originally highlighted. The segregated vision of America presented in *Carmen Jones* verges on the preposterous when even the scenes of urban streets and boxing arenas in Chicago fail to show a single white face.[42]

Perhaps the most suspect move the film makes is to replace the voices of the majority of the performers with those of classically trained singers. Billy Rose, who produced the musical on Broadway and orchestrated the film deal with Preminger, faced a great deal of resistance from Georges Bizet's estate in relation to both the film and stage productions of the musical. The central problem for the estate lay with the quality of the singing voices. As Jeff Smith observes, "Bizet's estate had no problem with African-American performers or with Hammerstein's approximation of a Negro folk dialect as long as the performers did not sound like African-American singers but adhered to the more 'universal' standards of classical vocal performance."[43] This contradictory requisition, which presented Rose with enormous dilemmas in terms of *Carmen Jones*'s production, points to the irresolvable confluences of high and low cultures within *Carmen* and the particularly convoluted racial politics of this version. Although the transplanting of the opera to a rural, segregated African American setting posed no threat to *Carmen*'s standing as a canonical work (a status that the opera had now achieved in spite of its controversial beginnings), the vocal performance of Bizet's score needed to maintain its operatic integrity for the project to have any legitimacy.

Despite the fact that Dandridge and Belafonte were highly accomplished performers in their own right, their voices were replaced in the film version by Marilyn Horne and LeVern Hutcherson. The rationale for this decision was that the rigors of the operatic style demanded professionally trained voices. Yet as Susan McClary points out, the singing voices in the film often seem to deviate somewhat from the perfect operatic form, sounding less full and less precise than in other performances. "It is as if Horne, who was brought in to sing a part presumably beyond the capabilities of the black actress, were trying to produce a sound quality she identified with untrained singers, so as to give the illusion of authenticity."[44] Marsha Siefert notes that Diahann Carroll and Harry Belafonte later produced recordings of the songs from *Porgy and Bess* (1959), another Preminger film in which the images of African American actors were accompanied by the voices of classical singers, suggesting that the justification for this displacement has less to do with musical ability and more to do with providing voices that were less overtly "ethnic" and more palatable to white audiences.[45]

*Carmen Jones*, as such, is a highly contradictory film. It amplifies *Carmen*'s key refrains (female sexuality, race, class, community) as they are woven into Bizet's musical motifs. Yet the segregationist casting, the stereotyped lyrics, and the substitution of voices work to obscure critical engagement with these themes, pushing them beneath the surface to create a fusion of high and low that rings false on a number of levels. Jeff Smith describes the contemporary experience of watching *Carmen Jones* as one of "cultural schizophrenia," referring to the unsuccessful resolution of the film's multiple levels of contradiction: "The film feels stuffy where it should be loose, measured where it should be swinging, note-perfect where it should be improvisatory."[46] This conflicted experience is triggered by the film's many clashing juxtapositions: folksy speech spilling into operatic musical numbers, excessively colloquial lyrics coupled with Bizet's familiar compositions, and black actors singing with voices that are coded "white."

It is difficult to determine whether, or to what degree, this schizophrenia is the result of an intentional artistic decision or is a reflection of the cultural climate from which it emerged. The conflicting interests involved in the production of the film certainly contributed to the maelstrom, as Preminger was forced to contend with restrictive demands from multiple parties. United Artists rejected Preminger's pitch for the film, doubting the financial viability of a film with an all–African American cast. The film was funded through an agreement between Preminger's own production company and Twentieth Century Fox; the budget for the project was extremely low for a musical, and Darryl Zanuck retained the right to approve the script and final edit.[47] Throughout the production, the film was challenged on numerous counts by the Production Code Administration, namely, for its "lustfulness" and its failure to assert a "voice for morality."[48] While Preminger was able to win most of these battles, he did make other concessions. According to Harry Belafonte, Preminger agreed to the use of operatic voice doubles as a means of "appeasing" the Bizet estate and securing the rights for European distribution (an attempt that ultimately failed).[49] As critics such as Jeff Smith have argued, this explanation for the use of substituted voices in the film fails to fully address both the selective use of substitution and the racially coded ways in which this substitution took place. It is nevertheless clear that the production of *Carmen Jones* was fraught with economic, industrial, and cultural conflicts, all of which are manifest in the film's construction.

While the inscrutable nature of *Carmen Jones* is in part a result of these demands, there is evidence that Preminger actively sought to integrate various versions of the *Carmen* text into his film, expanding the frame of reference from Hammerstein's stage version. In his adaptation of *Carmen Jones* to the screen, Preminger made drastic changes to the text; in his autobiography, he describes excising all of Hammerstein's text other than the lyrics and returning to Mérimée's novella as the basis for his script. He chose to reject as well the narrative formula of the musical film. "I had decided to make a dramatic film with music," he writes, "rather than a conventional film musical."[50] His goal, as such, was not to replicate the stage version or to adhere to the conventions of the musical genre, but rather to create a dialogue with *Carmen's* earlier refrains. Given Preminger's directorial style, one that addresses social conflict from the remove of an "objective" perspective, one might argue that his return to Mérimée, at the expense of Hammerstein's play or Meilhac and Halévy's libretto, has to do with a shared interest in providing a mediated reflection on strategies of narration and representation.

Preminger's *Carmen Jones* does not contain an explicit framing device, but it is rooted in a theatrical and overtly artificial musical style, one that stands in direct opposition to the unromantic grounding of the story in the dusty yard of the air force base and in the claustrophobic interiors of Chicago. We witness here one of Preminger's own refrains—the melding of a stylized mode of presentation with intrusions of the real. Dandridge's performance of "Dat's Love," for instance, takes place within the base's cafeteria, where the parachute workers and servicemen mingle. The familiar strains of Bizet's "Habañera" resonate strangely with Hammerstein's colloquial lyrics ("If I love you that's the end of you"). Dandridge is unrealistically styled in a tight red skirt and low-cut black blouse; her makeup and the colors of the outfits of her coworkers are surreally saturated. Yet as she moves about the cafeteria, the banal action of that space continues uninterrupted, with people eating and lining up at the cash register. The camera moves fluidly, following her as she picks up her tray, fills

Dorothy Dandridge in *Carmen Jones* (Preminger, 1954).

a coffee cup from an industrial-sized urn, and collects her meal ticket—in a speaking voice, she even pauses to order a chicken sandwich between verses. Preminger sets a surprising amount of the film on location. "Dere's a Café on de Corner" (the "Seguidilla" in Bizet's opera) takes place in a moving jeep, shifting first to a dramatic chase across the flatbeds of a moving train and then to the dust beside the tracks, where Belafonte wrestles Dandridge into submission. In other numbers, the sounds of the "natural" environment intrude on the aural space of the song. During Olga James's "My Joe," for example, we faintly hear the traffic and the people on the street who surround her.

There is a second tension struck in the film among the "real," affective issuance of the human voice in song, the highly visible bodies that visually perform this voice, and the clearly artificial and unconvincing bond that is asserted between them. Whether this disconnect was created consciously or unconsciously, the impact is uncanny. The misalignment of voice and body in *Carmen Jones* taps into one of *Carmen*'s most significant refrains: the artificiality and unreliability of the voice that narrates, speaks, and names. A double failure occurs in this articulation: the impossibility of speaking for oneself and the impossibility of representing the Other. Mérimée's *Carmen* is mediated by an archaeologist-narrator conducting historical research on Spain, and the final coda presents a vicious catalog of characteristics associated with Gypsy culture. In both instances, the narrator explicitly strains to find the language with which he can describe a people and a territory. The final coda, in particular, registers as an attempt to contain and diffuse the power of Carmen's story but one that fails miserably. No objective study of customs or the etymology of Gypsy slang can account for the affective power that the readers have encountered in the previous chapters. Mérimée makes it clear that those who seek to speak, who seek to represent, are unable to fully contain the stories that they relate and always are at risk of tipping over into the realm of the unknowable. He ends the final chapter of the story with a Gypsy proverb that serves, simultaneously, as a warning: "A closed mouth, no fly can enter."[51]

The mismatching of artifice and reality and of image and sound in Preminger's film performs a similar function. In each instance, we can identify a failure of narration. Voices (directorial, and musical) seek to name and to affix meaning. Each invokes an established language (generic formulas, conventions of cinematography and musical composition, character types, codified styles of vocal expression). Yet the representational conventions fail to adhere; they stutter. The strain of producing these effects, the labor of representation, is rendered visible. And the political power differential inherent to this process is also brought to light.

Indeed, the very act of vocal expression can be seen as an exercise in power. To speak is to assert, to command, and to claim. The voice acts; this power is reflected in our references to the "voice of authority." Yet the voice exists in a distinct realm from language (the "content" of vocal speech) and its position in relation to the body of the speaker is both diffuse and ephemeral. In his study of vocality, Mladen Dolar suggests that the voice creates an ontological crisis in its collapsing of interior and exterior:

> The voice cuts both ways: as an authority over the Other and as an exposure to the Other, an appeal, a plea, an attempt to bend the Other. It cuts directly into the interior, so much so that the very status of the exterior becomes uncertain, and it directly discloses the interior, so much so that the very supposition of an interior depends on the voice. So both hearing and emitting a voice present an excess, a surplus of authority on the one hand and a surplus of exposure on the other. . . . *One is too exposed to the voice and the voice exposes too much.*[52]

This double excess, the excess of authority and the excess of the interior exposed in the process, relates to the intermediary position the voice occupies between language and the body. For Dolar, the excesses revealed here are in fact the "cumbersome remainder" of signification. The musical moments in *Carmen Jones* reveal a similar significatory excess. By rendering the voice strange, artificial, and disembodied, Preminger compels it to reveal more than it could in a naturalized depiction. What the voice reveals here are the limits and the failures of representation.

What we find in *Carmen Jones* are hybrid, multifaceted modes of expression, voices, functioning on a range of registers (the cinematic, the musical, the gestural, the linguistic). These voices each draw on a wide range of representational refrains—refrains that include *Carmen*'s own historical repetitions as well as a larger history of representations of race and gender and of narrative and genre. Many of these refrains appear bent on asserting a territory, in particular codified notions of African American culture and music, of the black body and of gender and sexuality. Yet the articulation of these refrains falters as they transect with new milieus—they resonate dissonantly and, in doing so, make plain their own operational strategies. And many of these refrains are articulated via the ambiguous and power-laden excesses of the human voice. The various voices in the film (the literal human voices, the cinematic, the authorial) begin to take on an autonomous expressive quality removed from their significatory function—they begin to map out a new, hybrid territory. Nowhere is this dissonance more apparent than in the film's musical moments.

## Performing Playback: The Excesses of the Voice

Many critics have described the problematic use of *dubbing* in *Carmen Jones,* but this is a technical misnomer. While dubbing is the process by which voices are recorded in postproduction to match the flow of movements on the image track (particularly those of the actors' lips), playback requires that actors synchronize their actions to prerecorded music. Nearly all musical films utilize playback during production, and *Carmen Jones's* musical numbers, too, were recorded in advance of the shooting.[53] This is not to nitpick over semantics. The aesthetics of playback are central to my argument for several reasons. First, in understanding the racial politics of *Carmen Jones,* it is significant to note that the bodies of the black actors were forced to mold themselves around preexisting voices—a scenario that is far different from one in which singers synchronize their voices to the movements of the actors.[54] Second, the implications of playback as a practice extend to all musical films; playback, and the inherent schism it creates between voice and body, tells us something crucial about the operations of the musical film in general. This is not in any way to minimize the extraordinarily troubling politics of *Carmen Jones* and films that made similar racially motivated vocal substitutions. It is to suggest, rather, that the relationship between the voice and the body in musicals is anything but natural. On the one hand, the status of the voice within the musical number, situated within the orchestral track and recorded in impossibly close proximity, frees the body from the constraints of producing that voice; it can dance, leap, and transcend the constraints of the physical world. On the other hand, this separation renders the body highly substitutable and replaceable.[55]

Playback is de rigueur in all musicals, as it would be next to impossible to record a quality vocal performance synchronously, let alone with orchestral accompaniment. Despite the obvious artificiality of the musical's production numbers, there is nevertheless an aura of legitimacy that binds image to voice, regardless of their origins on separate recordings. Michel Chion describes our affective response to all audiovisual synchronization as "synchresis": "the spontaneous and irresistible weld produced between a particular auditory phenomenon and visual phenomenon when they occur at the same time."[56] The connection we make between simultaneous images and sounds occurs "independently of any rational logic"; our brains process these elements as continuous no matter how impossible the combination.[57] We might draw a correlation between the idea of territorialization and the grounding of voices to bodies in film, what Chion, following Marguerite Duras, calls the "nailing-down" of a voice to an image of a body. For Chion, this fixing reflects an ideological attempt on the part of mainstream cinema to mask the "seams" wrought through the process of production, the inevitable severing of the voice from the body during the recording and filming process, and the sutures of their rejoining via two separate tracks.[58] We thus link a voice with the person represented on screen, even when we intellectually know that this particular body did not produce this voice, or at the very least it did not produce it as we hear it. All musicals, and in fact all films, rely on our conditioned response to this phenomenon. The issue in *Carmen Jones* is clearly one of the political ramifications of replacing the voice of the body pictured, particularly when the replacement voice belongs to a body of a different race or is styled to sound as if that is the case.

The success of synchresis, in instances where playback is involved, depends on a visible, physical act of labor. Indeed, the conflicted responses that *Carmen Jones* elicits seem linked to the palpability of this labor within the musical moments in the film. Distinguishing the practice of playback from dubbing, Chion writes:

> In dubbing, someone is hiding in order to stick his voice onto a body that has already acted for the camera. In playback there is someone before us whose entire effort is to attach his face and body to the voice we hear. We're witnessing a performance whose risks and failures become inscribed on the film. No emotion arises from dubbing as such. . . . Playback is a source of a direct, even *physical* emotion. . . . Playback marshals the image in the effort to embody.[59]

The body, which becomes a puppet, labors toward a unity that is ultimately impossible. The gap, and the body's physical struggle to surmount it, offer a drama of intense conflict, desire, and thwarted identification. Given the fraught political nature of the embodiments performed in *Carmen Jones,* this labor becomes all the more poignant and disconcerting.

Joe's "Flower Song" scene, rewritten as "Dis Flower," presents a typical example. Joe pauses while working with a roadside crew, punishment for allowing Carmen to escape his custody, to contemplate the flower she gave him. The scene is set outside, near a body of water; the surface of the water ripples, and wildflowers and grasses shift in the wind throughout the performance. This outdoor setting, which registers as real for the viewer, is denaturalized by the intrusion of Hutcherson's operatic voice and its orchestrated accompaniment. Belafonte's voice, one quite familiar to contemporary viewers, is disturbingly absent. Yet his highly visible body, shirtless and glistening with sweat, works to perform the unfamiliar voice that it ghosts. Each breath the voice takes is amplified through Belafonte's visible, labored miming of it. The scene vacillates between hollowness, where the soaring voice seems at complete odds with the

Harry Belafonte in *Carmen Jones.*

image, and genuine emotiveness, where Belafonte's talent and charisma seem to harness and make use of the voice that is thrust upon him.

Throughout the film, it is significant to note that Belafonte and Dandridge perform both as actors and as listeners who carefully time their movements based on the nuances of the voices they, and we, hear. We encounter, as such, the double excess that Dolar identifies in the voice, the excess of authority that is imposed from the speaker and the excesses of the interior that are exposed in the process. Belafonte and Dandridge at once are subject to the voice that enters from the outside and become the visual, corporeal vehicle through which that interiority is registered. Yet there is also a register upon which their performances challenge the assertions of authority and amplify the discord hidden within it. As Dolan argues, the listener has a certain "power to decide over the fate of the voice and its sender; the listener can rule over its meaning or turn a deaf ear."[60] The voice of the speaker, too, tips its own hand. "It brings out more, and other things, than one would intend."[61] The vacillations between embodiment and distance in the "Dis Flower" scene or in Dandridge's "Dat's Love" may reflect an active movement between resistance and engagement. The lyrics of "Dat's Love" invoke doubly coded racial and gender stereotypes. As in the "Habañera," "Dat's Love" suggests that a woman in the throes of love is untamed, fickle, and drawn to those men who mistreat her. Her affections will spell certain death for their recipient. Yet as Dandridge moves her mouth and body around Horne's voice, commanding the visual space of the cafeteria and controlling the gaze of the camera, the song is imbued with both a defiant forcefulness and an empathetic vulnerability. Dandridge, through her gestures, changes the meaning of the prewritten words her body appears to speak. It is important to acknowledge here, too, the interpretive dimension added to these performances by Hutcherson and Horne, both extraordinarily talented vocalists who serve as critical speakers/listeners engaging with *Carmen*'s refrains.

The voices in *Carmen Jones* thus reveal excesses of meaning. These voices include not only the sonic and gestural voices of the performers but the authorial voices of the filmmakers that speak through them. Rick Altman uses the concept of ventriloquism to describe the general relationship between image and sound in narrative film:

> The sound track is a ventriloquist who, by moving his dummy (the image) in time with the words he secretly speaks, creates the illusion that the words are produced by the dummy/image whereas in fact the dummy/image is actually created in order to disguise the source of the sound. Far from being subservient to the image, the sound track uses the illusion of subservience to serve its own ends. . . . Cinema's ventriloquism is the product of an effort to overcome the sound-image gap, to mask the sound's technological origin, and to permit the film's production personnel to speak their sub-conscious mind—their belly—without fear of discovery.[62]

For Altman, sound uses the image ideologically, obscuring its own means of production by presenting a (false) visual source to the viewer. He further attributes a psychological dimension to this doubling or projection. Sound and image act as mirrors for one another, mirrors that, in their struggle to present an illusion of unity, reflect that which is repressed in the opposing track. This model resonates with readings of *Carmen Jones* as technological blackface, where the singers and the librettist "black up" their voices, using the silenced black bodies of the actors as their front.[63]

Curiously, however, the substitution of voices in *Carmen Jones* was not applied across the entire cast; most notably, Pearl Bailey and Olga James sang in their own voices. As Jeff Smith notes, this decision undermines the rationale for replacing the lead voices in the film. Olga James was a classically trained opera singer, so her voice was continuous with the white operatic voices, yet Pearl Bailey's was not.[64] Smith argues that Bailey and her one solo number, "Beat Out Dat Rhythm on a Drum," "bear the burden of *Carmen Jones*'s racial identity."[65]

Before turning to Bailey's performance, I would like to look at the way that *Carmen Jones* renders even Olga James's "authentic" voice—a voice that authentically issues from her body and is authenticated by her training at Juilliard—strange. Certainly, the knowledge that James is singing her own part changes the investment an audience places in that performance. Yet in James's solo aria, "My Joe," she sings in an interior monologue. This results in an

Olga James in *Carmen Jones.*

uncanny image: James's tear-stained face is stoically silent as she follows her own disembodied voice down the street, a voice that almost appears to dangle before her defiant gaze. James's voice rejoins her body later in the scene, but its mobility denaturalizes the physical connection between image and voice, to haunting effect. Voice and body here are transcoded and deterritorialized. Our movement "inside" James's Cindy Lou is paradoxically more intimate in that we hear her interior voice while her face becomes a separate, expressive surface. In this manner, the shot attains the status of an affection-image (a deterritorializing image that Deleuze describes as an immobile, reflective plane, abstracted from its spatiotemporal coordinates).[66] Yet this penetrating moment remains curiously open to the outside. As the camera glides in front of James in a single tracking shot, we see the naturalized movements of the world around her and are conscious of the sonic counterpoint of the street. Neither fully set loose nor fully grounded, the expressive strains in this musical moment reverberate against one another, generating, within the audience, an irreconcilable difference.

## "Beat Out Dat Rhythm"

"Beat Out Dat Rhythm on a Drum," by contrast, takes a more embodied approach to its visualization. The scene opens as Carmen enters Billy Pastor's club. The opening theme of Bizet's "Chanson Boheme" accompanies clusters of jitterbug dancers and a four-piece band on stage. The music halts abruptly as the band's drummer, Max Roach, breaks into an extended drum solo. The dancers accelerate their movements, and the crowd begins to chant, "Go Max" along with the beat, Frankie (Bailey) being the most enthusiastic among them, pounding her fists on the bar. Here Roach's drumming shifts awkwardly from the improvisatory, dynamic rhythms of his jazz solo back to the simple rhythm that provides the foundation for "Chanson Bohème." The drumbeats soften as Frankie begins to sing and gradually fade beneath the pizzicato strings that carry the beat for the remainder of the number.

Bailey sings in the tradition of the "hot mama," sensually, deeply, and with fluid jazz phrasing. Her voice is refreshing compared to the stiltedness of the other musical numbers in the film, and her own playback performance seems to minimize the distance between body and voice present in other scenes. Yet the lyrics and rhythm of the number embed this voice within their racially charged assertions. In this staging, the strained labors fall less on body and voice than within the beat of the music itself. Bizet's "Chanson Bohème" is a pastiche of Spanish-themed colloquialisms that sound completely out of place in the setting of a black jazz club. The dancers jump frenetically in the background with much gratuitous hip shaking, and the choreography is dissynchronous with the music in terms of beat and style. As overenthusiastic as the dancers are, the orchestra on stage appears wooden, static, and completely disinterested.

Given the lyrical thrust of "Beat Out Dat Rhythm," that the "bump bump bumping of the music" overrides any need for melody by stirring Frankie "deep inside her bones," the rhythmic construction of this number is perplexing. Hammerstein's lyrics are coupled with overtly stereotypical representations of the dancers to reinforce an image of African American culture as primitive, exotic, innately rhythmic, and inherently sexual.[67] Yet for all the talk of drums the song provides, drums are strangely absent from the orchestration of this number, buried beneath the strings and woodwinds. Aside from Roach's open-ing solo, the sound of the drums appears again only momentarily when Frankie grabs a drumstick and begins tapping along for several measures. This inter-vention is rather jarring, as Roach's own mallet strokes, mimed along with the playback orchestra throughout the scene, have been largely inaudible.

The decision to orchestrate the song in this manner seems odd, especially when more straightforward renditions of Bizet's opera have gone to lengths to emphasize the song's "primitive" rhythmic roots. Maria Callas's 1964 record-ing of *Carmen,* for example, features nuanced dynamic shifts during this aria, punctuated by a prominently featured tambourine.[68] The jangling rhythm of the tambourine escalates as Carmen sings about the hypnotic and arousing nature of Gypsy music, and the song builds to a fevered pitch. The flourishes

Pearl Bailey in *Carmen Jones.*

of the tambourine point precisely to the role rhythm and music play in securing our reading of Carmen as an exotic and sexualized Other. The use of a tambourine is key, not only because the instrument is referenced in the lyrics of
the song but for its links to ethnic dance and its roots as a folk instrument. Rosi
similarly highlights the percussive foundation of the song and the roots of the
beat in the Gypsy community. In his film, the song opens in the Gypsy camp,
where families eat and lounge by fires while young girls practice flamenco-like
steps. The Gypsies begin to clap, and this is the rhythm that carries us into
Lilla Pastia's hall, where Carmen and her friends begin to dance. Other instruments pick up on the beat, but even as it builds to its frenetic conclusion, it
remains firmly grounded in this folk sensibility.

"Beat Out Dat Rhythm" clearly attempts to echo coded assumptions about
music and racial identity, transplanting and extending them into a commentary about African American culture. Hammerstein's lyrics translate the tambourines of the Gypsies into the drums of jazz (which, the song implies, are
direct extensions of the "primitive" drums of Africa). So why is the actual beat,
the most territorial refrain of "Chanson Bohème," missing?

For James Baldwin, *Carmen Jones* engages in a strange, conflicted project.
It purports to relocate *Carmen* within a contemporary African American community, yet in doing so it systematically eradicates any semblance of actual African American culture, leaving a vacuous and false image. In his scathing review
of the film in *Commentary,* Baldwin writes:

> In *Carmen Jones,* the implicit parallel between an amoral Gypsy and an amoral
> Negro woman is the entire root of the show; but at the same time, bearing in

mind the distances covered since *The Birth of a Nation,* it is important that the movie always be able to repudiate any suggestion that Negroes are amoral—which it can only do, considering the role of the Negro in the national psyche, by repudiating any suggestion that Negroes are not white.[69]

Baldwin argues that *Carmen Jones* can make an analogy between a Gypsy woman and black woman only within the context of an individualized sexual morality tale and only so long as the parallel does not invite any larger connections about the racial politics of the opera and contemporary race relations in the United States. The musical must walk a razor-thin edge between invoking and repudiating markers of blackness; the difficulty of this task may account for its stilted stylizations and extreme musical conservatism.

By 1943, when the stage version of *Carmen Jones* premiered, the populist roots of *Carmen* had long faded from memory, and its refrains were resituated within the realm of high art. The invocation of *Carmen's* rhythms which had once existed as a multiplicity of conflicting references, recalled now a far more singular territory: the elitism of European opera. In terms of its musical interpretation of Bizet's master text, *Carmen Jones* seems interested in pursuing this refrain alone, for it engages with the rhythms and melodies of the opera with as little imagination and innovation as possible. Whereas the collage of speech and variations of popular song in Bizet's opéra comique might have allowed for legitimate rhythmic variation (albeit one that was highly politically charged), the structure of *Carmen Jones* falls closer to the realm of what Deleuze and Guattari would call "meter."[70] Meter functions on the level of linear, regimented time *(Chronos),* working like the bars in a musical score to measure and divide song into equal blocks. Perhaps one of *Carmen Jones's* greatest acts of violence is to reterritorialize *Carmen's* refrains, to eliminate their musical contradictions and force them into a plodding, measured meter (hence its stiffness where it should swing). Its regimentation seems to derive precisely from its anxiety about the "folk" it purports to give voice to: to allow legitimate dialogue between black musical voices and the refrains of the *Carmen* legacy would be to potentially unleash a critical rhythm that neither Broadway nor Hollywood could afford to risk. The repression of rhythm and the suturing of sound and image in the film may serve to replicate a metered tendency core to the *Carmen* narrative—to assert a homogeneous territory, a "noncommunicating milieu" that is unable to accommodate or acknowledge unexoticized racial difference.

As Kaja Silverman has demonstrated, the relations between cinematic bodies and voices typically assert gender identity in precisely this territorializing manner. Whereas the male authorial voice gains power when it functions in an omniscient, bodiless state, the female voice must always remain corporeally grounded. To permit female characters "to be heard without being seen," she writes, "would be even more dangerous, since it would disrupt the specular regime upon which dominant cinema relies."[71] There is a level on which such a grounding occurs within *Carmen Jones,* driven by a repressive rationale. The female voices are not merely harnessed to the body; in the case of certain bodies, the voices are vacated altogether, silently replaced by more obedient substitutes.

Yet this cannot fully explain the politics of substitution, mimicry, and embodiment that occur in the film. One must pay attention to the manner in which the black male body is subject to a similar specular fascination and the labor it undergoes in straining to attach itself to a voice—race here renders masculinity in a decidedly corporeal fashion. And just as Marilyn Horne was asked to "black up" her vocal performance, LeVern Hutcherson, an African American opera singer, had to force his own tenor voice into an unnaturally low register in order to sound more "authentic."[72] Moreover, there is a deeper level on which the affective experience of viewing these embodiments just does not work. The strain of embodiment is painfully apparent, and the parts remain unhinged.

Given the excessive artificiality of the film and the consistent misalignment of body and voice, I am not certain that process of gendered synchronization that Silverman describes is successfully reenacted in *Carmen Jones.* For many viewers (as evidenced in the responses of the critics referenced here), the simulacrum is far from convincing. It is unclear whether the phantasmic nature of the staging was driven by a deliberate social agenda.[73] Regardless, the net result is that the coexistent elements of the illusion begin to fracture and clash, exposing their fissures in some instances and in others creating monstrous new hybrids. The seams exposed include not only attempts to fix and define racial and sexual identity (a project shared by the *Carmen* narrative as a whole) but also the seams between voice and body at the heart of the cinematic illusion. Chion writes about the inherent "impossibilities" contained within the cinema's artifice of synchronization:

> The voice and the image can only appear as cut apart, they cannot consummate their reunion in a forever lost mythic unity. The talking film is but a jerry-rigged assemblage, and perhaps in this condition it finds its greatness. Instead of denying this rigging, it can choose it as its subject matter, taking that route, under the sign of the impossible, to the very heart of the effect of the Real.[74]

*Carmen Jones* asserts a rationale and an identity that its own images and sounds cannot realize. The unabashed manner in which this jerry-rigging is foregrounded in the film suggests that this tension is indeed the subject matter of the film. In this sense, though *Carmen Jones* does strike the viewer as affectively false, it is precisely this failure of self-identity and unity that makes the film meaningful.

The concept of fabulation, for Deleuze, can be linked to the relationship between image and sound in cinema.[75] When sound is dislocated from the image, it no longer functions to describe, narrate, or dictate meaning within the visual realm. Each element is freed to interact with the other in irrational, indeterminable ways; rather than prescribing meaning, fabulation opens sound and image to critical, multiple readings. *Carmen Jones* contains unwieldy, monstrous combinations that are enigmatic, multiple, and false. These include not only the sutured bodies and voices but also the imposition of the overly familiar music, the wooden dialogue, and the "paraphrasing of the real," all meant to elicit an imaginary, false narrative world. The simulacrum forged by these sutured elements can be read as an attempt to repress difference, to territorialize representations of identity, to ground *Carmen*'s refrains within the safe and familiar ground of metered convention. Yet the dissonance inherent in these combinations serves, in many ways, to falsify, or at least to denaturalize, any notions of realism or truth asserted by the narrative.

There is a definitive counterpoint present at nearly every moment in *Carmen Jones*—a counterpoint between voice and body, theatricality and the real—that establishes a dialogue between heterogeneous elements. It is a counterpoint forged through the interventions of a number of interlocutors (Preminger, the actors, the vocalists, the crew, each of *Carmen*'s authors) drawing on a wide range of habitual conventions (including conventions of literature, opera, musical theater, and film; of African American musical traditions; of Preminger's own filmography; and of a long history of representing racial and gender difference). What emerges in this mix is rhythm, difference, and a challenge to the strictures of meter. The fictional assemblage being forged here clearly does not fully rise to the ideal of the powers of the false as evoked by Deleuze in *The Time-Image; Carmen Jones* seeks to imagine a people, but it is not able to shake its expressive elements loose from the strictures of a major cinema. Yet its contradictory refrains surely do shift from the function they performed in their originary milieu, transcoding themselves in newly resonant, expressive combinations as they collide in this new setting. The role of signification (of language, speaking, and narrating) in other words, gives way to performative, affective expression.

The productive failure of *Carmen Jones* as a cohesive reproduction rests on the profusion of irreconcilable registers within the film. Each one of these registers (the discord between high and low culture, between the self and the exotic

Other, between voice and body, between speaking and singing) resonates clearly and directly with the whole body of texts that compose the *Carmen* oeuvre at the same time that they remain in perpetual discord with one another. The link between this film and each other *Carmen* iteration is not a single narrative or an identical melody but in fact these irrepressible dissonances. *Carmen Jones,* intentionally or not, reproduces and magnifies *Carmen*'s schizophrenic ruptures, exposing difference and incommensurability as *Carmen*'s most basic refrains.

## Counterpoint and Refrain

How, then, to understand the correlations among *Prénom Carmen, Carmen Jones,* and the refrains they echo? It might appear that the earlier, more territorial versions of the refrain (such as *Carmen Jones*) provide the raw material from which more artistically challenging works (such as *Prénom Carmen*) depart. The connection between these two modes of refrain is nevertheless far more mutual and deeply seated. "It is odd," Deleuze and Guattari note, "how music does not eliminate the bad or mediocre refrain, or the bad usage of the refrain, but on the contrary carries it along, or uses it as a springboard" (*A Thousand Plateaus,* 349). The creative, deterritorializing refrain could not in fact exist without that first territorial refrain. Following Brelet's discussion of the theme that arises from the popular melody, Deleuze and Guattari argue that the second form of the refrain (the refrain that deterritorializes and takes flight) marks not a complete rupture with the first (the refrain that territorializes and grounds). Instead, the deterritorializing refrain takes part in an intensive reengagement and mobilization of the first, "slipping through its net instead of breaking with it":

> We may say long live Chabrier, as opposed to Schoenberg, just as Nietzsche said long live Bizet, and for the same reasons, with the same technical and musical intent. . . . We do not need to suppress tonality, we need to turn it loose. We go from assembled refrains (territorial, popular, romantic, etc.) to the great cosmic machined refrain. But the labor of creation is already under way in the first type; it is there in its entirety. Deformations destined to harness a great force are already present in the small-form refrain or rondo. (350)

The relationship between the two refrains is inextricably knotted; the flight of the second is bound to the flight of the first. "Childhood scenes, children's games: the starting point is a childlike refrain, but the child has wings already, he becomes celestial. The becoming-child of the musician is coupled with a becoming-aerial of the child, in a nondecomposable block" (350). Both are one in the same movement, actualized out of the same material and the forces it contains. We might think of this in terms of the jazz improvisation: in the standards reworked on John Coltrane's album *My Favorite Things* (Atlantic, 1960), for example, Coltrane's most abstract flights away from convention always return to and build on the familiar refrains of Rodgers, Porter, and Gershwin. Rather than experiencing this movement as a grounding or a retreat, it is felt as an inspired and pleasurable deepening of the original works. Difference is not added to the refrain, it is teased out, transcoded, set loose, and integrated into a wider, more open assemblage.

Godard and Miéville's invocation of Preminger in *Prénom Carmen* functions similarly. During the shoot-out scene, for example, Joseph breaks off his embrace with Carmen X in order to tie her hands for their escape from the bank. The scene is a clear reference to the highly eroticized scene in *Carmen Jones* where Joe binds Carmen's feet and hands after wrestling her to the ground, a scene that registers as simultaneously real (it is shot on location, and the struggle is convincingly dusty) and utterly staged (the scenario oozes clichéd sexuality). In Godard and Miéville's adaptation, we are similarly off-put by the collision of reality (the uninterrupted operations of the bank) and the ludicrously accelerated seduction. As Joseph moves to secure Carmen X's hands, he says, "I should tie you up—it will look more real," a statement that feels less connected to the trajectory of the narrative than it is to a larger paradox regarding the status of reality as a performance. This act of fabulation picks up on the tonality already well articulated in Preminger's work, bringing that creative discord—that difference—more clearly to light and harnessing it toward different artistic ends.

Chion calls the unlinking of image from sound in film "audiovisual counterpoint," "an 'auditory voice' perceived horizontally in tandem with the visual track, a voice that possesses its own formal individuality."[76] Counterpoint here means more than audiovisual dissonance (the linking of images and sounds that clearly "don't belong" together); he cites *Prénom Carmen,* in fact, as a film that critics have read as contrapuntal in superficial, literal ways. In labeling the combination, for instance, of the sound of seagulls with the image of the metro train, as counterpoint, critics are often relying on symbolic interpretations of images and sounds, seeing them as fixed signifiers for particular ideas "at the expense of their multiple concrete particularities, which are much richer and full of ambiguity."[77] A more nuanced understanding of audiovisual counterpoint does not rely on a literal case of mismatched tracks but instead looks at the tangible ways unexpected combinations of expressive elements create rhythmic difference. Images and sounds may come from entirely different planes, yet they reverberate against one another, mutually transforming their structures and meanings through their physical combination.

Thus, *Prénom Carmen* does not "right the wrongs" of the *Carmen* legacy through its removal of the Bizet score or its use of seemingly disconnected images and sounds. Rather, Godard's fracturing of the multiple refrains of *Carmen,* the manner in which he has forced those refrains into a dialogue with other elements and melodies, reveals his deep engagement with the questions already contained in the heart of the myth. This engagement is realized through a combination of concrete sounds and images that, rather than merely contradicting or canceling each other, add to and speak through one another. Evoked both through reference and absence, the movements of *Prénom Carmen* radiate simultaneously outward and inward, concentrating, penetrating, and appealing to *Carmen*'s memories at the same time that they push forward into new circuits of recombination and thought. *Carmen Jones,* too, through its labored contradictions, creates a different kind of counterpoint. Representational elements are forced into uncomfortable juxtapositions, denaturalizing the preconceived meanings to which they normally refer, and opening a space for affective expression.

This reading of *Carmen* on film is by no means exhaustive. In particular, it has neglected the emotive contribution of music, especially the creative power of female voice, to the *Carmen* legacy—a voice that is disembodied in *Carmen Jones* and that does not sing in *Prénom Carmen.* Emotional affect in music has been consistently denigrated as subjective and feminine, a tendency central to the history and reception of *Carmen,* and a study of the politics of difference in the music of the story must certainly take this into consideration. I raise this point in conclusion not to question the integrity of the versions discussed here but to suggest that *no* version of *Carmen* could ever address the full range of questions, the cacophony of refrains, provoked by the story. Individual *Carmen*s cannot be read in isolation; we gain more when we view particular *Carmen*s alongside other artistic co-optations of that refrain (Geraldine Farrar's inspired vocal and silent film adaptations are a particularly poignant example). The power of *Carmen* lies in its function precisely as a refrain, a series of articulations that are always shifting, moving, and incomplete, forging rhythms *between* texts and between different sites of articulation.

# Three

# En Chanté: Music, Memory, and Perversity in the Films of Jacques Demy

She had had quite a long argument with her sister only the day before—all because Alice had begun with "Let's pretend we're kings and queens"; and her sister, who liked being very exact, had argued that they couldn't, because there were only two of them, and Alice had been reduced at last to say, "Well, you can be one of them, then, and I'll be all the rest."

—LEWIS CARROLL, *Through the Looking-Glass*

Henri Bergson's theories of perception, memory, and time fly in the face of our most commonplace assumptions about these processes. We presume that perception is the processing of stimuli by our sensory organs, that memories are highly individualized neurological images stored in our brains, and that time, despite our relative perceptions of it, unfolds as a series of moments that are strung like beads onto the thread of the past. According to Bergson, however, perception is a reflective interaction between the perceiver and the perceived, a reciprocal exchange that takes place in the space between them, not in the mind of the subject. The phenomenon of perception originates within the object itself; the entity that perceives this object registers or distills from it only those qualities that it finds useful. These qualities may convey an immediate usefulness, whereby the perceiver might perform some action in response to the object, or the qualities might resonate with memories of other objects and images perceived in the past. "Perception," Bergson writes, "is never a mere contact of the mind with the object present; it is impregnated with memory-images which complete it as they interpret it."[1] Recollection, like perception, is a process that is external to an individual subject or psyche. Although individuals may form memory images that are tailored toward their particular interests, these images for Bergson are distillations of a pure memory, a collective past that exists outside the human brain. The act of remembering does not

involve searching through the reservoirs of one's mind for the matching memory. Instead, to recollect is to leap outside one's self into the past carried along
by each passing present.

A Bergsonian understanding of memory and time reveals much about the
role temporality plays in musical cinema. There is an emphasis on collectivity
in musicals that is rarely found in nonmusical narrative films, the presence of
forces whose movements are larger than the individual. Narrative progression
is secondary to the production number that ruptures and suspends the plot.
Movement and transformation arise less from narrative causality than from
the rhythms of a musical, time-based logic. One sees this primarily in the force
of the song that sweeps characters up in its path, moving freely between them,
a kind of movement-of-world not unlike Bergson's description of the past as
a depersonalized presence that catalyzes feelings, actions, and creative thought.

Yet questions of history and the past are not easily addressed in a genre
that is often perceived as regressively nostalgic. Jacques Demy's musical films,
when contrasted with the works of his contemporaries, particularly those associated with the French New Wave, have been dismissed as naïve and apolitical.
"The fruitiest film ever made," one reviewer of *Les parapluies de Cherbourg*
writes, "like a French pastry . . . [it may be] little more than an elaborate con-
fection."[2] Terrance Rafferty says of Demy, "This auteur's sensibility obviously
lacks the invigorating rough edges we associate with the New Wave. . . . He
makes no intellectual demands on the viewer: he aims to seduce, not to challenge."[3] Rafferty compliments the unity of Demy's "idea of the cinema" and
"idea of the world"; that world, however, for Rafferty, is little more than a lovely,
isolated illusion. Demy does forge a unity between cinema and world; hardly
a meaningless ornament, however, this unity is as challenging and politically
relevant as the films of his contemporaries. Demy's world incisively collapses
the distinction between cinema and life, creating a realm of indeterminacy that
is far from insular. Like Jean-Luc Godard, Demy toys with the intersections
of life and cinema through unconventional juxtapositions of image and sound
and through self-conscious filmic references. His technique, however, is not one
of Brechtian distantiation.[4] Rather, Demy's intertextual references work to destabilize the viewer's relation to the film through emotional resonance. Demy
is less interested in breaking down the wall of identification than in plunging
inward, exploring the correspondences between the intensely personal and the
movements of the world.

This chapter points to several of the ways in which issues of temporality,
memory, and history surface in the films of Jacques Demy, building on Bergson's
*Matter and Memory* and Gilles Deleuze's writing on cinema. Of particular

interest are Demy's three musicals: *Les parapluies de Cherbourg* (1964), *Les demoiselles de Rochefort (The Young Girls of Rochefort)* (1967), and *Peau d'âne (Donkey Skin)* (1970). Each of these films glosses on the conventions of the musical genre in distinct ways, with the singing of dialogue in *Les parapluies,* the self-conscious inclusion of iconic American performers in *Les demoiselles* (which costars Gene Kelly), and the musical revision of the children's fairy tale in *Peau d'âne.* It is impossible to understand these films outside of Demy's larger body of work, however. His *Lola* (1961), *La baie des anges (Bay of Angels)* (1963), and *Model Shop* (1969) are similarly reliant on music in their creation of meaning and rehearse characters and themes from Demy's other films. The peculiar history that Demy invokes is constructed in large part in the spaces between individual films, both within his own oeuvre and through references to other texts.

Despite criticism of Demy's work as escapist and romantic, each of his films is firmly rooted in its geographic and temporal settings. With the exception of *Peau d'âne,* the cities in which the films take place (Cherbourg, Nice, Rochefort, Los Angeles) function almost as characters. Set in these border towns or ports of call, Demy's films are populated by dancers, sailors, single mothers, and precocious children. While the narrative might focus on personal relationships, these individual stories are always implicitly shaped by the flow of larger political shifts. The romances and players seem purposefully simplified or even clichéd at the outset, but the action that ensues, complicating these scenarios, is set in motion by the force of time and the transformations of the city and the larger world. The characters are always thrown off course by some external movement, most typically by war. History, in Demy's films, is not a backdrop for tragic love stories. Neither does the romance serve as a metaphor for historical and political events. Rather, the complex interplay between present and past in the film, the conflicting temporalities, and the flows in which the characters are caught all work to interrogate the very processes of remembering, feeling, and thinking.

Music plays a central role in Demy's films, functioning as the primary force that transects the registers of the individual and the world. Michel Legrand's scores (present in all of the Demy films I discuss here with the exception of *Model Shop*) refuse to take a subservient position in relation to the image, even in those films that are not explicitly musicals. The theme from *La baie des anges,* for example, is an incredibly short, excessively romantic passage that dramatically punctuates the soundscape of the film. The majority of the scenes contain no nondiegetic music at all, and thus the intrusion of the theme disrupts notions of realism and points to the role that music serves in narrative cinema. This self-consciousness, which nevertheless maintains a genuine emotional affectivity, demonstrates the complexity of Demy's project. The viewer is implicated in the journey that he constructs, placed in a paradoxical position of emotional identification and an acute awareness of the constructed nature of the film experience. Demy's films are as much about this process of "reading" or interpreting as they are about the specific narrative. His use of music crystallizes this project, mobilizing the audience's histories and memories in concert with the actual and fictional histories on the screen. In this way, Demy's use of music verges on what Deleuze would call an image of time.

I begin my study of Demy by discussing Bergson's theory of perception, memory, and time in relation to *Les parapluies de Cherbourg*. The intersection of actual and fictionalized histories present in Demy's films leads me back to Deleuze's writing on fabulation and the powers of the false, as presented in *Cinema 2: The Time-Image*.[5] Fabulation, or "storytelling," for Deleuze, is a powerful strategy for undermining repressive systems of thought. The presence of multiple, simultaneous "realities" within a work of art falsifies any single claim to truth or self-same identity. While all of Demy's films engage in acts of fabulation, his later musical works do so far more explicitly by retelling classical children's fairy tales. I examine Demy's *Peau d'âne* within the tradition of the fairy tale and its own complicated history of storytelling. I conclude by questioning one of the more curious themes that emerges in Demy's films—the "multiplication" of women through reflection, repetition, and doubling. The female double serves as one of Demy's most potent images of the false, one that can be read alongside Deleuze's writing on perversity and doubling in literature.

While I concentrate primarily on the body of work of a single director here, my objective is not to paint a picture of an individual auteur. Demy has clearly crafted his films with a distinctive perspective on temporality and history, but the musical images he works with resonate with and feed from those found in more traditional musical films. The complexity of Demy's style demands a careful exploration in its own right, and as such, most of this chapter is devoted to his films. In the conclusion of this chapter, I draw on examples from Hollywood films that might correlate with Demy's work (specifically, the dream ballet from *Oklahoma!* [Zinnemann, 1955]), with the hope that the questions I raise about history and time might be posed, in different contexts, in relation to any number of musical moments.

## History and Affect: *Les parapluies de Cherbourg*

*Les parapluies de Cherbourg* is Demy's best-known film and the work most typically referenced in discussions of Demy's sugary romanticism. The film is structured around the transformative power of time. The narrative is composed of three distinct acts, Departure, Absence, and Return. Set in the small port city of Cherbourg in 1957, the film traces the relationship between Geneviève Emery (Catherine Deneuve), the young daughter of a widowed umbrella shop owner, and Guy (Nino Castelnuovo), an auto mechanic who lives with his elderly Tante Elise (Mireille Perrey). Their passionate romance is cut short when Guy is called to serve in the war in Algeria. Devastated, the couple swears to wait for each other, and Geneviève spends the night with Guy before his departure. She soon learns she is pregnant, to the dismay of her mother (Anne Vernon). Madame Emery, fretful about her struggling shop, sells a necklace to a kind diamond dealer, Roland Cassard (Marc Michel), who is sympathetic to her plight and taken with Geneviève's beauty. He later proposes to Geneviève, who, hurt by Guy's inconsistent communication and the weight of his absence, succumbs to her mother's prodding and accepts Cassard. In 1959, Guy returns, embittered from the war, to find that Geneviève has moved to Paris, the umbrella shop has been turned into a laundromat, and Tante Elise is on her deathbed. He flounders about, drinking heavily, before noticing Madeleine (Ellen Farner), Tante Elise's lovely caretaker who has patiently and silently adored Guy from afar. Four years pass, and Guy now owns a gas station and lives with Madeleine and their young son. On a winter's evening, Geneviève and her daughter pull into the station, having made a detour through Cherbourg. She and Guy speak briefly, but he refuses to meet his own daughter, and they part, utterly estranged.

The narrative of *Les parapluies* is thus far from rose-colored and is filled with disillusionment, loss, and the personal tragedies wrought by war and capitalism. The charges of romanticism and frothiness that are directed at the film target its striking aesthetics: its intensely saturated color palate and the jazzy accompaniment of Legrand's score, to which every word of dialogue is sung. *Les parapluies* is not a traditional musical in that spoken dialogue does not give way to outbursts of song. There are few moments when the characters launch into an identifiable, distinct song in the film; the score consists instead of strung-together themes that are associated with a particular character or emotion and incessantly repeated.[6] The hyperstylization of this technique, which does not allow the audience to withdraw into the comfortable conventions of the traditional musical, takes on a further strangeness when the characters begin to sing about the most banal of subjects: paying bills, disputes at work, what type of gasoline to use. Combined with Bernard Evein's vibrant art direction, *Les parapluies* is an outrageous celebration of surface and style.

*Les parapluies* contains numerous moments of playful self-reflexivity. At the beginning of the first act, for example, Guy chats (sings) with his coworkers in the locker room of the garage about their plans for the evening. Guy is taking Geneviève to see *Carmen,* which inspires one friend to launch into Bizet's "Habañera" while another asserts his preference for film over opera, for "all that singing" gives him a headache. The overwhelming thrust of the film, however, is not an ironic gloss on cinematic conventions. The initial distance created by the film's stylization soon gives way to an utterly sincere meditation on the loss experienced by Guy and Geneviève. Rather than being undermined by the film's excessiveness, music, texture, and color elevate their romance, which is made all the more endearing and bittersweet by its ordinariness. Legrand's compositions play a tremendous role in revealing the tragedy of the everyday, particularly the love theme that accompanies Guy's departure at the Cherbourg train station, one of the few portions of the score that can be distilled into a recognizable song (nominated for an Oscar in 1965 under the title "I Will Wait for You").

The scene opens with a long shot of Geneviève and Guy seated at a table in the train station; the palette of the scene is awash in shades of green. The two have just spent the night together for the first time, and the music that carries us into the morning is the same song that swept them into that passionate decision, now rendered bittersweet. They declare their undying devotion to one another and swear to wait for the day they can be reunited. The exchange is at once clichéd and entirely heartfelt. The couple reluctantly moves outside, and the music crescendos as Guy boards the train. Geneviève pulls a blue scarf from her coat and tries to keep up with Guy as the train begins to churn forward. Their duet, which had followed the melodic line while alternating between the singers, shifts here. The orchestra swells, taking over the melody, while their voices, still following one another in a kind of call-response ("Mon amour," "Je t'aime, je t'aime, je t'aime"), assume harmonic, supplemental positions to that melody. Their voices fragment and become part of the larger instrumentation as their emotions escalate. The train speeds ahead of Geneviève, and she is swirled into the steam of the engine's wake, shrinking into the distance as the camera cranes upward and away.

Demy gives a nod to an entire history of melodrama in this scene and to hundreds of tearful cinematic train-station departures. But rather than distance the viewer through ironic intertextual reference, the invocation of cliché seems poised to heighten the emotional depth of the scene—an earnestness that perhaps lies behind the perception of Demy as naïve and sentimental. This is where Demy departs from New Wave directors such as Godard or Truffaut. His fascination with the musical certainly exhibits the reflexivity and love for American cinema that are part of the New Wave sensibility. But Demy's use of references is markedly different from Godard's; the allusion is never made at the expense of affectivity. Although reflexivity was important to Demy, to rely on reflexivity alone is to create work that is, in his view, "stuffy, frozen, and often annoying."[7] References and memories in Demy's films extend beyond the parameters of the narrative, but they do so in ways that deepen, rather than inhibit, the emotional relevance of the image.

Demy's sincerity serves as a means of implicating the audience in the cycles of recollection his references set into motion. These references are most often extradiegetic, and the music that instigates flights into reverie, even when diegetic, is meant to trigger an emotional response from the viewer. Obviously, Demy is not unique in this way, as every film is created for an audience and every film score is created for the ears of the filmgoer, not the characters. What is different about Demy's approach is the strange middle ground he creates between an awareness of the falsity of the film experience and an endorsement of that same experience as incredibly real and deeply moving. He does not achieve this by asking the viewer to observe the characters' journeys as they recollect the past. By and large, the characters remain deeply rooted in the present, and even though they refer to the past, those moments remain irrevocably lost and serve to demonstrate the cruel reality of the here and now. Instead, Demy forces the viewer to become aware of the pleasures and discomforts of his or her own cycles of perceiving, remembering, and feeling.

## Perception, Action, Recollection

The work of Henri Bergson suggests new ways of understanding the complexity of Demy's construction of time and memory. Demy seems particularly attuned to the relationship between objects, images, and processes of recollection, weaving these elements together in ways that resonate with Bergsonian (and Deleuzian) theories of temporality. For Bergson, perception and memory cannot be thought of in dualistic terms. It is counterintuitive, he argues, to assert that an object exists entirely outside of perception or exclusively within the mind of the perceiver. He writes in *Matter and Memory*:

> Matter, in our view, is an aggregate of "images." And by "image" we mean a certain existence which is more than that which the idealist calls a *representation*, but less than that which the realist calls a *thing*—an existence placed halfway between the "thing" and the "representation." (9)

The implication of the "in-between" space Bergson designates is far-reaching. It suggests a model of perception that is not only reciprocal but that also extends through time. Memory takes up the image, and through a process of mutual transformation, penetrates the material object itself.

Bergson's emphasis on the complex nature of the image manifests itself, in part, in an interest in physical phenomenon and human physiology. This does not mean, however, that the key to perception lies within any physical function. He systematically refutes scientific claims that the brain stores memories and images within itself. Rather, one can best understand the interplay between perception and memory if one thinks of them in terms of their temporality. The body, Bergson writes, is an image like any other image object. What differentiates a living being from other objects is its ability to initiate action in relation to the image objects that surround it. Within the chain of effects caused by the interaction of objects with each other, living beings create zones of indeterminacy, shifting the flow of effects when they decide whether or not to perform an action in relation to a particular object. A bird can eat a seed or not eat a seed, a girl can throw a rock or not throw a rock, and depending on the choices made by each, different chains of events will follow.[8] The body for Bergson "is an instrument of action, and of action only" (*Matter and Memory,* 225). Raw perception, as such, takes place always in the present and is only concerned with action a body may exert upon the realm of objects that it perceives (229). The (ideal) present, as rooted in the body, can be summarized as existing in a sensory-motor state (240).

Although memory arises from perception, it cannot be described as a "weakened" present moment that the body retains. The mechanisms of recollection serve an entirely different function. Memory can be loosely split into two types: voluntary or motor memory and spontaneous memory (85). Motor memory can be linked to the present, perceptual reality of the subject. These memories are likened to learned perceptions that attain meaning through a repetition that divorces them from their original occurrence (e.g., typing, or tying one's shoe). Conversely, spontaneous memory is geared not toward action but toward reflection. These images remain fixed in their localized pasts; they are at once highly personal and independent from individual will (88). Spontaneous memories exist below the surface of the action-motivated reality of the present. Hemmed in and fettered by motor memory, spontaneous memories flash forward; if not maintained in equilibrium, they have the potential to "distort the practical character of life, mingling dream with reality" (84).

These descriptions, for Bergson, are of "two extreme forms of memory in their *pure* state," ideals that operate in tandem in actual practice (88). The realization of their interplay is mapped out in his diagram of the circuits of memory and perception. The smallest circle in this figure (AO) contains the object itself and what Bergson calls its "after-image": "a *reflection,* in the etymological sense of the word, that is to say the projection, outside ourselves, of an actively created image, identical with or similar to, the object on which it comes to mold itself" (102). From this inner circuit, which is closest to a pure state of perception, memory and reflection fling themselves outward, on the one side (B–D) as echoing memory images and on the other (B′–D′) as reflections of those images that penetrate the object, "creating anew not only the object perceived, but also the ever widening systems with which it may be bound up" (105). The registers of memory and physical reality that these circuits represent are dependent on one another and return with each repetition to the same object. Each repetition also contains a difference, a change that is mutually transformative and that blurs the distinction between those "pure" states: "any memory-image that is capable of interpreting our actual perception inserts itself so thoroughly into it that we are no longer able to discern what is perception and what is memory" (103).

The difference contained in each expanding repetition is critical in this regard, for each change implies a movement in time. Yet the temporal movement of these ripples should not be understood merely as a progression from the present (at the center) to various points in the future or a regression into the past. Rather, perception proceeds through shifts in *duration,* freezing or mobilizing sensations as dictated by the demands of each individual situation, a "moment" captured in the fold of each expanding circuit (208). The notion of duration is key here, as it differs tremendously from traditional understandings of temporality. The concept of time, for Bergson, has already been colonized by that of space in that we understand time only as it is spatially mapped, in measurable, divisible, isolated moments (seconds, minutes, years). Duration,

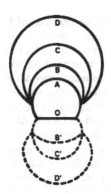

Henri Bergson's model of reflective perception. Expanding circuits of memory (B, C, and D) arise from the circuit closest to immediate perception (A), containing both the object (O) and its afterimage. These memory circuits are reflected by virtual circuits that penetrate into deeper strata of reality (B', C', D'). From Bergson, *Matter and Memory.*

by contrast, is indivisible, multiple, and conditional. One cannot measure duration against some immutable, universal notion of time. Within perception, Bergson figures time as a relative quality:

> In reality there is no one rhythm of duration; it is possible to imagine many different rhythms which, slower or faster, measure the degree of tension or relaxation of different kinds of consciousness and thereby fix their respective places in the scale of being. (207)

Duration, then, is flexible and nonlinear; it is contingent on the various virtual and actual images between and through which it emerges.

For memory to become attuned to more "relaxed" states of duration, which we might associate with the outer circuits of the memory image, it must disengage itself from the realm of action and the demands of the present. Bergson describes memory as a process that occurs at the intersection of two axes. The first axis is spatial. We can understand line AB as containing "all simultaneous objects in space," all physical matter, in other words, that exists at a given time. Line CI represents a temporal axis across which are spread all of our successive recollections. Point I, then, is the intersection between our physical interactions with the material world (that which we are perceiving or might potentially perceive), and the whole body of our past experiences, that which we have already perceived (142–44). Point I is consciousness, the meeting of memory with matter, the individual with the world. It is not a fixed point, however, but a nexus that is continually in flux, moving, processing, responding, and acting according to shifts in its spatial and temporal contexts.

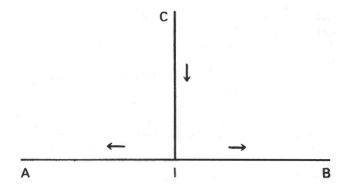

Bergson's model of the actual and virtual axes of perception. Line AB represents the actual, or spatial axis, which contains all simultaneous objects in space. Line CI represents the virtual, or temporal axis, which contains the successive range or our recollections. Point I, at the intersection of these axes, is the point of consciousness. From Bergson, *Matter and Memory.*

Looking at these axes set into motion, temporality could be represented by the cone SAB, point S being the present moment, the place of interaction that is continually propelling forward, while the body of the cone is the accumulated past. Point S is the highly concentrated realm of action and immediacy. Plane AB is the realm of pure memory, a virtual presence that is carried along as the base for existence. Within this cone are an infinite number of strata between the two extremes (A′B′, A″B″). Each level of the cone represents a different level of concentration between purely active sensation and pure memory (162). Our lives are primarily experienced in the most immediately concentrated section of the cone, focused on the demands of the present. Yet the past always persists in a virtual state. To recall is to remove oneself to a certain degree from the realm of action and to leap into this past. One will inevitably actualize memory images that are colored and often distorted by one's individual present situation. Nevertheless, even faulty recollections are sparked by contact with a past that exists outside individual will. Memory, for Bergson, does not exist within us, we exist within it.

The virtual past is analogous to our commonsensical understanding of space. Although we cannot see all the objects in the world when we are inside a windowless room, we still understand that they exist; their relation to us is thus virtual. The past, for Bergson, similarly maintains a presence even when

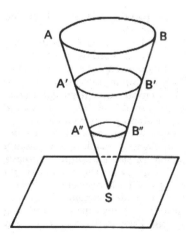

Bergson's model of the image of the body as the location for sensory-motor phenomena. Cone SAB represents the totality of accumulated recollections within one's memory. Base AB remains motionless, in the past. Point S is the concentrated image of the body, always situated in the present. Point S is continually moving forward across plane P, the images that constitute one's actual representation of the universe. From Bergson, *Matter and Memory*.

portions of it are inaccessible. Our recollections can move freely to different strata of the past as our needs dictate or, like Proust's madeleine, as certain stimuli propel us. That the past exists not as a time line but as a concurrent whole complicates our understanding of the self as a cohesive being. We are in fact many simultaneous beings (the child, the adult), all drawn from different layers of the past and all present, in different concentrations, at once.

To recollect, then, is to remove one's self from the active demands of the present and to plunge into the virtual plane of the past. The opening of *Les parapluies* is suggestive of such a leap. The first frames open, through the expanding iris of a sepia-tinted circular vignette, on a shot of Cherbourg's harbor. As Legrand's love theme is introduced in a simplified, solemn form, the camera pivots 90 degrees downward, looking directly on the cobbled street below.[9] The street is slick with rain, and the open umbrellas of the people passing by become highly orchestrated abstractions. There is a certain indeterminacy that emerges here between people and objects; the people *are* umbrellas from this vantage point, and we observe that their individual movements are part of a highly patterned system of movement.[10] There are forces at work that compel their comings and goings, forces of history, time, and politics that transform people, objects, and spaces just as the music compels the dance. "The sung action," Deleuze says of the film, "becomes a movement of city and classes."[11] Demy has shifted the plane of our perception, suggesting, perhaps, that we are to watch what follows from a position detached from the realm of causality and the linear progression of action. We have moved away from the sensory-motor plane and toward that of pure memory.

According to Deleuze, the cinema can operate to various degrees along either spatial or temporal axes. When films concentrate less on immediate causality and more on reflection, they begin to move according to the dictates of time. Time-driven films allow for the presence of multiple temporalities, images drawn from different strata simultaneously. This does not mean the use of flashbacks or other devices that merely manipulate time in the service of furthering the plot (the spatial plane). Narrative causality gives way in time-based films to the more fluid movements of time. The past becomes multiple, indeterminable, contradictory. It "overflows" the circumstances of the individual and becomes something larger, something collective, a "memory-world."[12]

The narrative development of *Les parapluies,* though chronological, is marked less by action and progression than by loss, delay, and the failure to overcome difficulties. Bill Marshall and Sylvie Lindeperg see this aspect of Demy's approach as firmly rooted in the context of postwar France. Modernization and the Americanization of the French economy in the 1960s were wreaking huge changes, particularly on middle-class existence; small businesses were being swallowed up by larger corporations, and consumer and commuter cultures were proliferating in small port cities like Nantes, Cherbourg, and Rochefort. The political climate in France was escalating toward major upheaval, and the war in Algeria loomed as a violent marker of colonialism's failings.[13]

*Les parapluies de Cherbourg*'s suspended durations and thwarted actions are in many ways a response to the alienation caused by these material conditions. The film presents a deeper challenge to linear progress, however, one that is based in both its musical nature and its intertextual references. Time appears not only in the progression of months and years but also in the surfacing of multiple, frequently incommensurate presents. Demy makes continual references to other films, often his own, through narrative scenarios, character's names, visual repetitions, and musical cues. One of the most significant references in *Les parapluies* is the diamond dealer Roland Cassard, the same character, played by the same actor, Michel, who was the alienated romantic youth in Demy's 1961 *Lola*. Cassard's entrance in the film is underlined by his musical motif, exactly the same Legrand theme that buoyed his tragic loss in the earlier film. The inclusion of Cassard and his theme complicates our emotional response to a character that might otherwise be vilified. Demy explicates Cassard's history in the film's only flashback, which consists of direct visual references to *Lola*—a film that itself pays tribute to Max Ophüls's *Lola Montès* (1955) and Josef von Sternberg's *Der blaue Engel (The Blue Angel)* (1930).

Anouk Aimée in *Lola* (Demy, 1961).

The sequence begins in the Emery flat, where Cassard had just finished dining with Geneviève and her mother, a somewhat awkward meal during which they celebrate the Feast of the Epiphany. Geneviève retires, as she is not feeling well, and Cassard stays to ask Madame Emery for her daughter's hand. Madame Emery is taken aback by this unexpected request, and Cassard begins to tell her about his past. As he speaks, the score shifts into the *Lola* theme, which, as in the original, consists primarily of strings (in contrast to a number of the more brassy, jazz-infused themes in the film). Cassard's voice is soft and proceeds haltingly as he recounts the story of the one woman he once loved, Lola, who did not love him in return. The image cuts to le passage Pommeraye in Nantes, a central location in the earlier film, the site where Roland and Lola rekindle their relationship, and later where Lola leaves him. We see the arcade of shops in color now, but the camera slowly circles the balcony in much the same way it did in the earlier version. And it is the familiarity of the music that most concretely and affectively connects this new Roland—a character who could not be more different from his first incarnation—with our investment in that previous emotional loss. Cassard's voice occupies the melodic line as he narrates, a haunting and simple passage that cycles—ascending, swelling, and then retreating—much like the camera, in a seemingly endless round, returning always to the same three notes.

Such recyclings and temporal displacements proliferate in Demy's films, most explicitly in the repetition of characters, names, settings, and images. There are layers of coincidence, resemblance, and chance. Yet there are just as frequently missed meetings, misrecognitions, secrets, and an abundance of concealed pregnancies. And always there is war. If Demy's films are marked by repetition, it is not a repetition that asserts the solidity of that which reappears. Absence, violence, and failure render recurring elements unfixed and destabilized. Characters are transformed by time and love and emerge as entirely different people.

Repetition is essential to the particular temporality Demy forges. Musical themes, characters, names, or situations recall earlier films, yet these recollections are always marred by their profound difference—the same song, the same character has changed and fails to adhere to our memory of what it should be. While these elements might emerge in a kind of round, the circle is never completed. Elements are constantly metamorphosing in Demy's work, surfacing in endless variations that rarely result in a cohesive whole.

How can we understand Demy's work in relation to history and Bergson's virtual past when these cycles of recollection remain immersed in the realm of fictionalized fantasy? If *Les parapluies* is driven by the historical materiality of

1960s France, its hyperstylization could not be further removed from the reality of Cherbourg. Demy is infamous for his Herculean efforts to transform reality to fit his cinematic vision: unable to afford large-scale sets for *Les parapluies,* the production literally painted large portions of the real city in the Easter-egg hues of the film.[14] A more fundamental fabrication occurs on the sound track: all of the musical dialogue was prerecorded, and the actors synched their movements to voices that were not their own. Demy's portrait of Cherbourg is utterly false. This falsity, however, is the film's greatest strength not only in terms of its sheer beauty and lyricism but also in terms of the challenge it presents to the viewer.

## Fabulation and the Powers of the False

Time-based cinema, for Deleuze, "prevents the past from being debased into recollection. Each sheet of past, each age calls up all the mental functions simultaneously: recollection, but equally forgetting, false recollection, imagination. . . ."[15] The falsity of the recollection-image, half remembered or misremembered, contradicts and destabilizes other memory images. Rather than a fixed, dead representation (some sort of "true" image we can refer to), the past is drawn into an active engagement with the demands of the present, the conditions that cause us both to recall and to falsify. The Bergsonian leap into the virtual is not a quest for the true image of the past. To leap is to engage in a creative act, to think, to be freed from the immediate to forge something new from the provocations of memory. In blurring the distinctions between reality and fiction, fantasy and memory, art moves from the static realm of representing history into that of creation, unleashing images that only become meaningful when they generate thought, in other words, when we take them up, question them, and open them into new circuits of action and reflection.

The power of the false can present itself, as discussed in the previous chapter, through the autonomy of sound and image. Each track presents a contradictory reality that invalidates any singular claim to truth. Demy's use of sound and image is not as immediately radical as the films of Marguerite Duras or Hans-Jürgen Syberberg, films Deleuze discusses as examples of the powers of the false. But there is a discrepancy in Demy's work between the breeziness of the sound track, which in this instance corresponds directly to the colorful flatness of the set, and the banality or outright darkness of the issues the plot confronts. The lack of distinction between humans, objects, and surfaces in the image also works to falsify. "You'd think the wallpaper was bent on world conquest," writes a skeptical reviewer of *Les parapluies,* and there is indeed an abundance and intensity to the mise-en-scène of Demy's musicals that borders on aggressivity.[16] The surfaces multiply, overwhelm, and dwarf the actors, whose own costuming is often hyperstylized and utterly divorced from the reality of middle-class existence in Cherbourg, Rochefort, or Nantes. In *Les parapluies,* Geneviève bemoans being cooped up in "this dreary shop," yet her resistance to the banality of petit bourgeois existence is radically undermined by the riot of colors and patterns that fill the set and by the lilting melody that speaks through her.

One of the darker false images Demy crafts occurs in *Les demoiselles de Rochefort.* Madame Garnier (Danielle Darrieux), mother of the twin daughters at the center of the narrative, reads/sings a disturbing newspaper story to the regulars who have gathered in the *friterie* she owns. "Someone butchered a dame / By the chateau in Etiquette Lane," she begins.[17] The body of a sixty-year-old "ex-Folie Bergère chorine / And one-time beauty queen" was found hacked to pieces in a wicker basket. The woman's stage name was Lola-Lola. "Does anyone remember a Lola-Lola?" Garnier asks, and while no one in her shop does, the viewer is likely to recall Marlene Dietrich's character fitting that name and description from von Sternberg's *Der blaue Engel.* For a tangential storyline that has little to do with the central narrative, this scene seems excessively long, lingering over every gruesome detail. The tone is at odds with the

Catherine Deneuve and Anne Vernon in the "dreary" umbrella shop in *Les parapluies de Cherbourg* (Demy, 1964).

stories of idealized love and missed connections that dominate the film, as is the flippant manner in which the characters sing about the grizzly act. "She was assembled like a puzzle kit," a waitress gushes, and while the characters in the shop soon turn their attention to other matters, the next scene cuts to an image of the wicker basket on the street and the impossibly colorfully clad crowd that has gathered to catch a glimpse of the crime scene. The policemen sing lightheartedly as they try to disperse the gawkers, "Don't make us club you on the ear." The crime becomes fodder for a flirtatious exchange between Solange and the sailor/artist Maxence, who stroll away from the corner singing about which hair color one prefers in the women to whom one takes an axe.

There is a great deal about this sequence that is disturbing: the obvious titillation the townspeople share in discussing the incident, the bright music and trite verse used to narrate it, and the horror of the crime itself, which seems utterly gratuitous. Moreover, none of the characters seems at all unnerved to learn that the killer was a friend of the family, who had only the night before made a show of slicing a cake for them with a giant knife. The jarring and inappropriate nature of this narrative twist is clearly intentional and very much in line with the juxtapositions of the profound and the mundane that mark Demy's oeuvre. Such moments can easily be read as Demy's indictment of bourgeois capitalist modernity. Yet they also cannot be understood outside the context of the larger film, which as a whole exudes an irrepressible joy that nearly explodes in its celebration of the beauty found in the movements of the everyday.

Perhaps we can best understand the story of Lola-Lola's murder in *Les demoiselles* in terms of the contradictory processes of perceiving and recollecting it sets in motion. The tension in this scene is caused by conflicting memory images that falsify one another through their coexistence. Our memory image of Marlene Dietrich's Lola-Lola cannot be reconciled with the Technicolor image of the wicker basket that holds this Lola-Lola's dissected body or the cheerful song that narrates her murder. Yet the invocation of Lola-Lola's name forces the recollection, the leap, to the Lola-Lola of the past; both entities are present at once, and the impact of each memory image is radically transformed.

We might associate such contradictory, simultaneously present moments with the concept of fabulation, a function of storytelling. Fabulation, as the process is described by Bergson, is an act of mythmaking within closed social structures, one that serves to reinforce cultural codes, behaviors, and customs through the creation of fictional beliefs (e.g., spirits, animism, gods). For Bergson, fabulation is a component of religion and an outgrowth of intelligence at the same time that it works against the individualistic inclinations of intelligence—it "counters intelligence's anti-social tendency" to create vivid fictions that will inspire individuals to act in a manner conducive toward a larger social good.[18] In other words, fabulation creates fictions that interpellate the individual and write them into the narrative of the larger social order.

While fabulation serves a primarily conservative function in this scenario, one that is quite similar to that of habit as outlined by Hume, as both Ronald Bogue and John Mullarkey illustrate, there are aspects of Bergson's formulation that suggest a creative potential. Fabulation, as Bergson describes it, arises from a trauma or shock—an encounter with the unexpected—resulting in an immersive, "voluntary hallucination" that can temporarily circumvent the powers of reason, offering a spiritual or animistic recuperation of the unknown.[19] This fabulation function, for Bergson, is opposed to creative emotion, which generates the possibility of a dynamic, open society via "a break from the closed circle of what seems possible and a disconcerting jump into the apparently impossible."[20] Yet as Mullarkey argues, Bergson's description of fabulation as a hallucinatory image that mediates between perceivers and their relation to the flow of images that surround them resonates strongly with Bergson's description of perception as a whole. In each instance, the image generated is a fiction meant to "carve out events from the 'continuity of the real.'"[21] Fabulation here is the creation of something new, a difference, born out of sensation and affect. While that image can be recuperated, it might also be used to illuminate, and to reanimate, that encounter with the unknown while at the same time creating a rupture or suspension in the linear flow of time.

Ronald Bogue notes that Deleuze combines Bergson's formulation of fabulation with that of creative emotion, that libratory leap into the impossible. Alongside the closed forces of custom and habit, we have the possibility for the generation of the new, of difference, which for Deleuze springs directly from that encounter with the accidental, that affective shock.[22] Deleuze's evocation of fabulation, in the course of his writing, took on an increasingly political dimension, linking fabulation with the formation of collectivities and with the imagining of history. "We should take up Bergson's notion of fabulation," Deleuze stated in an interview, "and give it a political meaning."[23] Fabulation is central to the concept of a minor literature as developed by Deleuze and Guattari—through fabulation, those who are marginalized can invent themselves, they can illuminate and mutate the molarizing forces that oppress them and imagine future lines of flights, new assemblages, and new collectivities.

Fabulation, for Deleuze, has an enormous political potential, especially as it can work to destabilize territorial or molar notions of identity and history. D. N. Rodowick describes the political role that storytelling plays in forging a connection between the individual and the collective:

As narration or fabulation, this is neither a psychological memory where the individual recalls a repressed history, nor simply a historical memory as the representation of the occluded story of a people. Rather, it entails a serialism that transforms the individual at the same time as the collective. This double-becoming intertwines two discursive series in a free indirect relation: communication between the world and the I in a fragmented world, and communication of the world and the I in a fragmented I, which must find common points of articulation.[24]

Although Rodowick discusses fabulation in the context of postcolonial African cinema, I argue that a similar process takes place in Demy's films. This is not to say that the musical is a minor cinema—clearly it is not. Musicals are most often the hallucinations of a firmly entrenched culture industry; they typically banish historical trauma from their narratives or recuperate it with images that reinforce the stasis of the status quo. And while Demy's films, too, are not produced from a marginalized position, I suggest that the fictions they offer do create legitimate realms of indeterminacy (between singing and speaking, people and objects, the singular and the collective, reality and fantasy) that throw static notions of history, memory, and truth into question. Demy interrogates, as well, the complex relations between the personal and the political within the larger flows of history.

It is interesting that Bergson's reflections on creativity and the arts privilege music as an emotive form that can exceed representation over the novel, a fabulative form more prone to the systemization of a closed society.[25] Yet the musical is nothing but the combination of the fabulative nature of the narrative with the abstracting force of music. The narrative of the musical is explicitly the telling of a fable, and the stagings of the numbers, as has been illustrated in the discussions of cliché and stereotypes in early chapters, make use of habitual forms of representation. At the same time, the musical moment can make use of the temporal force of music in ways that transport the fabulative out of a closed system. Demy seems particularly attuned to this dynamic, utilizing the affective power of music and the suspended tableau of the musical moment to illuminate precisely the falsifying and multivalent nature of the tales he sets to film. Within the worlds he creates, the individual and the whole are autonomous and interconnected at one and the same time, a paradox that Demy explores through fragmentation, repetition, and the force of music that is constantly surging forward.

## Tableaux Vivant and Donkey Skin Tales

Demy's 1970 film *Peau d'âne* is the first of a series of fairy-tale musicals he created in his later career. It is the most bizarre and least accessible of the films I discuss here and perhaps brings these themes of fabulation and falsity to their pinnacle.

The story of *Peau d'âne* was written by Charles Perrault, who is often credited with founding the literary genre of the fairy tale with his collection of stories *Histoires ou contes du temps passé,* or *Contes de ma Mère l'Oye* (The Stories of Mother Goose) in 1697. *Peau d'âne* was one of his earliest stories, first published in 1694 as a witty verse on the subject of incest. Woven from a number of folk and religious sources, the evolution of *Peau d'âne* has much in common with the history of *Carmen:* multiple retellings across several countries as well as mixtures of high and low elements and of speech and song. While these are qualities shared by most fairy tales, the origins of *Peau d'âne* are particularly complex. The story, in its originary versions, tells of a daughter who flees from the incestuous advances of her father. She meets with different fates in various versions (death, marriage, reconciliation with her father); she disguises herself in different animal pelts in some stories (bear, donkey) or none in others; and the moral of each story shifts depending on context (from the prohibition of incest in some cases to the undermining of familial authority in deference to the church in others).[26] The basic narrative was so commonly told that fanciful stories of all sorts were referred to by the generic category of "Donkey Skin Tales." However, the central problem the story addresses—the desire of the father for his own daughter—has caused varying levels of discomfort for storytellers in different contexts. Of all of Perrault's fairy tales, *Peau d'âne* is reproduced the least frequently, almost never in verse, and subsequent versions often downplay any illicit desire on the part of the father or excise this aspect of the narrative altogether.[27]

Demy's version of the tale remains close to Perrault's, maintaining his dry wit, foregrounding the incestuous designs of the father, and returning the musical rhythms that were lost when Perrault's original verse was translated to prose. *Peau d'âne* tells of a King (Jean Marais) whose wife has fallen ill. From her deathbed, she solicits a promise from him to never wed again unless he can find a bride who surpasses her beauty. The King, brokenhearted, tells his only child, the Princess (Catherine Deneuve), that he never wants to see her again as she reminds him of her mother. The King's advisors eventually press the King to find a new queen, as the State requires a male heir. Unwilling to break his promise, the King is unable to find a woman who approaches his first wife's fairness until his advisors show him a portrait of his own daughter. The King hears his daughter singing in the courtyard and is utterly enchanted. He commands his daughter to marry him, and she protests, conflicted by her love for her father and her fear that the union would be wrong. Frightened, she runs from the castle to seek the advice of her godmother, the Lilac Fairy (Delphine Seyrig).

Her fairy godmother convinces her that the feelings of love she has for her father are confused and that to marry him would be "unlawful." To avoid his advances, she tells the Princess, three times, to request a gift so unattainable that she will be able to avoid her father's advances. The daughter requests first a dress the color of the weather,[28] then a dress the color of the moon, and finally a dress the color of the sun, but each time the King succeeds in providing these gowns, each more luminous than the last. With each gift, the Princess wavers; her own feelings of love for her father are fueled by the depths of his devotion. The godmother remains firm and commands the Princess to demand the thing that is most precious to the King: his magical donkey, who defecates gold coins and jewels and as such provides the primary source of the kingdom's wealth. The Princess demands that the donkey be slaughtered and the hide brought to her; to her shock, the King complies, and the Princess is left with no alternative but to marry her father. She consults her godmother one last time, and on her advice, cloaks herself in the donkey skin, smearing her exposed skin with cinders to appear like a peasant, and flees into the forest with a magic wand and an enchanted trunk holding her dresses and jewels.

The Princess (Catherine Deneuve) and her fairy godmother (Delphine Seyrig) consult in the Princess's boudoir in *Peau d'âne* (Demy, 1970).

After traveling for some time, carried by her godmother's magic carriage, she arrives in a village in a neighboring kingdom. An old woman, perhaps a cohort of her godmother's, who has the odd habit of spitting toads when she speaks, gives Donkey Skin (as she is now referred to by those she meets) work laundering rags and cleaning the pigsty. Donkey Skin is ridiculed and shunned for her pungent, abject, hairy state. She silently bears the abuse of all the other townspeople, yet one day, when the Prince is passing by the hut in the forest where she lives, he catches a glimpse of Donkey Skin clothed in one of her celestial gowns. The Prince asks the villagers who the gorgeous girl who lives in the forest is, and they tell him it is only the filthy scullion, Donkey Skin.

The Prince returns to his castle and becomes ill with longing, refusing to eat until his love for the girl in the golden dress can be fulfilled. His mother frets over him, until he asks for the one thing that will ease his suffering: a cake made by the hands of Donkey Skin. His servants rush to the hut in the woods, and Donkey Skin prepares a magical cake for the Prince, slipping a ring from her slender finger into the batter. The Prince finds the ring and announces that he will wed any woman in the kingdom who can wear the tiny ring. Every maiden in the kingdom tries to don the ring, but to no avail. The last maiden to appear is the lowly Donkey Skin. When the Prince places the ring on her finger, she flings back the donkey's pelt and emerges in her dress the color of the sun. The Prince's family is thrilled and throws a tremendous wedding ceremony, attended by the Lilac Fairy and her new husband, the Princess's father.

Demy's gloss on this fairy tale is incredibly whimsical, and while it remains true to the worldly tone of Perrault's original version, it does away with any pretense of a moral or lesson. The King questions his desire, but is advised by his wise man that all daughters want to marry their fathers and that the wise man himself would surely marry his own daughter if he had one. Not only is the father's incestuous desire thus sanctioned, but Demy suggests that this desire is reciprocated on the part of the daughter. Her song, which seduces the father, speaks about love as a form of madness. "It cries, it sings, it swears false oaths," she sings, while accompanying herself on an organ that sounds like a haunted calliope. The tune itself echoes earlier Legrand compositions, descending a minor scale, only to cycle back upward, repeatedly. The Princess's voice is lilting and clear, buoyed above the harshness of the organ, and we can hear the twittering of the white doves that flit around her in the garden, as well as the sound of their beating wings. Yet despite the romanticism of the setting, and the jewellike quality of the Princess's voice, the song is a seductive, dissonant descent into perversity. The scene is framed by the King, who gazes at his daughter out the window, and we find ourselves participating in his growing desire, a desire that is at once utterly mad and completely logical. If the music alone was not enough to ensure this scene's depravity, the impact is sealed by the Princess's giant blue parrot, who croaks out the final lines of the song.

The Princess, upon hearing of her father's desire, is ready to commit herself to him on more than one occasion, and it is only the intervention of the Lilac Fairy that stops her. But the Fairy's instructive song about the perils of incest is exposed as disingenuous by the conclusion of the film, motivated not by moral dictates but by the Fairy's own romantic designs on the King. The Princess looks more than slightly miffed when her father and the Fairy arrive at her wedding, as the Fairy informs her in a strained whisper, "I'm marrying your father. Try to look pleased." Even the romance between the Princess and the Prince is tinted with shades of decadence. Their first duet, enacted through their fantastical meeting within a dream, is beautifully orchestrated. The lovers' voices chase one another, then swell together in a complex harmony. Yet the lyrics are not typically romantic. The couple declare that they will now "do whatever is forbidden," smoking pipes, going to snack bars late at night, and devouring large pieces of cake served to them by waiters with the heads of antlered stag.

Certainly, the mise-en-scène of this film, which borders on the psychotropic, adds to the ambiance of decadence and excess. Everything in the kingdom of the King and the Princess is marked by an intense blue hue: the clothing of the royal family, the horses, and the servants, the lower ranks of which have blue hair and skin. When we are later introduced to the handsome Prince, his kingdom is similarly saturated with red. The sets, which are constructed like *tableaux vivants* sprung from the pages of a book, are incredibly fantastical and clearly artificial. Moreover, they work to dissolve the distinction between people, animals, and objects at every opportunity. People and animals alike are marked by this impossible, uniform coloring. The King's throne is an enormous reclining white cat on whose furry back he sits. The Princess's bed is covered by a mossy green spread speckled with clumps of flowers and is flanked by life-sized sculpted stag. The Red King and Queen throw a party for their son, the Ball of the Cats and the Birds, where the guests wear outrageous feathered and furred masks. And the Princess's metamorphosis into Donkey Skin subsumes her body into the beast's hide and toothy, long-eared head.

Demy engages in a more fundamental transformation of Perrault's text in his use of temporal anachronisms. The Lilac Fairy, who is well versed in the ways of the future, makes frequent historical slips. She has given the King a book of poetry from the future "written by the poets of tomorrow," which he uses to court the Princess. The Fairy, when having difficulty with her powers,

The King (Jean Marais) on his cat-throne in *Peau d'âne*.

complains that a spell can weaken like a battery, much to the bewilderment of the Princess. The most outrageous of these anachronisms occurs during the wedding celebration at the end of the film, when the Fairy and the King descend into the courtyard of the castle in a helicopter. This playful juxtaposition of temporally disjointed elements reinforces a Bergsonian reading of Demy's use of time, memory, and history. Multiple layers of time exist simultaneously, and the contradictions between these layers are productive. The leaps and connections that are made through nonlinear temporal associations generate new trajectories of thought and provide the foundation for the creativity.

We might thus characterize Demy's work as being structured around the tension between a range of dualisms: the past and the future, the animal and the human, fate and free will, passion and duty, the animate and the inanimate, reality and fantasy. Rather than reinforcing binary oppositions, Demy's films concentrate on the indeterminate or mixed ground that lies between them. Every aspect of his films, the musical films in particular, seems fixated on this realm of the uncertain. The mise-en-scène of *Les parapluies, Les demoiselles,* and especially *Peau d'âne* can be read as elaborate *tableaux vivants,* breathing pictures that collapse depth into a flat surface and blur the distinction between living beings and objects. Conceiving of Demy's films as *tableaux vivants* provides a means of conceptualizing the film's contradictory tendencies in relation to the questions of immobility and movement that frame Deleuze's writing on the cinema.[29]

Eleanor Kaufman makes a similar link between Deleuze's work on cinema and the *tableau vivant* through a reading of Pierre Klossowski. Klossowski, whom Deleuze refers to in many of his works, perhaps most extensively in an appendix to *The Logic of Sense,* returned continually to the image of the *tableau vivant* in his novels, drawings, and philosophical writings. In each of these media, Klossowski exhibits an interest in what Kaufman calls "the way immobility highlights an unbroachable disjunction between bodies and their gestures."[30] Klossowski describes this quality as a kind of solecism, a suspended gesture that presents simultaneous, contradictory messages within the image.[31] Within a series of photographs and drawings that illustrate his *La monnaie vivante,* for example, the positioning of bodies, and in particular of hands, can be read as both inviting and repelling certain actions. Numerous disciplinary categories are blurred here as well, as Klossowski's fiction is overtly philosophical, his drawings accompany and refer to his written work, and the subjects of each resonate with his personal life and history. As Kaufman notes, the images in *La monnaie vivante,* which is a "quasi-economic treatise," include photographs of his wife, Denise Morin-Sinclaire, the inspiration for the character Roberte in his erotic fiction, shown in provocative poses reminiscent of scenes from these novels. In one photograph (taken by Pierre Zucca), a man places a crown on Morin-Sinclaire's head. The gestures within this image are, for Kaufman, fraught with contradiction: "With her body, she leans backward to accept the coronation yet with her hands extended before her torso she defends herself from some unseen onslaught in front of her, while simultaneously, and by way of a slight curvature of the right hand, gracing that same offender with a gesture of waving or beckoning."[32]

For Klossowski, the contradictory gestures of the *tableau vivant* have little to do with bringing a still image to life. Instead, they represent, via the surface and the limits of the body, the process of turning the mobility of the world into an image, "of life giving itself as a spectacle to life; of life hanging in suspense."[33] The distinction to be made here is that one cannot easily differentiate between image and world. The living beings who reenact a famous painting are always already a potential image or spectacle, while the painting itself is never fully removed from the dynamic movements of the world. For Kaufman, the orchestrated melding of movement and immobility associated with the *tableau vivant* is one and the same with Deleuze's reading of the cinema. The *Cinema* books, she argues, elucidate a similar tension between mobility and suspension, exploring the limits of time as both the present of action and the nonspatialized duration of the time-image.

To return to Bergson's model of perception, one might say that Deleuze is exploring the contradictory moment when a living being perceives the flow of the world that surrounds it. The being creates a perception-image that is an immobilized slice of that world, a means of distinguishing between objects so that the being can act upon, and in effect survive within, the movements of the world. The contradiction is that the perception-image is never fully immobilized, as it both enables movement on the part of the being and gives rise to the series of memory images that ripple outward into the dynamic movements of time. Similarly, the movements of the world always maintain the potential of being extended into immobile images. There is no clean break between image and movement. The limits of each exist as a mutual penetration or a contradictory gesture that both immobilizes and flows freely: hence Deleuze's paradoxical description of cinema as a movement-image.[34] The concept of the time-image, too, marks a contradiction as impossible as a dress the color of time. To search for an image of time is to explore the highly charged intersection of the axes of time and space, a site at which the sensory-motor schema and the multiple layers of the virtual past infect one another with their simultaneous movements into and away from one another.

Kaufman makes an extremely compelling argument in this essay, one that resonates with Demy in rather unexpected ways. She notes that Klossowski's *tableaux vivants* are explicitly geared toward the exploration of sexuality and the limits of the human body. In building her argument, she cites a passage from Jean-François Lyotard's "Acinema" in which he discusses the *tableau vivant* in relation to the Swedish practice of posering, where women are hired to assume various erotic poses at the direction of clients who are not permitted to touch the women in any way. A similar practice provides the entire premise for *Model Shop,* where Anouk Aimée's Lola works as a model for hire in a sleazy studio in which clients direct and photograph women in the risqué poses of their choosing. The scenes within the shop where Lola meets her love interest George (Gary Lockwood) exhibit a dramatic tension between stillness and motion (the living enactment of a fixed pose), invitation and withdrawal (the provocative nature of the pose in contrast to Lola's cool demeanor), and action and passivity (Lola takes control of the scene when George is too nervous and uncomfortable to direct her). The series of contradictions invoked here are carried over into the types of temporal contradictions typical of the Demy oeuvre. Lola shares her photo album with George, a series of stills, immobilized memory images from the earlier, fictional motion picture.

Like *Model Shop, Peau d'âne* engages in overt *tableaux vivants,* where the illustrations of a fairy-tale book spring to life, extending their paradoxical movements into larger paradoxical formulations of time. Deleuze writes about the way in which Orson Welles's use of deep focus becomes a kind of temporal-ization, where multiple sheets of the past are simultaneously present within the foreground and background of a single shot; Welles revealed how "spatially distant and chronologically separate regions were in touch with each other, at the bottom of a limitless time which made them contiguous."[35] These sheets, however, contradict and destabilize one another, resulting in utter indetermi-nation and the demise of rationality. The collapsed space of Demy's *tableaux vivants* serve a similar purpose, revealing through a flat surface coexistent tem-poral planes that contradict one another. This indeterminacy is echoed by the myriad tensions that compose the visual plane and by the disjointed move-ments of voice and music that work at times in concert and at times in dis-harmony with the image. The contradictory tensions of the suspended gesture are much like the simultaneous invitation toward identification and the shock of disconnection that mark Demy's style in general.

Deleuze discusses the *tableau vivant,* or what he calls the "frozen scene," directly in relation to Pierre Klossowski's erotic fiction, drawing on similar ter-minology of contradiction and indeterminacy.[36] His interest in Klossowski's suspended stagings, however, relates directly to Klossowski's use of the body. The indeterminate space of the frozen scene is fraught with inconsistencies that actively resist the formation of self-same identity and larger systems of repre-sentation and control. It is significant to note that they are also marked by perversity and excess. The appeal of the *tableau vivant* is the challenge it pres-ents to the human body, which is stretched to its limits in Klossowski's work and placed at the nexus of any number of organizational regimes: sexual, his-torical, theatrical, economic. The body expresses resistance by successfully co-habitating these incommensurate positions at once, perhaps because it does so in ways that are often disturbing and threatening. This perversity is central to the radical disjuncture that drives every level of the *tableau vivant.* I offer that Jacques Demy's cinematic style, despite its innocuous and frivolous appear-ance, is similarly marked by a deep-seated perversity. Although this perversity is not always explicitly erotic, it is one that demonstrates a fascination with the surfaces and limits of objects and bodies. And not unlike Klossowski, Demy's solecisms return again and again to the figure of the female body as a site of inherent spectacle and contradiction.

## The Lady Multiplies: Doubling and Perversity

Of all the recurring images and themes in Demy's films, one is perhaps the most persistent and the most curious—the doubling and multiplying of the female image. As mentioned previously, this occasionally takes the form of characters who reappear in subsequent films, asserting the existence of a fictionalized past. At the same time, the unsentimental manner in which both the character and the world have transformed during the elapsed time between films undermines the memory of that past and reveals the unfixed nature of identity. The Lola of Demy's 1961 film is not the same Lola of *Model Shop;* her face is the same, and she carries a photo album of stills from the earlier film, but she is colder, disillusioned, and no longer swayed by the romantic promises of young American boys with convertibles. The new Lola replicates perfectly the image of the old Lola, but they bear little resemblance to one another in terms of a sameness of identity.[37] In Platonic terms, Lola is a false simulacrum, a bad copy.

This kind of doubling is not limited to the female characters, as we have seen in the case of the Roland Cassard character. The Prince in *Peau d'âne,* too, splits into a dream double that runs off with the Princess's dream double while they sleep. But the female characters in general seem much more prone to such fracturings and duplications. Jackie (Jeanne Moreau) in *La baie des anges,* torn apart by her dual addiction to roulette and to her young companion, chases after him, and for a split second, her image is multiplied into a hundred Jackies reflected in the mirrored pillars of the casino. Other doubles are more firmly embodied. Mothers repeatedly speak of their own romantic entanglements, which we see echoed in the actions of their daughters *(Lola, Les parapluies, Les demoiselles de Rochefort).* The sisters Solange and Delphine in *Les demoiselles* are continually depicted as light and dark mirror images of one another, a comparison that is heightened by the knowledge that the actresses Deneuve and Dorléac are real-life sisters and that Dorléac was killed in an automobile accident shortly after the film's completion. And Lola-Lola's memory, as discussed earlier, is grotesquely butchered into literal fragments. Yet the most explicit and spectacular case of doubling occurs in *Peau d'âne* when Deneuve appears simultaneously as both Donkey Skin and the Princess in the dress of the sun, joining in song with herself as each girl sings and prepares a magical cake.

In this scene, Donkey Skin has retreated into her hut to bake a cake for the Prince while his servants wait outside. She thumbs through a magical cookbook that she pulls from her enchanted trunk. Beneath the listing for Rum Alaska, she finds a recipe for a Cake of Love. Donkey Skin waves her magic wand, and the dress the color of the sun slides out of the trunk and over the body of the Princess, who is now standing beside Donkey Skin. The two identical beings begin to sing, Donkey Skin reading the recipe while the Princess prepares it. One might suppose that the reasoning behind this duplication is

The twins (Catherine Deneuve and Françoise Dorléac) in *Les demoiselles de Rochefort* (Demy, 1967).

to emphasize that the beautiful Princess's hands, rather than those of the filthy Donkey Skin, must be the ones to prepare the cake. Yet this is not borne out by the emotional trajectory of the scene, which strives to emphasize the sameness of the two women and the common ground between them. Donkey Skin, not surprisingly, is hardly abject; other than a few smears of dirt on her cheek and the disconcerting donkey skull atop her head, she is incredibly beautiful. The Princess, too, has no difficulty rolling up her sleeves to knead the dough or clean the kitchen. It would have been simple for Donkey Skin to transform herself into the Princess and back again, and it would have been far simpler for the production to shoot the scene in this manner. One is left with the feeling that the joy of the task at hand exceeds the ability of one entity to perform it; it causes her to multiply into two selves that burst into simultaneous song (much like the chick that bursts from the egg that the Princess cracks while baking the cake).

The twinned form of the woman may say something about the concept of the self that typically emerges from fairy tales and musicals. The doubling that occurs in this scene has nothing to do with unveiling the "true" identity of Donkey Skin/the Princess. Indeed, it confronts us with the incommensurate coexistence of the two beings who in fact are defined solely through their

The Princess and Donkey Skin sing a duet and bake a cake.

masks and veils (the dress that shines like the sun and the donkey pelt). Indeed, the two figures, connected by the song they sing, are less "beings" than "becomings," processes of metamorphosis moving away from the fixed identity "woman" toward a becoming-donkey and a becoming-celestial. For all the disguised and revealed identities woven into the narrative of *Peau d'âne,* all that is exposed in the end is a proliferation of empty veils.

Deleuze, in *Difference and Repetition,* opposes forms of repetition that assert sameness and self-identity to those that reproduce difference. The distinction leads us back to Bergson's model of memory as a cone. Superficial repetitions of the same remain bound by the horizontal axis; elements are divorced from their temporal evolutions and are reproduced as identical appearances. Repetitions that leap into the layers of the past, however, recognize the totality of time and the fundamental differences that occur between those successive layers. "Difference itself is therefore between two repetitions: between the superficial repetition of the identical and instantaneous external elements that it contracts, and the profound repetition of the internal totalities of an always variable past, of which it is the most contracted level."[38] The dynamic, time-oriented repetition opposes the repetition of representation, where one element comes to stand for, replace, or explain another. This more profound repetition allows for multiple simulacra that contradict and falsify one another, "a clothed repetition of which the masks, the displacements and the disguises are the first, last and only elements."[39]

The kinds of repetitions that emerge across Demy's films, and in particular within *Peau d'âne,* have a great deal in common with the second form of repetition that Deleuze describes. Despite the work these repetitions do to destabilize identities, however, they appear to fixate on the category of female identity when enacting their multiplications. In *The Logic of Sense,* Deleuze finds patterns of doubling, and specifically female doubling, in the literature of Lewis Carroll and Pierre Klossowski. Carroll's Alice continually undergoes doubling transformations (changing size, passing through the looking-glass) and encounters doubles (the kings and queens, Tweedledum and Tweedledee, the March Hare and the Mad Hatter) that embody the forked time of becoming. Within this forked movement, processes of change and transformation move simultaneously toward the future and into memory images that reside in the virtual past. Deleuze writes:

> This is the simultaneity of a becoming whose characteristic is to elude the present. Insofar as it eludes the present, becoming does not tolerate the separation or the distinction of before and after, or of past and future. It pertains to the essence of becoming to move and to pull in both directions at once: Alice does not grow

without shrinking, and vice versa. Good sense affirms that in all things there is a determinable sense or direction *(sens); but paradox is the affirmation of both senses or directions at the same time.[40]

The doubling in Carroll's stories, like the doubling in *Peau d'âne* and in the larger oeuvre of the fairy tale, is strategically nonsensical. The playfulness and joy it exhibits is in affirming that good sense is utterly incapable of describing what we inevitably experience through the paradoxical and contradictory movements of our own becomings.

Yet the play that occurs here is not all light and innocence. The repetition that resists sameness and resemblance necessarily involves the transgression and dissolution of the boundaries of subjectivity. Deleuze writes about the hesitations and suspended scenes that mark Klossowski's trilogy of philosophical-pornographic novels, *Les lois de l'hospitalité.* The novels are rife with numerous doublings, in particular the multiplication of the female protagonist Roberte. Roberte's husband, Octave, engages in the ultimate hospitable act. He offers his wife for the sexual enjoyment of all the guests that enter his home, obliging her, as such, to duplicate herself into an endless series of doubles that can fulfill this demand. As Deleuze writes, Octave "attempts to multiply Roberte's essence, to create as many simulacra and reflections of Roberte as there are persons establishing relations with her, and to inspire Roberte to emulate somehow her own doubles."[41]

There is something profoundly disturbing about the duplication of Roberte as a sexual "gift." But the formulation that Klossowski offers is, potentially, not as sexist as it might first appear. As Kaufman notes, the figure of the sexually aggressive woman has a long and complex political history in French pornography, and there are decisive moments when Roberte challenges the logic of the masculine demands made of her. The perversity of Roberte and Octave's arrangement further strike a blow to the doctrines of the institution of marriage. And the excessiveness of both Octave's request and Roberte's compliance becomes a means of perverting the repetition of exchange.[42] For Deleuze, this suggests a mode of repetition diametrically opposed to the repetitions of resemblance and equivalence. Roberte's body, rather than becoming a commodity, is a gift that is freely given. The impossible multiplicity of that body and the impossibility of reciprocating its generosity threaten to undo the structures of equivalence that provide the framework for our cultural economy.[43] Moreover, Deleuze notes, Octave is equally implicated in Roberte's doubling. He never owns her image fully, for "he also knows well that, as a result of his observation, he loses his own identity, sets himself outside of himself, and is multiplied in the gaze as much as the other is multiplied under the gaze."[44] What we find here is a repetition of pure difference, one that defies singular notions of identity or resemblance.

The particular form of doubling that Klossowski presents extends beyond the sexual theater in which it is framed. There is a perversion, for Deleuze, that is inherent to the suspended gesture, one that relates directly to the processes of hesitation that mark both the physical and intellectual development of living beings. The capacity for reasoning develops via "fits and starts," just as the biological formation of an embryo goes through stages of indeterminacy—"a butt of a limb is determined to be a paw before it is determined to be the right paw."[45] For Deleuze, this corporeal indeterminacy is fundamentally perverse:

> What is perverse is precisely this objective power of hesitation in the body: this paw which is neither left nor right; this determination by fits and starts; this differentiation never suppressing the undifferentiated which is divided in it; this suspense which marks each moment of difference.[46]

The perversity of Klossowski's *tableaux vivants,* then, is based not solely in their sexual content but in the links that they make between the indeterminacy of the individual (female) body pushed to its limits and the profound indeterminacy that enables life itself. They reveal the perversity foundational to the body, as well as to reason, language, and representation, which for Deleuze are also driven by the creation of doubles and simulacra.

The musical as a whole is marked by a proliferation of doubling, especially female doubling, fraught with contradiction and the perverse violation of boundaries. Certainly, the spectacle of the Berkeleyesque musical moment reproduces the female body endlessly, eradicating the distinction between body and object, rendering the body an accumulation of disconnected parts, and flattening the female form into a sexual fetish.[47] Female characters in musicals double, too, in ways quite similar to Demy's films. In the dream ballet sequence in *Oklahoma!,* Laurey (Shirley Jones) dreams a dance (choreographed by Agnes de Mille) in which she explores her anxieties about her two competing suitors.

Such dances were common problem-solving devices in musicals during this period. What is unusual in this film is that Laurey splits in two on the screen, meeting a dream double who performs the dance for her. Upon sniffing a bottle mysteriously labeled "Elixir of Egypt," Laurey falls into a trancelike dream and sings to her double (the dancer Bambi Linn) before touching her hand and launching the double into the fantasy dance. The dream Laurey first engages in a joyful duet with her principle love interest Curly, also danced by a double (James Mitchell) in Zinneman's film. The duet evolves into a danced

Shirley Jones and Bambi Linn in the dream ballet from *Oklahoma!* (Zinnemann, 1955).

marriage ceremony, which is cut short when Curly is transformed into Jud (Rod Steiger, notably not a double), the degenerate and violent farmhand who lusts after Laurey. While Laurey is fearful of Jud while awake, her double is allowed to experience the realization of the raw sexuality that Jud represents. She is manhandled by Jud, who chases her into a brothel where she is confronted by a line of coarse burlesque dancers. The sequence ends when Jud strangles Curly, the culmination of Laurey's deepest fears about the consequences of her sexual awakening.

There is of course a technical justification for Laurey's doubling, as "dream" characters are often used in stagings of *Oklahoma!* when the lead performer's dancing skills are not up to the task. Yet as is the case with vocal doubling in *Carmen Jones,* such explanations fail to address the excessive rift that these doubles cause in the flow of the films. The dark sexual desires and fears that the dream Laurey sets loose are at complete odds with the veneer of innocence and respectability that surround the real Laurey and that set the tone of the musical as a whole. The dark sexual fantasy that the double enables is not fully resolved by the narrative's glossy synthesis, for the impact of that threat feels far less fantastical than the choreographed gaiety of the film's wakened world. The double in *Oklahoma!* appears to have explicit psychological overtones, indicating the return of the repressed or a nightmarish wish fulfillment. The entire ballet is a confrontation/duet with Otherness, and much like the mythology of the film as a whole, serves as an allegory of the subject's treacherous journey into adulthood.

Similarly, the psychoanalytic implications of *Peau d'âne,* with its explicitly incestuous royal drama, are difficult to ignore. Fairy tales quite often follow the adventures of a young female protagonist, the not-fully-formed girl whose trials allegorize the foundation of subjecthood. The figure of the girl becomes a neutral surface on which identification is projected, a girl "identified with the phallus but also deprived of a penis."[48] The desexualized nature of the narrative, contained within the bubble of the children's fairy tale or the sanitized Technicolor musical, elevates the female protagonist to an iconic status that indirectly reaffirms her status as the sexual object par excellence. Alice, Laurey, and the Princess are all androgynous, childlike avatars who undergo an oedipal crisis, a process of becoming via fantasy, from which they emerge as fully formed subjects within the laws of propriety and sense (Alice wakes from her dream, Laurey and the Princess are wed to suitable male love interests).[49]

While it might be tempting to thus read tales such as *Peau d'âne, Oklahoma!,* or *Through the Looking-Glass* as variations on an oedipal drama, for Deleuze, such interpretations are of little use, for "it is well known that the encounter between psychoanalysis and the work of art . . . is not achieved by 'psychoanalyzing' the work."[50] At issue here, for Deleuze, is a fundamental misunderstanding of the function of the work of art. Art is not a static text that can be psychoanalyzed as if it were a subject. Neither is the work of art a fixed reflection of the inner state of the artist-as-subject. The artist should not be conceived of as a patient, nor should the work of art. The usefulness of psychoanalysis in the realm of art for Deleuze occurs in the case of great artists who use their art to explore the symptoms woven into the structures of our larger culture. "Artists are clinicians," he writes, "not with respect to their own case, nor even with respect to a case in general; rather, they are clinicians of civilization."[51]

How do we make sense of the double without "psychoanalyzing the work," and how can we understand the role of the artist as clinician? Of utmost importance to Deleuze's formulation here is the relationship between the double or simulacrum and the outside. The doubles that appear in these works are never the outward projection of some interior state. Indeed, for Deleuze models of the human subject built on interiorization and exteriorization fail to grasp the fragmented nature of selfhood. The self is never hermetically removed from the movements of the world, and the establishment of boundaries between the two is a convenient abstraction. Like Bergson's model of the intellect or the spatializing modality of the sensory-motor schema, it is an abstraction that is necessary for survival. Nevertheless, psychoanalytic models that describe the subject as a singular being marked by an interior splitting inhibit more fluid understandings of the subject in relation to the world. *All* is outside for Deleuze, for the self is always a conglomeration of multiple elements actively engaged with the elements that surround it. As Brian Massumi describes Deleuze and Guattari's formulation of the self,

> A human subject in the broad sense is a superindividual composed of a multitude of subindividuals comparable to muck and sedimentary rock, but doubled by surplus-value layers of larval and fledgling selves.[52]

Each subject is always already multiple, yet the concrete person that emerges from this "muck" will conform, under normal circumstances, to the practices and categories of subjecthood dictated by a given civilization. But there is a potential and a risk for this coherence to fall apart:

> The person always has the potential to reconnect with its impersonality to become a subject-group: singular, orphan, atheist, inhuman. Since a person is only as stable as its constituent contractions—that is, metastable—it can be precipitated into a crisis state despite its best intentions.[53]

This potential is of great political import, for it suggests an alternative to the repressive structures of identity and representation that discourage multiplicity. For Deleuze, it is a potential that all selves have access to, and the double provides a powerful tool toward the actualization of this crisis.

The double, then, is not the repressed subconscious brought to the surface because the self is never a closed system, a single entity split into stratified parts. The fractured state of the self is instead a proliferation or assemblage of elements that exist *beside* one another, simultaneously. The double is the image not of submerged sameness but of difference and all those fledgling selves. For Deleuze, the double "is an interiorization of the outside. It is not a doubling of the One, but a redoubling of the Other."[54] Deleuze is drawing from Foucault's work in which the simulacrum challenges Cartesian understandings of identity and being to assert the uncertainty of becoming and the unthought. "The unthought," Foucault writes, "is not lodged in man like a shrivelled-up nature or stratified history; it is, in relation to man, the Other: the Other that is not only a brother but a twin, born, not of man, nor in man, but beside him and at the same time, in an identical newness, in an unavoidable duality."[55] If one were to claim some sort of "truth" or "essence" to a being, it could only be the failed coherence of self-same identity in the face of the radical, creative potential of the unthought. The double is the actualization of this alien Otherness.

Thus, the artist does not delve inward into herself, nor does she expose the subconscious of her fictional characters. The great artist will break the chain of representation and sameness to unleash the phantasm of difference, rupturing identity and setting into motion new lines of flight. Such an act requires a leap outside, a loosening of the contractions of action and the present, to allow for the image of the Other, the simultaneity of multiple temporalities, and the recognition of the self as a conglomeration of multiple, simultaneous, composite selves. As clinician, the artist motivates this leap by recognizing the relationship between the individual and the outside. More important, the unthought that is invoked is not the unthought of the individual but the unthought of civilization. The double does not bring to light the unconscious of the subject; it raises "the visible to the invisible," bringing the realm of the everyday in contact with the "repressed" differences and paradoxes of the larger world—"This is the object of the novel as a work of art, and what distinguishes it from the familial novel."[56]

The role of the artist, for Deleuze, is to break down the oppositions between self/other, mind/body, interior/exterior, and self/world that have dominated Western thought. The artist does not do this to "cure" the world; Deleuze suggests a far more threatening proposition: "The artist is not only the patient and doctor of civilization, but is also its pervert."[57] The figure of the pervert invoked here is not a degenerate or a subject possessed by an illicit desire. For Deleuze, the pervert poses a challenge to discourses of control and to systems of representation that seek to categorize desire and delineate bodies and subjects. He writes:

> The concept of perversion is a bastard concept—half juridical, half medical. But neither medicine nor law are entirely suited to it. . . . It seems that we seek the reason for its quite ambiguous and contingent connection with law as well as with medicine in the very structure of perversion. The point of departure is as follows: perversion is not defined by the force of a certain desire in the system of drives; the pervert is not someone who desires, but someone who introduces desire into an entirely different system and makes it play, within this system, the role of an internal limit, a virtual center or zero point.[58]

The artist as pervert induces the crisis state that upsets the coherence of the subject and sets its constituent components into dialogue with the elements of the world. This is a political move, the introduction of a force that destabilizes not the individual but the very structures that define our civilization.

The *tableau vivant*, through its hesitations and contradictions, becomes a playground for perversity, for revealing the porous boundaries between the categories that govern our systems of thought. *Peau d'âne*, far more than Demy's earlier musicals, escalates the fracturing of time and the dissolution of resemblance into perversity. It is the playful, pleasurable simultaneity of innocence and incest that feels perverse in this film, an effect that is wrought by its status as a musical. The story is a song to be sung to and repeated by children, and by all accounts, the film has been embraced by children and parents alike. Demy offers no moral and goes to great lengths to undermine the implied indictment of taboo found within Perrault's original version. He celebrates the incongruities of the fairy tale and, with Legrand's score, weaves those contradictions into a whole that refuses to resolve them. The perverse doubling in this film occurs not only on the level of narrative but also through its indeterminate images and its bifurcations of temporality and history. Image, music, and narrative become a play of surface that joyfully defies boundaries of identity, familial propriety, humanness, history, and common sense.

In his essay on Klossowski, Deleuze points to the connection between vision and sound in relation to movements of differentiation and collaboration. "The function of sight," Deleuze writes, "consists of doubling, dividing, and multiplying, whereas the function of the ear consists in resonating, in bringing about resonance."[59] I see image and music functioning in Demy's films in precisely this manner, enacting the disconnection between image and sound that is foundational to fabulation and the time-image. The flat surfaces of Demy's images are filled with textures and colors that eradicate the distinction between animate and inanimate objects. The complex choreography of these elements further violates these boundaries and, like the *tableau vivant,* operates via the tension between fixity and motion. Hesitation is core to Demy's style, emerging across multiple registers in terms of the hesitations and missed connections in the narrative and the hesitation between movement and stillness in the image itself. There is a further tendency toward multiplication and doubling in the image that fundamentally destabilizes Cartesian and psychoanalytic theories of subjectivity. The candy-colored surface of Demy's images seems to resist notions of depth and interiority, creating instead a perverse dance in which the boundaries of self and world are entirely indeterminate.

The function of music, it seems, is to then forge the resonant connections between these fractured and destabilized elements. Music, speech, and sound are often used to deny and resolve difference and fragmentation in the image by fixing meaning and establishing closure, but in Demy's films, music denies closure and celebrates difference. Rather than reestablishing the unity of the subject, music works as an innovative force, creating new correlations that cross the boundaries of history and corporeality. Music in Demy's films, and in the musical in general, is the force that propels us into temporal and logical leaps. The refrains of each theme suggest links to people, places, and feelings, sending us into the plane of recollection. Yet that refrain comes unhinged, floating uncannily above the street that has transformed, the love that has dissipated. Music teases out the multiple temporal layers of an event, memories that uncomfortably coexist within a present situation but often remain buried and forgotten. Perhaps most important, music functions as a force that overwhelms and overflows the individual through waves of reciprocal transformation. Love, pain, and the monotony of everyday material existence are not opposed to the loftier realms of history, politics, and critical thought. Music, instead, maps their resonant connections. The collisions between the private and the public, the real and the fantastic, enact a mutual fragmentation that marks both the incommensurability and the interdependence of self and world as well as the schizophrenic multiplicity of either of these states (individual and whole).

There is a degree to which the perversion of indeterminacy and the resonations of the leap are qualities shared by all musical films. Yet the question still remains, Why does the image of the female body serve as the privileged site for the musical's fabulations? Deleuze's most direct response to this line of inquiry is cryptic and not particularly satisfying: "As a general rule, only little girls understand Stoicism; they have the sense of the event and release an incorporeal double." He makes the allowance that on occasion "a little boy is a stutterer and left-handed" and as such has access to the modality of contradictory surfaces and simulacra.[60] It is unclear if Deleuze, whose discussion here involves Carroll's (potentially perverse) fascination with the figure of the little girl, presents this statement in a playful manner that he does not intend us to interpret literally. Nevertheless, his language here raises further questions about the potentially gendered nature of several of his formulations, in particular the process of "becoming-woman," a concept addressed in detail in the next chapter.

## Four

# Becoming-Fluid:
# History, Corporeality,
# and the Musical Spectacle

History becomes "effective" to the degree that it introduces discontinuity in to our very being—as it divides our emotions, dramatizes our instincts, multiplies our body and sets it against itself. "Effective" history deprives the self of the reassuring stability of life and nature, and it will not permit itself to be transported by a voiceless obstinacy toward a millennial ending. It will uproot its traditional foundations and relentlessly disrupt its pretended continuity. This is because knowledge is not made for understanding; it is made for cutting.

—MICHEL FOUCAULT, "Nietzsche, Genealogy, History"

In "The Mass Ornament," Siegfried Kracauer describes the spectacle of the Tiller Girls, a franchise of dance troupes that performed synchronized routines in geometrical formations. Kracauer writes:

> These products of American distraction factories are no longer individual girls, but indissoluble girl clusters, whose movements are demonstrations of mathematics . . . One need only glance at the screen to learn that the ornaments are composed of thousands of bodies, sexless bodies in bathing suits. The regularity of their patterns is cheered by the masses, themselves arranged by the stands in tier upon ordered tier.[1]

For Kracauer, the fragmentation and abstraction of the body that takes place in the Tiller Girls' performance echoes the abstract regimentation of industry. Kracauer draws a distinction in his reading of this spectacle between two levels of reality, one being the structural, historical truth of a given culture, the second consisting of external "surface-level expressions."[2] The "girl cluster," as a surface-level expression, is a prismatic ornament that exposes the logic at the heart of capitalist rationality.

A "girl cluster" from Busby Berkeley's "By a Waterfall" number in *Footlight Parade* (Bacon, 1933).

Throughout "The Mass Ornament," one can trace the mutual influence of these two layers. The pure externality of surface-level expressions, for Kracauer, provides "unmediated access to the fundamental substance of the state of things."[3] In the case of the Tiller Girls, the illumination that takes place is of the empty abstraction of the capitalist *Ratio;* the spectacle fragments and mechanizes the body while refusing "that reason which arises from the basis of man."[4] Despite their superficial appearance, such surface-level expressions provide us with an image of reason that we can use to analyze and interpret the deeper status of our present situation.

When looking at musical spectacles like the one described here, Kracauer's provocation forces us to confront some rather difficult questions. Even if one is skeptical of the visual parallel that he draws between the "girl cluster" and the factory, the potential connection between aesthetics and politics that he suggests is compelling. Given the difficulty of discussing the fantastical aspects of the musical in relation to history, Kracauer's model of the ornament complicates readings of the musical spectacle as sheer escapism. Can such spectacles be described as "surface-level expressions," and if so, what is the nature of the reality that lies beneath them? Kracauer's formulation seems to arise from a Marxist distinction between base and superstructure and may resonate with psychoanalytic models that regard the surface as a series of signs symptomatic of underlying conditions. Are these the models Kracauer draws upon, or are there alternative ways of reading his formulation?

Moreover, how do we address these musical spectacles in terms of gender? Kracauer describes the body found here as sexless, but it is always decidedly female. In what ways do gender and sexuality play into the musical's presentation of the body, and if a capitalist rationale does lie at the heart of the musical ornament, is gender a critical cog in that machine? And is it possible to formulate a feminist reading of the synchronized girl cluster that finds more than the fragmentation and exploitation of the female body? Are these expressions inherently repressive, or might they hold some productive potential?

The distinction that Kracauer draws between surface and depth appears entirely at odds with Deleuzian theory, which celebrates fragmentation and rejects understandings of the real as something that exists behind or beneath a veil of signs. Deleuze asserts that cinematic history cannot be described as a chronological evolution; neither is cinema an "aesthetic reflex," a mirror image of a historical moment. The power of the time-image, in fact, rests in its incommensurability with a teleological History; it is discontinuous, interstitial, and it serves to destabilize and falsify notions of identity and truth. As demonstrated in the previous chapter on the *tableau vivant,* Deleuze argues that the surface encompasses all and that representational analogies drawn between various elements assert false and reductive resemblances at the expense of difference. But the concept of reality that Kracauer presents is far more complex than it might first appear, and the relation between this reality and its surface expressions is not one of resemblance or representation. I argue that reading these two divergent thinkers alongside each other will illuminate not only the nuances of their theories but the problem of the musical spectacle.

One of the primary tensions driving this project relates to the contradictory tendencies of musical films, films that simultaneously verge toward creative differentiation and the repetition of the mass-produced same. I have argued that it is possible to read this tension in productive ways and to see the musical's brief gestures of rupture as artistically, politically, and philosophically significant. In this chapter, I cast this question in a slightly different manner. How do we read the musical spectacle in light of its origins in the capitalist culture industry? More specifically, do the sounds and images of that spectacle emerge not in spite of, but precisely because of, these political and cultural conditions? By acknowledging these conditions, is it even possible to locate a creative potential within the musical spectacle? If the musical is the ornament of modern industrialized society, is its significance merely a dystopian image, a visible symptom of our alienated conditions? Or might the musical ornament serve some other function?

My inquiry is driven by two extraordinarily different sets of examples, both of which feature highly spectacular musical ornaments. The first set comprises the musical films starring Esther Williams, films that spotlight the champion swimmer in synchronized extravaganzas much like Kracauer's description of the Tiller Girls. Williams's films are exceptional both for the impossible otherworldliness of their musical productions and for the extreme rupture between narrative and number imposed by their watery nature. I am interested here in the unusual nature of Williams's work and in the role that water plays in transforming the time and space of the musical spectacle. At the same time, Williams's filmography is incredibly formulaic. The flimsy premises for each of her films are repetitive and relatively exchangeable. Fixated by design on the bathing-suited female body, Williams's films were often thinly disguised marketing tools for swimwear, aboveground pools, and vacation destinations. Indeed, the Williams films are driven by fairly base presumptions: attractive female athletes hold a certain fascination with audiences of the 1940s and 1950s; plots involving swimsuits allow for the maximum display of the female body; "wholesome" girls and chlorinated waters simultaneously sanitize and contain that body's threatening sexuality; and underwater photography is a technological novelty that will hold audience attention.[5] As unapologetically exploitative and market-oriented films, Williams's body of work highlights the capitalist rationale at the heart of the spectacle's will to entertain.

In stark contrast, *The Hole,* by Taiwanese director Tsai Ming-liang, presents an apocalyptic vision of Taipei racked by a mysterious virus, a narrative curiously interrupted by intensely stylized musical performances. These performances, which are for the most part entirely unaccounted for by the "real world" of the narrative, feature the female protagonist, Yang Kuei-Mei, lip-synching to songs by Grace Chang (Ge Lan), a Hong Kong musical star of the 1950s and 1960s. Tsai extends the musical's prototypical break between narrative and production number into an insurmountable gulf. The reality of the musical's narrative world, which is often entirely fantastical and saccharine, becomes a dystopian nightmare in *The Hole.* Modern life, defined by alienation, disease, and despair, is entirely at odds with the optimism and beauty of the songs that invade it. These songs are themselves trite, Western-style pop songs culled from frothy pop musicals that, much like the films of Esther Williams, were formulaic vehicles for their female star. Chang's films similarly made few attempts to veil their celebration of capitalist ideals and Western trends, as the English translations of several of her titles indicate (*Mambo Girl* [Yang, 1957], *Air Hostess* [Yang, 1959], *Our Dream Car* [Yang, 1959]).[6] Tsai's use of the musical spectacle is complex and ambiguous, suggesting at once the bankrupt abyss of industrialized urban life and the liberating power of the musical baubles that this world has produced.

There are several points of resonance between these seemingly distinct sets of films. In terms of their musical style, both feature production spectacles that are relatively autonomous. Tsai offers no immediate justification for the jarring insertion of musical numbers, and while several of Williams's films involve the production of a water ballet, the link between narrative and number is so preposterous that these justifications are rendered completely hollow.[7] Both *The Hole* and the Williams films prominently feature the spectacle of the female body, and as distinct from the more anonymous girl cluster described by Kracauer, combine elements of abstraction and fragmentation with the fetishization of the singular female star. Perhaps most significantly, water plays a critical role in each set of films, utterly transforming the temporal and spatial planes along which they unfold.

Grace Chang in *The Wild, Wild Rose* (Wong, 1960).

It is my contention that the aqueous spaces invoked by Esther Williams and Tsai Ming-liang forge a hybrid field in which the multiple tensions of the musical film are crystallized. In reading these groups of films beside each other, I suggest that the spectacle typified by Esther Williams is a refrain that is reworked in *The Hole*. In each, the surface of the human body becomes a malleable, permeable entity that resonates with the larger body of industrialized society. The multiplication of the body in Williams's films takes place through the ambiguity of surfaces and spaces, through the hybrid status of Williams as a star, and through the reflection of her form by its many abstracted doubles. Yet in Tsai's work, the human body is mutated and divided by alienation and illness, and then doubled through phantasmatic spectacles. Water serves as a transitional body that both links and fragments the body of the city and the body of its inhabitants. Tsai explores this dynamic and the shared corporeality of people and urban spaces with a keen awareness of the politics of gender and sexuality. This theme reverberates throughout the body of his work, which much like the work of Jacques Demy, is built upon the repetition of key images, characters, faces, and temporal refrains.

The ambiguous nature of the spectacles I examine here are key to understanding their status as historical images. In stating this, I am not suggesting that they are reflections of cultural conditions or metaphoric representations of historical moments. Rather, the historical image is a provocation, a stimulus that startles or unsettles us, making something that was previously imperceptible perceptible. The modality of the historical image is entirely contingent on the modalities that define its context; even when the image ruptures or breaks from prevailing structures, it is impossible to conceive of it outside of these conditions. Engagement with such an image becomes a means of generating new thought, of rethinking history.

This chapter, then, addresses a number of threads simultaneously: the ambiguous nature of the musical spectacle; the relation between these spectacles and notions of identity, place, and history; and the provocations these relations pose to those who encounter them. I draw on a number of conceptual models as I map these interwoven threads: Kracauer's "The Mass Ornament" and *Theory of Film: The Redemption of Physical Reality*, Deleuze's distinction between movement-image and time-image, Deleuze's and Foucault's adoption of Nietzsche's genealogical history, and Deleuze's work with Guattari on the notion of becoming. The surface-level expression of the musical spectacle actualizes the very real connections between individual and social bodies, between the general and the particular. Hardly a static reflection of a preexisting state, however, the musical spectacle and indeed popular music in general contain the potential to transform these conditions. Looking at the challenge to boundaries of interiority and exteriority that Williams and Tsai pose, I suggest a new model for understanding the force of the musical spectacle. Born out of the contradictory tensions of creative difference and repressive sameness, the musical spectacle is like the hint of a tune that enters us from outside, dissolving identity but also working to free us from its grasp.

## The Musical Spectacle as Implied Dream

The finale of Esther Williams's first feature film, *Bathing Beauty* (Sidney, 1944), begins with an elaborate, out-of-water prologue. A tight shot of Harry James's trumpet opens onto his full orchestra playing on a series of pristine white steps at the edge of an enormous pool. Rows of women in gauzy pink dresses and flowered headdresses dance beside the band, and the entire scene is perfectly reflected in the waters below. Suddenly, the dancers dash to the right of the frame, revealing another wide expanse of stage and pool, where Xavier Cugat and his orchestra launch into a choreographed "battle of the bands" repartee with James. As the medley unfolds, the first row of dancers strip off their pink robes, unveiling shimmering pink and blue swimsuits beneath. The camera cuts to a navel level shot in front of the line of women, who dive sideways into the pool one after the other like a cascading row of dominoes.

After a slow crawl across the length of the pool, the swimmers point their hands upward, leading the camera back to James's trumpet. To the beat of the "One O'Clock Jump," the dancers in and out of the pool echo each other's jazzy kicks, splashes, and arm movements. They multiply on each side of the water's surface to create increasing confusion as to the limits of the space in which they dance. All at once, however, the swimmers and dancers part, and the music wafts into a smoothly orchestrated arrangement of Strauss's "Blue Danube Waltz." The camera pans up as the waters empty before a pedestal framed with giant seahorses rising from within the stage. Esther Williams, cloaked in a silver suit and crown, steps from the platform and, as ladies-in-waiting take her robe and sash, dives alone into the pool.

From this point forward, the production continues through a series of movements that shift between Williams diving and surfacing, while the chorines periodically emerge in synchronized lines and whirlpools of kicking legs. The shots progress through playful visual associations. At one point, Williams swims into an underwater camera holding a lone water lily. The camera pulls back from what is now a gigantic flower on the surface, in the center of hundreds of girls floating in concentric, kaleidoscopic rings. Back underwater, Williams propels herself through a tunnel of rotating girls, linked from shoulder to foot in a twisting, corporeal passageway that never stops to breathe. At the climax of the number, Williams kicks past fountains shooting huge plumes of water and flames into the air. She rises again on a pedestal within the circle of water and fire and girls, and we see for the first time several silhouetted audience members applauding at the edge of the frame.[8]

This scene, which is typical of an Esther Williams musical number, makes use of excessive compositions, much like the Busby Berkeley–style girl cluster. The play between surface and depth, and the ambiguity that the camera delights in forging between them, is the governing principle in the Williams number. Yet the appeal and marketing of Williams centers on her fame as a championship swimmer, and she is clearly featured as a solo performer, resulting in far less democratic stagings than the typical Berkeley number.[9] Her role as an avatar, leading us through the various settings of the sequence, undermines the sheer abstraction of the multiplied female form. Rather than a surface of indistinguishable doubles, we follow a singular protagonist through an odyssey. This odyssey, despite its circuitous path, could be interpreted, in certain instances, in terms of its narrative or problem-solving functions (especially, in the finale, when Williams invariably encounters her love interest in the depths of the pool).

Deleuze's reading of the Berkeleyesque production number, which draws on language very similar to Kracauer's, suggests that it is the impersonality and abstractness of the spectacle that makes these compositions so evocative:

> In Berkeley, the multiplied and reflected girls form an enchanted proletariat whose bodies, legs and faces are the parts of a great transformational machine: the "shapes" are like kaleidoscopic views which contract and dilate in an earthly or watery space, usually shot from above, turning around the vertical axis and changing into each other to end up as pure abstractions.[10]

Deleuze sees the impersonal multiplications that occur in the kaleidoscopic image as key to understanding its function. The musical spectacle, for Deleuze, is an "implied dream," a dream-image within the film that is not bound by the narrative rationalization of an individual dreamer whose reverie we witness. In the musical, the dance is our dream, and the movement between dream-world and "reality" is, to greater or lesser degrees, open and ambiguous. The significance of the musical number rests in its rupturing of the sensory-motor situations that define the movement-image. While the dream-image does not attain the state of pure virtuality and indiscernibility that, for Deleuze, define the time-image, the dream-image does mark a significant movement in that direction. Within the musical spectacle, the actions of the individual are subsumed by the indeterminate and depersonalized movements of the world.

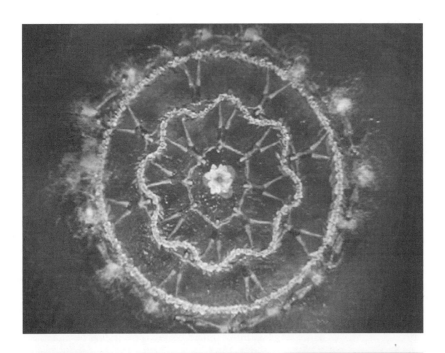

Esther Williams in the water lily sequence from *Bathing Beauty* (Sidney, 1944).

Nevertheless, it is not impersonality alone that gives the spectacle access to this larger movement. Deleuze notes:

> Of course, even in Berkeley, and all the more in musical comedy in general, the dancer or couple retain an individuality as creative source of movement. But what counts is the way in which the dancer's individual genius, his subjectivity, moves from a personal motivity to a supra-personal element, to a movement of world that the dance will outline. This is the moment of truth where the dancer is still going, but already a sleepwalker, who will be taken over by the movement which seems to summon him.[11]

The power of the great musical is to reveal a "plurality of worlds," juxtaposed and unresolved. The passage between divergent worlds is a dreamlike movement that renders the boundaries of those worlds indistinguishable. Thus, the protagonist's dance is not driven by the sensory-motor situation (by action or causality). For Deleuze, the problem-solving function of the number (a song that fixes a narrative conflict) seems entirely secondary to this movement of world that subsumes individual agency. The dancer is swept up by a force larger than herself; like the elaborate conveyer belts and platforms that move Berkeley's chorines, even the solo performer becomes a puppet for the force that moves through her.[12] Williams, as a swimmer pulled by the movements of water and music, becomes the catalyst for our shift between various planes and registers.

Deleuze refers specifically to the "degree zero," the moment of stuttering, where the movements of the character shift from between worlds. Fred Astaire, for example, exhibits an imperceptible shift between walking and dancing, whereas Gene Kelly uses the faltering step or the found object as a springboard into the dream dance. The kind of movement at play in the Berkeley/Williams number is clearly different from that found in dance-oriented films, which often call upon a more organic or integrated relationship to the performed music. Both Astaire and Kelly sing, for instance, and they are almost always partnered with singers (or at least with partners who are made to sing). The dances are composed around pauses and climaxes in which the individual or the couple halts to break into song. Such moments imply a full embodiment of the music; the song rises up, through dance the emotions take possession of the body, and the lyrics burst forth through the voice in a gesture of seeming spontaneity. Even when the dancers do not sing in musical films, their movements express a visible and often audible physicality that fixes the body to the flights of music. The clearest instance of this is the tap dance, where the clicks of the dancer's feet punctuate and flirt with the accompaniment. In more balletic numbers, too, one is made aware of the grace and athleticism of the body and its singular, expressive relationship to shifts in the music. The emphasis on weighted, energetic corporeality expresses the interpretive power of the individual body as it resonates with the music.

By contrast, the Berkeleyesque spectacle uses the body in an abstract choreography of objects and spaces, a choreography that itself is part of a larger movement toward contradiction and indiscernibility. The body here is less an interpretive instrument than a vessel or decorative surface. Before the final water ballet of *Neptune's Daughter* (Buzzell, 1949), for example, we are shown a brief glimpse of a backstage interaction between characters (during which, in a matter of seconds, the conflict that drove the film for ninety minutes is resolved). When the music begins, we are transported to an unworldly, impossible space. Impeccably coordinated swimmers unfurl long bolts of colored fabric in a seemingly endless pool. A spotlight isolates Williams in the water. The twisting, smiling body we see beneath the overhead camera is completely divorced from the character she has played throughout the film. The cuts between subsequent tableaux in the number maintain a certain continuity, but one that is irrational and playful. Williams, alone, dives beneath the water only to enter into a calisthenics routine with twenty or so underwater dancers. Their movements here, while elegantly athletic, seem driven less by personal agency than by the forces of water and music. When Williams surfaces, suddenly, the dancers have vanished, and she is in the arms of her love interest, Ricardo Montalban. The scant dialogue that occurs emphasizes the utter unreality of the space that has been created—what Deleuze would call an "any-space-whatever." As Williams breaks through the surface of the water with Montalban, who has materialized out of nowhere, she asks:

> "Where did you come from?"
> "South America," he replies.

The Williams spectacle is governed by irrationality, by an excessive objectification of the human body, and by the dissolution of logical spatiotemporal coordinates. Indiscernibility and ambiguity reign, pushing the movements found in the performance-based musical number into the realm of disembodied abstraction.

Given its propensity for the irrational, there is little concern within the musical comedy to reconcretize imaginary events within an everyday world, at least not in one that is realistically believable. While two distinct registers of fantasy and reality most often exist, the joy of the musical emanates from their conflation and confusion. The opening titles in *Bathing Beauty* make the collapsing of reality and fantasy explicit:

> We don't know if this story actually happened—But if it *did* happen—it couldn't happen in a nicer place than California.

Clearly, such fantastical formulations are inextricably linked to the historical moments in which they are produced, conditions that play a large role in shaping the worlds these films dream. But Deleuze's concept of the dream-image poses a significant challenge to our commonsensical understandings of history.

First, it provides us with a way of rethinking the fantastic elements of a film according to Bergsonian distinctions between time and space. Deleuze invokes Bergson in the *Cinema* books to supplant chronological history with a temporality that is eternally splitting into the past and the indefinite future. Rather than a time line, we are confronted by coexistent, incommensurate sheets of the past. The distinctions between movement-images, recollection-images, dream-images, and time-images center on this question of temporality, each containing varied "pressures" of time. Neither time nor history can be represented. Instead, cinema at its most creative seeks to resist the entombing of a fixed History, opposing it with time as difference and the never-ending processes of becoming. This does not preclude a historical analysis of the spectacle, but it would reject models that view these elements as passive "mirrors" of historical conditions or as ungrounded escapist fantasies.

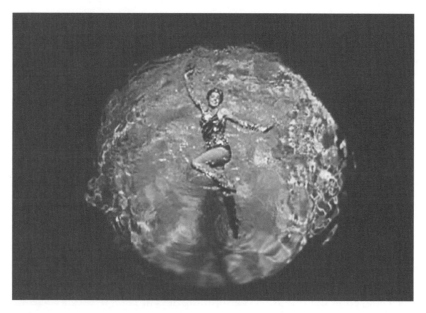

Esther Williams in *Neptune's Daughter* (Buzzell, 1949).

Second, the dream-image throws into question the location of the "real" within film, linking it not to the "real world" of the narrative, or even simply to the historical conditions that produce the film as a cultural object. Instead, Deleuze uses the concept of the implied dream to focus on the indiscernibility between states and on the actions of movement that flow between them. This is not to suggest, of course, that Deleuze does away with the notion of reality or history when discussing cinematic fantasy. To elucidate the complex ways Deleuze formulates history and the real, I return to Kracauer's work on cinema and physical reality.

## Surface-Level Expressions and Physical Reality

Kracauer's later work in *Theory of Film* further develops his assertion in "The Mass Ornament" that the popular image might give us access to new understandings of the "fundamental substance of the state of things." He discusses the ways in which films, unlike photographs, "represent reality as it evolves in time."[13] Distinguishing between "revealing" functions of film, which are bound up within the formal structure of filmic techniques, and "recording" functions, which consist of cinematic subjects, objects, and movements immediately apparent to the eye, Kracauer sets up a model of surface and depth, which again places the dance image on the level of surface expression. His concern is no longer with the dance spectacle as an "aesthetic reflex" of the rationality of a historical moment but with the way in which filmmakers such as René Clair or performers like Fred Astaire guide movements "along the divide between the real and the unreal" (43). What interests Kracauer here is the slippage of the dance from reality to fantasy. In Clair's work, he notes, ordinary characters whom one might encounter on the streets of Paris appear to fall in and out of complexly choreographed movements, shifting from dancing to walking in the matter of an instant. What is essential for Kracauer is that the dance emanate from material reality. The "imaginary universe" into which the characters dance, he argues, "reflects throughout our real world in stylizing it. What dancing there is seems to occur on the spur of the moment; it is the vicissitudes of life from which these ballets issue" (43).

Deleuze draws on language similar to Kracauer's in his discussion of the dream-image, focusing on the divide between real and dream worlds. Yet the reality Kracauer invokes is distinct from Deleuze's. In *Theory of Film*, Kracauer distinguishes the musical film from other forms of narrative cinema. The musical is a collage of divergent elements—visual, musical, theatrical, and narrative—in continual flux. The musical "pretends to unity and threatens to fall into pieces," Kracauer writes, "no one could honestly say that a musical makes sense" (146). He locates the primary tension within musical films as occurring between the production numbers and the narrative threads that weave them together, between "the realistic and the formative tendencies." Kracauer explicitly links musical spectacles with this formative tendency, whereas realism is expressed by "the musical's stubborn, if halfhearted, insistence on a plot of a sort which loosely interlinks real-life happenings" (148). On first reading, this link between a "realistic" narrative scenario and a more general concrete "reality" seems facile and reductive and might account for the severe criticism heaped on *Theory of Film* since its publication. But the tension Kracauer isolates here, and the notion of reality he discusses, is more complex than it might initially appear.

Kracauer's discussion of the goals of cinema relates directly to the "'right' balance" between realistic and aesthetic movements. He acknowledges that the musical expresses little interest in finding balance and indeed appears to favor the fantastical over the narrative in its overall thrust. He offers a counterargument, however, suggesting that the musical "keeps these performances apart as isolated entities, thus avoiding uncinematic fusions of music and film—fusions, that is, in which free creativity wins out over the concern for our visible world" (148–49). Kracauer, contradicting his earlier reading of the Tiller Girls, seems to denigrate fantastical musical spectacles, finding them at odds with physical reality. Nevertheless, he sees the spectacle as a crucial component of the cinematic approach, provided it works in concert with the recording function of the realistic tendency. Because the musical is driven by precisely this tension between spectacle and reality, Kracauer argues that the musical is particularly attuned to the fragmentary and contradictory nature of reality, which he sees as similarly divided by contradictory tendencies. While films of operas, for example, merely visualize theatrical performances, thus remaining fully subsumed in the spectacle, "musicals prefer a fragmentized whole to a false unity" (149). By highlighting contradiction and duality, musical films occupy a median ground between the fantasy of the pure spectacle and the details of everyday material reality. The tensions inherent to the musical are one and the same with the tensions of the world, and the musical's refusal to resolve these tensions reveals more about the world than do works that adhere to only the formative or the realistic tendency. Furthermore, the production number, for Kracauer, provides the very shock that unravels false notions of unity and universalizing truths— what Hanns Eisler calls the "stimulants" that rupture the flow of the narrative (149). Thus, while Kracauer separates the spectacle from reality in a manner that might be viewed with suspicion, for him the spectacle remains a powerful disruptive force, revealing the fragmentary nature of lived experience and provoking an active interpretive response from the viewer.

I suggest that certain resonances appear between Kracauer and Deleuze in terms of their methodology. Despite the significant differences in their projects and in their historical contexts, both thinkers construct their philosophy through the opposition of dualisms that are never resolved through synthesis. In their writing on cinema, both Kracauer and Deleuze emphasize that the primary interest is not the purity of an extreme state, nor a dialectic resolution, but rather the zone of indeterminacy that lies between those poles. Both also suggest that there is an affinity between the general and the particular, between foundational structures and surface-level expressions, that is concrete, experiential, and never metaphorical. The world of aesthetics, particularly the cinematic world, is filled with signs that make the imperceptible perceptible. This is not a representation so much as it is a provocation, a shock that provides access to a new modality of thought and that speaks of the indeterminate, undividable flow that is historical reality. Kracauer and Deleuze alike recognize the pervasiveness of capitalist, repressive thought and its infiltration into the artistic realm. Acts of creation are our only means of resistance to this repressive rationality. For both theorists, film in particular is a potent tool that can provoke the interpreter to forge new modes of thought. It is important to note that Kracauer sees history and photography as productively outside the realms of art and philosophy, while Deleuze champions art as philosophy and philosophy as art. But Deleuze's collapsing of terms challenges prevailing views of both art and philosophy in much the same way that Kracauer positions history and photography in an in-between, indeterminate space.

Both Deleuze and Kracauer attempt to wrest history away from universalizing narratives to introduce it into the flows of everyday life. For Kracauer, the minutia of physical reality to which film bears witness is the base substance of that lived experience, the *Lebenswelt*. The image of physical reality does not reveal its "truth," however, for such a claim to truth would be a retreat into frozen universals. Nor does the materiality of the physical world mark an escape from repressive social structures; like the mass ornament of the Tiller Girls, the historical image will make the embedded nature of these structures all the more apparent. For Kracauer, film, photography, and history offer instead an image of reality attuned to its conflicted nature. These images reveal the excesses of universal narratives and systems of control, the inevitable by-products that become the seeds for resistance. Rodowick notes, "The very forces that tend to paralyze social life, to reify it and give it the form of an object, are simultaneously, for Kracauer, the forces that energize it and generate in the *Lebenswelt* the constant possibility of unforeseen, even revolutionary, potentialities."[14]

## History and Genealogy

Deleuze, I argue, is in agreement with many of Kracauer's central objectives. Yet to grasp the specificity of Deleuze's project, which does depart from Kracauer in many respects, it is essential to understand Deleuze's theorization of history in the context of his rereading of Nietzsche. As D. N. Rodowick indicates in *Reading the Figural,* French philosophy in the 1960s and 1970s took a sharp turn away from structuralist models, a move that in many ways was invigorated by a resurgence of interest in Friedrich Nietzsche.[15] In particular, Deleuze's and Foucault's readings of Nietzschean history suggest provocative new ways of understanding the relationship between philosophy, history, and art.

As Foucault argues in "Nietzsche, Genealogy, History," a genealogical approach to history refuses to search for points of origins and refutes any universalizing notions of "truth." Departing from Nietzsche's concept of "essential" history, Foucault's genealogical critique is an active practice, one that engages with the base, corporeal elements of existence in order to dispel false unities and fabricated identities. Because it opposes a sweeping History that would fix and entomb events within a chronological trajectory, the practice of effective history demands a new means of perceiving and conceptualizing, a historical "sense" that involves "all the connotations of the term: meaning, logic, perception or perspective, instinct, sensibility, reason."[16] This historical sense counters the pillars of Platonic history (reality, identity, and truth) with parody, dissociation, and the "sacrifice of the subject of knowledge," or the powers of the false.[17] Genealogical history thus opposes itself to the search for origins and to the teleology of metahistories by unearthing multiple, contradictory points of emergence. Rather than a hermetic, unified narrative, the descent that this genealogy traces is continually branching and open to chance and the accidental:

> To follow the complex course of descent is to maintain passing events in their proper dispersion; it is to identify the accidents, the minute deviations—or conversely, the complete reversals—the errors, the false appraisals, and the faulty calculations that gave birth to those things that continue to exist and have value for us; it is to discover that truth or being do not lie at the root of what we know and what we are, but the exteriority of accidents.[18]

The modality of the genealogical critique plays a central role in Deleuze's work on cinema, even when it is not directly acknowledged as such. He does not, however, approach the cinema as a text or historical object to be analyzed. Rather, the cinema, like philosophy, is a creative process that can act to excavate, to provoke, to make the previously imperceptible perceptible. Engagement with the cinema becomes a means of generating new thought, of rethinking history. The question is how to understand the modality by which a film operates. Does the film structure its sonic and visual elements according to associative links, or through differentiation and incommensurability? Does it build its narrative through chronological progressions or through discontinuities and chance? Is identity asserted as a unified whole, or is it dissociated, contradictory, and multiple? Does the film aspire to unveil the truth, or does it wage a battle against universals through fiction and farce? These are the questions that lie at the heart of the distinction between the movement-images and time-images.

## The Virtual and the Actual in Cinema

Deleuze's writing on the cinema forges its own highly specific, and somewhat indirect, formulation of history. His distinction between the movement-image and the time-image is, however, linked to a concrete historical moment, the climate of disillusionment after World War II. The importance of this moment is not technological, nor does this moment represent a simple shift in prevailing aesthetic practices. If there is a shift in expression that can be linked to a historical time and place, the connection lies in the emergence of new ways of thinking articulated, albeit quite differently, in a number of different registers (film, literature, painting, science, music, philosophy). This new modality of thought does not burst forth fully formed but evolves through the active resonations between these registers, each articulation provoking a shift in the others.[19]

Deleuze's seeming devaluation of the sensory-motor situation and the movement-image reflects less a dismissal of a particular aesthetic practice than a suspicion of modes of logic that operate through abstraction or resemblance. The image of time that breaks free from the sensory-motor situation does not break free from narrative.[20] It begins to forge associations between images that proliferate into newly differentiating images, and it begins to generate new kinds of fictions, fabulations, that undermine notions of truth or reality. The image that approaches an autonomous duration delves into the very matter of film itself, the pure optical and sound situation. This is significant for Deleuze, for it marks a shift in the relationship between the cinema and world, moving from the spatial axis of the sensory-motor situation, where time and space are governed by preexisting abstracted measure, to the temporal axis of duration, where one can make creative leaps and associations between the images of the virtual past. The "real" here, if one can even use such a term, is not opposed to the virtual. Rather, the virtual signals a molecular association with the elements in the world free from the confines of false models of representation and self-same identity. The crystalline circuits of the virtual and the actual within the time-image are, as such, a political ideal. The practice of time-based cinema, like the practice of philosophy and the practice of genealogical history, should strive toward the open-ended and unpredictable processes of excavation and creation.

What Deleuze proposes here cannot be reduced to a question of form, but he does gesture toward an artistic approach or style that resists universalizing abstractions. Very few films, of course, can achieve this ideal. When Deleuze outlines, for example, the contradictions of the dream-image, he demonstrates how, while they might approach a representation of time, they are nevertheless hampered by a certain logic that the time-image transcends. In most cases, this is exhibited by the image's failure to fully free itself from linear temporality. If this were the only distinction, we could identify time-images by purely formal means (the absence of narrative). This is obviously not Deleuze's goal; he does not advocate a particular school of filmmaking, and, in fact, he does not refer to a single film that is completely abstract. The key to the importance of the difference between movement-images and time-images can be found in the indiscernibility between the actual and the virtual.

Once again, Deleuze builds this distinction on a Bergsonian model of temporality. Bergson distinguishes between the "actual" present and the "virtual" pure memory. Pure memory, he argues, could have no impact if it did not engage with a material present:

> The memory-image itself, if it remained pure memory, would be ineffectual. Virtual, this memory can only become actual by means of the perception which attracts it. Powerless, it borrows life and strength from the present sensations in which it is materialized.[21]

The virtual, as Bergson defines it, cannot be confused with its colloquial usage, as something "not real" or "imaginary." The virtual does not resemble the real in that it is not a set of infinite "possibilities" waiting to come into existence. The virtual always exists as the past, and is, in fact, the precondition for the real in which it is "materialized." Perception itself, if we return to Bergson's diagram of the process (see chapter 3), can only occur as a result of two movements, one emanating from the physical object (B'–D'), and the other from virtual memory (B–D). The virtual and the lived present of the physical world are thus inextricably bound.

Yet the realm of physical sensations cannot be conflated, in Deleuzian thought, with the real. The direct time-image, Deleuze writes, "is virtual, in opposition to the actuality of the movement-image. But, if virtual is opposed to actual, it is not opposed to real, far from it."[22] "The real" is not a term that Deleuze invests with a great deal of interest, finding it linked to static notions of existence. By contrast, actualization is a *process of becoming;* it possesses a unique duration, and its dynamism allows Deleuze to conceive of entities as movements and forces rather than essential beings. Virtuality is real in that it exists, but it is not actual, for it is a potentiality that has not yet been mobilized by the processes of actualization. At the same time, one cannot read the virtual as some kind of possible, predetermined future that is waiting to come into being. The virtual can never resemble the actual, for one can never predict the ways in which the forces of change and differentiation will bear out in the process of actualization. One might compare the possible with the seventeenth-century model of the homunculus, a miniature, preformed man that is planted in the womb, whereas the virtual might coincide with genetic models, where the code of DNA might or might not bear out its potentialities throughout the course of living.

These distinctions play out directly in Deleuze's theory of cinema. According to Deleuze, each time the dream-image comes closer to the time-image, a failure occurs in terms of the relationship between the actual and virtual images it contains. Dream-images and recollection-images do engage in an exchange between the actual and the virtual. They exist, in fact, as virtual images, which then "are linked with the actual optical or sound image (description) but which are constantly being actualized on their own account, or the former in the latter to infinity."[23] The difficulty with the recollection-image and dream-image is that they both work through this process of association and linkage, bringing together "the actual image and *other* virtual images, recollections, or dreams, which thus become actual in turn."[24] In a "pure" time-image, "the actual image must enter into relation with its *own* virtual image as such . . . to the extent that there is no longer any linkage of the real with the imaginary, but the *indiscernibility of the two,* a perpetual exchange."[25]

The image, as a product of simultaneous currents of the actual and virtual, comes closest to a pure state when those circles of actualization and virtualization center on that image or object *in itself.* The layers of memory and materiality that emerge can thus expand on and explore that object to the fullest possible extent, without inhibition. The linearity of the narrative, as such, presents one kind of intrusion, the introduction of a second object to which the dream or flashback becomes linked. The virtuality of the dream-image is truncated; it no longer extends itself into the image-in-itself to be folded back and further expanded into deeper realms of virtuality and actuality. Instead, that virtual any-space-whatever is presented as a reflection of a different object, in this case, the result of a sensory-motor, narrative-driven link.

It is important to emphasize that the failure of the musical spectacle to unhinge itself from associative links is not merely a question of the relationship between narrative and number. The time-image, too, tells a story, but it does so via the Nietzschean powers of the false—through acts of fabulation. Musical spectacles are undeniably fabulous and fantastical by nature, yet they are rarely permitted to fully excavate the bodies and spaces they set into motion. The fabulations of the time-image revel in the farces, dissociations, and sacrifices of the genealogical critique, whereas the dream-image is ultimately contained within frameworks of identity and truth.

## The Million-Dollar Mermaid as Dream-Image

The movie musical as a genre seems designed to toy with an indiscernibility between the present and past, virtual and actual. Its images ripple outward with no conceivable sensory-motor motivation. The musical spectacle introduces a profound discontinuity into the chronological flow of the film, a stuttering in which causal associations are replaced by dissociation and impossibility. And the image of time that the musical spectacle offers exists in fluid layers of simultaneous present-past-future. Yet in the process of their actualization, the disturbances that occur in the musical appear to be of a distinctly identifiable sort. Discrepancies, discontinuities, and falsifications proliferate in Esther Williams's films, but certain reconciliations are also at work. As with most musical comedies, dreamlike departures are brought into being by the narrative trajectory that will later subsume them; this framework almost always involves the development of heterosexual romance, and the final synthesis takes place with a marriage. In both *Neptune's Daughter* and *Bathing Beauty*, for example, the teleology of the romance not only frames the dream but springs forth directly from its any-space-whatever: Ricardo Montalban, in the first instance, and Red Skelton, in the second, burst out of the irrational space of the pool, halting the dances and bringing the films to a close.

The significance of these types of intrusions goes beyond that of a general narrative linkage. Certainly the sociopolitical factors contained within an image can further impede its disruptive potential. In *Neptune's Daughter,* the framing device is not only the inevitability of heterosexual romance but also the blatant marketing of the swimsuit as commodity. Following the trials and tribulations of two swimsuit company executives (Williams and Keenan Wynn), the film prominently features Cole bathing suits and even posters used by Cole in actual magazine advertisements.[26] In fact, the commodity itself is promoted as an essential factor in the unfolding of the romantic narrative (Wynn, who serves as both the narrator and capitalist/romantic rival in the film, addresses the audience directly at both the opening and closing moments of the film to tell us "a story about a guy, a girl, and a bathing suit"). The central conflict of the plot is whether Williams will chose Wynn, her business partner, as a love object, thus preserving her career as entrepreneur/spokesmodel, or the sexy and mysterious Montalban. The finale of the film asserts the supremacy of love over career while simultaneously framing the extravaganza as a performance staged for potential swimsuit purchasers. The melding of economic and sexual interests culminates in a convenient display of Williams's body and a catalog of suits all inextricably linked to one another in a happy ending. Such "material" concerns not only fix the dream-image temporally within the narrative time line but also significantly color the fantasies that they offer us by repressing difference and imposing cohesive models of identity.

The female musical star is capitalism's ornament par excellence. Her body, whether multiplied or singular, is displayed as a surface of contradiction and fascination that is ultimately unified and contained by the twinned metanarratives of capitalism and heteronormativity. There is no doubt that the dream-image of the musical spectacle is almost invariably encapsulated within these types of universalizing frameworks. That said, one might still legitimately question how successful or complete this encapsulation is. The cliché of the musical, especially less-polished novelty musicals such as the Williams vehicle, is that its narrative framework is a poorly executed, unconvincing excuse for the production number, the number being the only reason audiences watch musicals in the first place. The experience of watching musicals frequently confirms this disparity, as the numbers are typically far more engaging, pleasurable, and memorable than any other aspect of the film. At least for this viewer, the hasty romantic synthesis at the musical's conclusion arrives as an unpleasant and insincere intrusion. Indeed, despite the musical's undeniably conservative leanings, the force of the production number remains stubbornly resistant to closure.

Paradoxically, the musical number remains particularly open-ended when contending with issues of identity. Anxieties about racial, ethnic, and, above all, gender identity dominate musicals. As Rick Altman demonstrated in *The American Film Musical,* the musical's raison d'être is to resolve these anxieties through romantic and musical synthesis.[27] Yet, by merely giving voice to these anxieties, the musical introduces images of difference and contradiction that, particularly because they are introduced through music and movement, can hardly be contained by the slap-dash conclusions that are offered. Recent criticism suggests that the celebration of contradiction in the musical, which often overpowers heterosexual union, is the mark of a camp sensibility, a strategy both of resistance and survival employed in particular by the gay directors, choreographers, set designers, writers, and other workers who played such a central role in the musical film industry.[28] Matthew Tinkcom uses the term "passing" to describe the encoded and veiled meanings of the musical, reflecting a gay sensibility that nevertheless is able to slip beneath the radar of the Hollywood film industry.[29] D. A. Miller, in his exploration of the affinity between Broadway musicals and gay men, describes a similar process of negotiation: "The musical thus let itself be colonized, or camouflaged, by the same narrative naturalism from whose tedium and tyranny its real merit was to keep alive, so long as it was vital itself, the prospect of a liberation."[30] There is indeed something decidedly and delightfully queer about musicals. The absolute excesses of the spectacle can, in this context, be read as explicit, if incomplete, affronts to heteronormative demands. The final shot of *Neptune's Daughter,* for instance, dollies in on the happy, heterosexual couple in an embrace—yet we see, before the camera closes in, that they are flanked by an admiring group of shirtless men dressed in short pink satin swim trunks and white captain's hats. In song and dance, fixed notions of identity, particularly gender identity, are joyfully subverted into dissonant formulations: cross-dressing, disguise, mistaken identity, and improper coupling proliferate within the musical's farce. In effect, the indirect and open nature of the camp sensibility allows for any number of irreverent readings and for a free play of multiple differences unhinged from fixed notions of identity.

When the female star, or the female body, becomes the site for the musical's complex negotiations, the contradictions of "passing" are articulated in paradoxical ways. Femininity is exposed as conflicted and performative, a masquerade that can be adopted at will. Yet such performances rely on specular apparatuses that tend to affirm objectifying presumptions about female identity. To pose this dilemma in terms of the questions raised in chapter 3, the image of the girl cluster shares much in common with the device of female doubling and with the modality of the *tableau vivant.* Like the *tableau vivant,* the Berkeleyesque spectacle obscures the distinction between motion and stillness, surface and depth, object and living being. Space, time, and scale are unhinged from the axis of linear causality and become a playground for free association. The female form in the musical spectacle is a sheer surface, an abstraction and an empty mask. The gestures it offers are decidedly contradictory, appearing to be obsessed with the female body as a sexual object yet eradicating any sensuality or eroticism through abstraction. Feminist debates about the Berkeleyesque spectacle highlight these vexing incongruities: is the

Ricardo Montalban, Esther Williams, and their entourage in *Neptune's Daughter.*

image utterly sexist, or does its exaggerated fascination with gender *as* an image debunk essentialized notions of gender? If one answers, "both at once," what are the implications for our understanding of gender, and gender in the realm of the arts? Can the contradictions of the *tableau vivant* or the musical spectacle be mobilized as a political tool?

## Liquid Perception and Monstrous Hybridity

The title number in *Dames* (Enright, 1934) begins in the boardroom of an imaginary entertainment corporation. Stodgy male investors interrupt one another as they debate the key ingredient of a moneymaking stage show: music, story, publicity, and so on. Dick Powell, the male lead in the film, breaks up the argument as he bursts into song:

> Who writes the words and music for all the girlie shows?
> No one cares and no one knows.
> Who is the handsome hero some villain always frames?
> Who cares if there's a plot or not, if it's got a lot of dames.
> What do you go for? Go see the show for?
> Tell the truth—you go to see those beautiful dames.[31]

On cue, a bevy of chorines enter the room, to the obvious delight of the investors. After Powell gives further evidence of the "dame's" box-office power ("Your knees in action, that's the attraction"), the camera spins into a spectacular Busby Berkeley production.

This theatrical prologue (which itself, curiously enough, is ostensibly part of a stage show) gives way to an unbounded, undefined space in which close-ups of the faces of individual "dames" sweep into tableaux of multiple, indistinct chorus girls, shifting in geometric formations—all floating above the strains of the show tune. Certain moments in the production pander to an ironic play on stereotypical, voyeuristic fantasies about femininity (an endless sea of bathtubs and vanities where the chorines splash bubbles and hide behind powder puffs). Yet the larger movement of the number is toward complete abstraction, even as it maintains an ocular obsession with the female body. The black-stockinged legs of the girls scissor and split into kaleidoscopic circles. The camera glides through squared-off tunnels created by the girls' bent bodies. Although the framing devices insist this is all part of a theatrical show, the spaces Berkeley maps out are utterly impossible. In the final moments of the song, hundreds of girls appear to smile and kick from the boxes in a mammoth gridlike construction. Before one can even begin to comprehend the workings of this architecture, Dick Powell's head crashes through the entire image as if it were a piece of paper, singing the last refrain.

This scene typifies Berkeley's directorial style. The "dames" are indeed the raison d'être of the show and form the exclusive object of the camera's gaze. The female body is multiplied into endless rows of identical, smiling, and always white women. Their movements are largely catatonic, for the choreography involved is undertaken primarily by the camera or by mechanized platforms that transport the female figures. Feminist critiques of the Berkeley style have highlighted the gender (and racial) politics of such spectacles, pointing to the multiple registers on which women are fragmented, frozen, objectified, and reduced to vapid doubles and exchangeable currency, and conversely, to the ways in which the exaggerations of such spectacles play into feminist camp sensibilities.[32] Rather than rehearsing these arguments, I examine the peculiarity of the Williams, water-based Berkeleyesque spectacle, read in light of the questions of female multiplicity raised in the previous chapter. These spectacles share much in common with the *Dames* sequence, with two notable exceptions: Williams as a star figure is never flattened into the indeterminate mass of the girl cluster, and the mechanics of water alter the spatial and temporal staging of these musical scenes. Williams emerges from these scenes as a contradictory, hybrid figure.

Dick Powell in *Dames* (Enright, 1934).

Berkeley directed several of Williams's musical performances, and the entire Williams oeuvre has a similar aesthetic to Berkeley's earlier productions. Framed around entirely implausible backstage premises, the Williams films exhibit the extreme discontinuity between narrative and number that mark films like *Footlight Parade* (Bacon, 1933) and *Dames*. Yet the narrative demands of water-based storylines are even more forced than those of the backstage musical, and the aquatic nature of their production numbers creates new possibilities for cinematic movement that complicate the already complex structures of the "dry" Berkeley. There is a different kind of physicality in a Berkeley/Williams number than is found in other types of musical performances. Most significant, the music itself, while rhythmically bound to the image, seems in all other ways outside the hermetic world of the image. The accompaniment is often less energetic or emotive, for the complex shifts between visual tableaux demand smoother orchestrations. Within the aquatic spectacle in particular, the floating body is silent, removed, and sealed off—we never hear the sounds of splashing, and there is not the same direct connection between the performing bodies and musical shifts as there is with singers and dancers. The figures are indeed propelled by depersonalized forces, and their movements are thus open to greater flights of irrationality. At the same time, their dance is more scripted and less open to improvisation or to elements of externally introduced change (music, found objects) that can be found in the dance film. The image evolves and mutates as if in an otherworldly globe, accompanied by and synchronous with music that nevertheless exists in a wholly different place.

Martin Rubin similarly comments on the affinity Busby Berkeley had for aquatic settings and the transformative opportunities they offered:

> One major advantage of aquatic spectacles is that they offer Berkeley the opportunity to redouble the sequestration inherent in the backstage format. The swimming pool functions as a stage-within-the-stage that further differentiates spectacle space from narrative space. Water itself is a literally different element from the terra firma of the narrative, with tangibly distinct laws and properties, as well as built-in opportunities for such prime Berkeleyesque qualities as fluidity, mutability, surprise, and amorphousness.[33]

Berkeley had first experimented with aqueous choreography in the "By a Waterfall" sequence in *Footlight Parade,* one of the most spectacular and ambitious productions of his career. In this sequence, the temporal and spatial acrobatics of his previous stagings have yet another axis to toy with: the surface of the water, which becomes a gateway to an underwater world, a threshold to be penetrated in multiple directions, and a smooth canvas on which geometrical body compositions can be mobilized. Water becomes a convenient device for extremely revealing costuming, as the anonymous female body remains Berkeley's primary fetish. Indeed, it is difficult to avoid the concept of the fetish when confronted with the finale of "By a Waterfall," in which chorines are hoisted onto the spinning tiers of a giant fleshy fountain, with arcs of water cascading from between their spread legs.

In his discussion of "liquid perception," Deleuze argues that the use of water as a theme builds on the capacity of liquid environments to abstract and decenter movement, to create an environment in which the "perceptions, affections and actions" of the landlocked world are seen as transformed, alien from those of the water.[34] These liquid environments allow for irrational, impossible locations that are not governed by the dictates of narrative or causality. Referring to the centrality of water in the work of Renoir, Epstein, and Vigo, Deleuze writes:

> Finally, what the French school found in water was the promise or implication of another state of perception: a more than human perception, a perception not tailored to solids, which no longer had the solid as object, as condition, as milieu. A more delicate and vaster perception, a molecular perception, peculiar to a "cine-eye."[35]

Liquid perception, for Deleuze, marks a significant movement away from the sensory-motor situation in that it offers us not only an alternative spatiotemporal world but also an alternative modality for perceiving. While Esther Williams shares very little in common with Vigo or Renoir, her aquatic performances do suggest a new, water-based form of perception. Given the highly coded ways in which the watery spectacle figures femininity, however, I suggest that the in-between liquid space of the Williams films cannot be separated from the curious hybridity of Williams as a performer.

Esther Williams is a peculiar musical star, known not for her singing or dancing but for swimming—or perhaps more accurately, for the image of her body in a swimsuit. Her body itself is marked by a number of contradictions. Esther Williams's fame as a competitive swimmer invokes a certain anxiety about the muscular female body. The success of Williams as a celebrity, however, rested on her ability to reintegrate and resolve these apparent contradictions. While this resolution was partially resolved by the manner in which she swims in the water ballet, using slow "feminine" gestures that work to display the body and deemphasize its strength, there were other registers in which this hybridity was foregrounded. "The discourse surrounding Esther Williams," Catherine Williamson writes, "more successfully repressed the gender anxiety over 'female athlete' by displacing it onto a humorous blurring of genus."[36] Publicity press describing Williams as a "Cinemer-maid" or as "a cross between Lana Turner and a seal"[37] suggests, for Williamson, a curious supplanting: "Within the complex hybrid that is the young starlet Esther Williams, 'Lana Turner' is the ultra-feminine bomb-shell, the seal (and not, say, Johnny Weissmuller) is the one with the muscles."[38]

While references to Williams as half-woman and half-beast might indeed be a strategy of displacement, I argue that such formulations do little to ease fears and instead cast Williams as an even more conflicted figure. Imagined as part human, part animal, part male, part female, Williams's body is undeniably a site of both anxiety and fascination. Williams's persona on land is decidedly more awkward and wooden than her underwater self. While clearly shapely in a manner befitting a pin-up star, Williams's frame was larger and more athletic than many female ingénues, and she towered over several of her costars—a forceful visual presence that compounds the contradictions indicated in her press coverage.[39] The rupture between aquatic and dry worlds in Williams's films is dramatically heightened by these shifts in her performance and her visual framing. Sound plays a monumental role in indicating duality as well. Williams on land projects an image of absolute ordinariness highlighted by her stilted speaking and singing voice. Yet in the space of the underwater performance, another Williams emerges. Her body here is utterly silent and ungrounded, a sheer surface that twists and conforms to the mutating tableaux of the spectacle. To call her a fish out of water is to extend our understanding of her hybridity to include not only her feminine and masculine attributes but also her more global otherworldliness.[40]

Hybridity and multiplicity are hardly unique to Williams as an icon, but they present themselves within her image in a highly specific manner. Williams's body is the nexus of a number of competing discourses and forces, the combination of which blurs the boundaries between the male and the female, the human and the animal, the dry and the wet. If we are to read the musical spectacles of the Williams films as dream-images, Williams's unusual corporeality contributes greatly to the disruptive nature of these scenes and to their (albeit compromised) challenge to fixed notions of identity. To understand the political implications of these disruptions, especially in terms of their relation to the body, it may prove productive to read them in the context of Deleuze and Guattari's concept of becoming. The process of becoming, which indeed digs itself into the materiality of bodies, is in many ways an extension of a genealogical approach. If the purpose of historical knowledge, as Foucault describes it, is for "cutting," becoming is a means of severing the bonds of molar identity in order to forge new strategic alliances. Becoming is a means of actualizing the potentialities that a genealogical critique unearths, utilizing them to transform the conditions of the present and to begin lines of flight into the future. Although becoming is clearly a real transformation that must be initiated through real bodies, and as such is never metaphorical, Deleuze and Guattari do speak of literary and cinematic examples that elucidate the nature of the process. While films and characters in themselves cannot be deemed "becomings" (as becoming is a process and never a thing), art can serve to incite actual transformations by mapping new sets of associations through different sets of bodies.

## Becoming-Animal, Becoming-Woman

Deleuze and Guattari outline a series of different becomings in *A Thousand Plateaus,* beginning with a discussion of "becoming-animal." They describe the process as a strategic alliance formed between distinct "molar" (stratified, territorialized, and fixed) identities. This alliance is not one of imitation nor one of a procreative synthesis; becoming is an event, a verb, a block of duration, a transitory symbiosis between molar entities that takes place on a mutually transforming, molecular level. In a novel by Vladimir Slepian, for example, a man realizes that he is always hungry, and as he believes this hunger is not befitting of man, he decides he should become a dog. He sets about this not by trying to resemble a dog but by analyzing the various qualities of dogness, recognizing the limits of a dog's body, discovering what it is that dogs are capable of (what dogs do), and integrating these functions into his own body. The man thus places shoes on his hands to make them more like feet, and when he finds he cannot tie the shoes, uses his mouth as a muzzle to complete the task.[41] The mutation that takes place here is a monstrous union between humanness and dogness, a union that is always incomplete and part of a never-ending process of recomposition.

Becoming is thus always a becoming-other. It involves the meeting of two disparate entities who form an alliance or assemblage toward the realization of some goal. Becomings reassemble the core components of these molar identities, the very specificity of their bodies, forming unnatural unions that rupture, transect, and take flight from those stable positions. Becoming is transitory, but it is never imaginary (*A Thousand Plateaus,* 238). Deleuze and Guattari speak of the couplings of orchids and wasps as one such alliance. Orchids depend on wasps to transport their pollen, and wasps in turn depend on orchids to feed them. Although clearly from distinct species, both the orchid and the wasp have evolved in a mutual symbiosis that is registered in the very shape of their bodies—a physical, mimetic correspondence, "a becoming-wasp of the orchid and a becoming-orchid of the wasp" (10). Insect and flower form a heterogeneous chain, an assemblage that is in effect a machine in that it actualizes concrete change. Deleuze and Guattari describe becoming both as a line that passes between two points (rather than connecting them) and as a block that "constitutes a zone of proximity and indiscernibility" between the two entities (293). Becoming is thus neither a wasp, an orchid, nor a wasp-orchid (nor man, dog, nor man-dog). "The line, or the block, does not link the wasp to the orchid, any more than it conjugates or mixes them: it passes between them, carrying them away in a shared proximity in which the discernibility of points disappears" (294).

The movement that is becoming is always political for Deleuze and Guattari. Because it creates an indiscernibility between molar identities, and because it initiates unnatural couplings between otherwise distinct groups, becoming is a powerful means of dismantling those identities. Becoming is always a becoming-minoritarian, and it opposes the unified subject with the notion of multiplicity. Each molar identity is molecularly reassembled through its encounter with another, and thus while it makes sense for a dominant identity such as man to enter into a becoming-woman or a becoming-animal, it is impossible for a minority identity to become-man. To become-man would be to reassert "the molar entity par excellence," whereas becoming-other always takes flight from molarity (292). Becomings, according to Deleuze and Guattari, proceed via stages, and it is necessary to initiate a molecular deterritorialization by becoming the other that is closest to you. Within *A Thousand Plateaus,* this demand results in a curious hierarchy of becomings, an ordering that seems at odds with the cataclysmic dismantling of identity that Deleuze and Guattari propose. This hierarchy, which extends ultimately to a becoming-imperceptible, necessarily begins with what Deleuze and Guattari call a becoming-woman.

"Although all becomings are already molecular, including becoming-woman, it must be said that all becomings begin with and pass through becoming-woman" (277). Becoming-woman, as the first stage of becoming, is a process that even actual molar women must undergo. Indeed, women must first become-woman to initiate larger series of becomings, "in order that the man also becomes- or can become-woman" (275–76). To become-woman is not to literally become a woman or even to imitate a woman, for it obviously would be unnecessary for an actual woman to make this change. The exact nature of a becoming-woman, however, as distinct from a more generalized becoming-other, is not entirely clear. While Deleuze and Guattari insist that this means entering into proximity with womanness, tapping into the speeds and slownesses of the duration that is a molecular femininity, it is difficult to determine how such an undertaking would take place. Moreover, the few indications they offer as to the specificity of the feminine conform to troubling stereotypes. Female haecceity is decidedly flighty: "What is a girl, what is a group of girls? . . . A girl is late on account of her speed: she did too many things, crossed too many spaces in relation to the relative time of the person waiting for her" (271). Femininity is always multiple, contradictory, and open to the schizoid logic of madness. Women, Deleuze and Guattari suggest, are paradoxically transparent and inherently secretive. Men, they argue,

> adopt a grave attitude, knights of the secret. . . . But they end up telling every-thing—and it turns out to be nothing. There are women, on the other hand, who tell everything, sometimes in appalling technical detail, but one knows no more at the end than at the beginning. They have hidden everything through celerity, by limpidity. They have no secret because they have become a secret them-selves. (289)

Deleuze and Guattari do draw heavily from the writing of Virginia Woolf in outlining the permutations of various becomings, particularly becoming-woman (276–77, 280). Yet they refer to the becoming-woman of male authors as well (Lewis Carroll, Marcel Proust, Henry Miller, D. H. Lawrence), a process

Deleuze and Guattari describe as "stealing" the bodies of female characters in order to transform the masculine being (276).[42] This occupation of the female body is especially troubling, particularly when the womanhood it lays claim to resembles a masculine projection of femininity as impenetrable, elusive, and fickle.[43]

Not surprisingly, the concept of becoming-woman has met with suspicion from some feminist scholars. The privileging of becoming-woman as the first threshold in larger series of becomings presents the central difficulty for many critics, especially the demand that women, whose status as subjects has been so historically unstable, must be first to relinquish subjectivity. Is the role of woman in becoming-woman being invoked symbolically, and if so, is it not thus merely a male fantasy of femininity as a sea of mutability? If becoming-woman is not a symbolic exercise, how has the nature of femininity been determined? And in either case, what are the implications of becoming-woman for real, embodied women? Luce Irigaray is vociferously critical of Deleuze and Guattari's formulation of "becoming-woman," the "body without organs," and more generally of the proliferations of difference that Deleuze and Guattari gesture toward without the specific acknowledgment of sexual differences. For Irigaray, Deleuze and Guattari colonize the concept of woman, divorcing her from her corporeal flows and eradicating her subjecthood in order to make her a metaphorical vehicle for inherently masculine objectives.[44] Alice Jardine similarly reads Deleuze and Guattari's formulation within a history of philosophies that attempt to erase femininity and undermine the legitimacy of active female subjects:

> But to the extent that women must "become woman" *first* (in order for men, in D + G's words, to "follow her example"), might that not mean that she must also be the *first* to disappear? Is it not possible that the process of "becoming woman" is but a new variation of an old allegory for the process of women becoming obsolete? There would remain only her simulacrum: a female figure caught in a whirling sea of male configurations. A silent, mutable, head-less, desire-less, spatial surface necessary only for *His* metamorphosis?[45]

The concerns expressed by Irigaray and Jardine are serious ones. At the same time, there is a degree to which they underestimate the potential Deleuze and Guattari might have for feminist projects. Despite some significant problems with the manner in which Deleuze and Guattari frame the concept of becoming-woman, their objective is clearly to dismantle binary notions of gender, and indeed of the gendered subject itself. When they speak of stealing the female body, it is because the patriarchal order has already abducted it:

The body is stolen first from the girl: Stop behaving like that, you're not a little girl anymore, you're not a tomboy, etc. The girl's becoming is stolen first, in order to impose a history, or prehistory, upon her. The boy's turn comes next, but it is by using the girl as an example, by pointing to the girl as the object of his desire, that an opposed organism, a dominant history is fabricated for him too (*A Thousand Plateaus*, 276).

If becoming-woman must come first for Deleuze and Guattari, this may be because the imposition of binary gender in Western culture is the first stage in the formation of the oedipal subject. This is not a denial of gender difference but an acknowledgment of the centrality of gender to the structure of contemporary capitalist society. To become-woman is to refuse the history and teleology of the molar woman and molar man, a paradoxical project initiated through the very multiplicity and mutability associated with femininity as a construct.

In effect, Deleuze and Guattari may draw on gendered stereotypes strategically, attempting to mobilize the patriarchal refusal of the female subject into an attack on subjectivity in general. Brian Massumi writes:

The feminine gender stereotype involves greater indeterminacy ("fickle") and movement ("flighty") and has been burdened by the patriarchal traditions with a disproportionate load of paradox (virgin/whore, mother/lover). Since supermolecularity involves a capacity to superpose states that are "normally" mutually exclusive, Deleuze and Guattari hold that the feminine cliché offers a better departure point than masculinity for a rebecoming-supermolecular of the personified individual.[46]

This reframing clarifies the location of becoming-woman within the political context of the *Capitalism and Schizophrenia* volumes—which is not to gloss over the problematic aspects of becoming-woman as Deleuze and Guattari propose it. Nevertheless, their larger project provides a provocative model for resistance, one that has many correspondences with feminist objectives. As Elizabeth Grosz notes, the most significant of these may be the break from psychoanalysis, the rejection of traditional notions of representation, the replacement of an "either-or" relation of binarisms with a "both-and," and with a reconceptualization of bodies as complex assemblages of forces and flows.[47] Although Deleuze and Guattari do not pursue the implications of these concepts for feminist projects, the tools they provide have a provocative potential.

If the notion of becoming is extreme, it is because, like the time-image, it is the limit toward which hybrid and negotiated movements aspire. Resistance, for Deleuze and Guattari, begins necessarily from an embodied, territorialized position. While they speak passionately about lines of flight, these flights are not meant to transcend the body. Indeed, while such flights are almost inevitably reterritorialized in the end, they can result in demonstrable changes in the nature of that territory. Becomings are elusive, but they are the accidents and fabulations that change the course of the larger whole. Brian Massumi writes:

> Stopping the World As We Know It, at least one of its spatiotemporal coordinates, is a prerequisite for setting up the kind of actual-virtual circuit crucial to the political imagination. Tactical sabotage of the existing order is a necessity of becoming, but for survival's sake it is just as necessary to improve the existing order, to fight for integration into it on its terms. These are two sides of the same coin, and they should be practiced in such a way as to reinforce rather than mutually exclude one another.[48]

Because the ultimate limits of becoming—what Deleuze and Guattari call "the three virtues": imperceptibility, indiscernibility, and impersonality—would disintegrate any stable lived identity or body, survival as a living being requires some degree of recuperation within the confines of a molar existence. Becoming, as such, will never be fully divorced from territorialized existence, nor should it if it is to maintain any real political viability. Becoming as a process cannot be inhibited by the boundaries imposed by molarity, but the radical ruptures that result from becomings nevertheless provide a means of changing the conditions and parameters of the molar identities from which they take flight.

If we were to speak of a becoming-other of Esther Williams, it would most likely be not a becoming-woman but a becoming-fluid. Her body enters into a relation with water, an assemblage that multiplies the body and opens it to new paths of movement. There is a viscosity to the aquatic spectacle that opposes and permeates boundaries. Female corporeality and water become a musical machine that introduces discontinuity into the ideological space of the narrative, forcing time and space to enter into new types of configurations. Given their tendencies toward the specularization of the molar identity of woman, however, Esther Williams's becomings retreat and are recuperated before they are fully set into motion. Yet perhaps we can read this fluid corporeality as a refrain that reemerges, radically transformed, within the films of Tsai Ming-liang.

## Becoming-Fluid: Tsai Ming-liang's Corporeal Cinema

Tsai Ming-liang's films are about bodies, bodies adrift in urban landscapes and the architectural bodies that comprise the city itself. Time is a palpable presence in his work, frozen into long blocks of suspended duration. Characters are ceaselessly waiting and consumed with the drudgery of monotonous, bodily tasks (eating, sleeping, peeing, fucking, bathing, cooking, vomiting, masturbating).

The landscape of Taipei that Tsai presents is a labyrinth of banality and hollow consumption. Empty corridors of shops, video arcades, food courts, movie theaters, and massage parlors are interspersed with elevators and escalators that go nowhere. Tsai's films are marked by distinct and persistent repetition. We see the same actors, in particular his muse Lee Kang-sheng, appearing in scenarios that resonate strangely with subtle shifts in content and context. The actors Miao Tien and Lu Hsiao-ling, for instance, are cast as Lee's parents in several films (*Rebels of the Neon God* [1992], *The River* [1997], *What Time Is It There?* [2000]), but the relations among family members are markedly transformed in each instance. The actors themselves change in the interval between films, physical shifts that the viewer is highly attuned to as the camera devotes such close attention to the nuances of each actor's body. The spaces of the city are similarly addressed in patient detail, and particular types of spaces recur consistently, with subtle shifts in color and décor. The pacing of Tsai's approach heightens the connection between bodies and environments. Nothing ever happens beyond the slow revolutions of these interdependent yet isolated elements, and they become the sole focus of the camera's gaze.

If history has a presence in this realm of suspended time, it is a history that is refracted through the crystalline image of time that Tsai presents, an image obsessed with the specific speeds and slownesses of the everyday. Tsai's films are primarily fictional, but his approach continually blurs the boundaries between fiction and reality. The banality of the scenarios, the lack of action, the use of single real-time takes, the familiarity of actors, and the use of autobiographical situations contribute to this ambiguity. Tsai relies primarily on nonprofessional actors, many of whom he encountered in his everyday life, cast as characters quite similar to their real-life selves. Lee's nickname, Hsiao Kang, is used as his character name in several films (*What Time Is It There? The River, Vive l'amour* [1996], and *Rebels of the Neon God*) and the apartment interior the films repeatedly return to is his family's actual apartment in Taipei (the giant fish in the aquarium depicted in *The River* and *What Time Is It There?* is his actual pet, as well).[49] Tsai is not attempting to replicate reality through a fictional representation, nor does he deviate from reality through fictionalizations that are intended as overt historical commentary. His approach instead seems driven by a sincere attempt to understand the larger conditions of the world through a contemplation of the everyday. This contemplation is not mere observation but also a creative, incisive intervention. The durations of life provide the materiality for artistic expression, in Tsai's case, forging associations between surfaces of divergent bodies and spaces. If the minutia of the everyday is captured in the surface-level expression of Tsai's compositions, the reality it reflects reverberates on multiple registers: the reality of contemporary Taipei, of personal isolation, of particular character types, of the actors themselves, as well as the reality of cinema itself, which always maintains a self-conscious presence in Tsai's work.

Tsai's films are noticeably devoid of scored music, which he perhaps avoids due to its artifice.[50] The primary exceptions to this rule are his quasi-musical features *The Hole* (1998) and *The Wayward Cloud* (2005).[51] Part of the French-funded series *2000 par vu . . ., The Hole* was one of seven films commissioned to imagine the last day of the century. The film opens seven days before the end of the millennium, and the city of Taipei is devastated by a mysterious illness, "Taiwan Fever," resulting in the evacuation of certain quadrants of the city. Victims of Taiwan Fever begin to behave like cockroaches, scurrying across the floor on all fours and hiding in moist dark corners, a becoming-insect that apparently leads to an irretrievable loss of identity. Although the illness is apparently spread through the secretions of roaches, garbage pickup and water services are being discontinued in the quarantined areas, perhaps in an effort to force residents to leave. Throughout this crisis, Taipei is besieged by a ceaseless, torrential rain. The film takes place entirely within the confines of a large public-housing complex, where several residents remain despite the evacuation. The nameless "man upstairs" (Lee Kang-sheng) works in a small grocery stand in a corridor of shuttered shops within the apartment building. He unrolls the metal gate and mans his store each day, futilely, it seems, for his only interaction each day is with a stray cat he feeds in the hallway, and he only encounters one potential customer during the course of the film.[52]

Beneath the man's apartment, the apartment of "the woman downstairs" (Yang Kuei-mei) is plagued by horrific flooding. A plumber searching for the source of the leak leaves a massive hole between their apartments. The hole becomes a vexed threshold of exchange throughout the film, a voyeuristic peephole and a passageway for sounds, dirt, fluids, scents, and insects. The relationship between the man and the woman remains anonymous and somewhat antagonistic throughout most of the film, despite a deepening fascination with one another. This fascination, which remains ambiguously asexual, appears to be born purely from their mutual alienation and boredom, and from their eruptions into each other's spaces through the hole. The woman vainly attempts to maintain the boundaries of her porous apartment as it falls to pieces around her. She stockpiles giant bags of toilet paper to stem the flow of water, which appears to be seeping in through every wall. Her wallpaper is falling off in sheets, and she sits on the toilet with a plastic bowl on her head to catch the dripping water from above. The man's apartment is utterly dry, yet his actions have

Lee Kang-sheng in *The Hole* (Tsai, 1998).

deleterious effects downstairs. When he turns on his faucet, the woman's tap water stops running, and his toilet leaks into her bathroom. The flows through the hole are even more pointed, and at times antagonistic. On the first evening after the hole appears, he arrives home drunk and vomits through the opening. The next day, he sits on his floor and watches the woman until he is hit in the face with a cloud of insecticide. The woman attempts several prophylactic measures to seal the hole; she calls several plumbers and covers the hole with packing tape. These attempts are each impeded to some degree by the man. He pretends not to be home when the plumber rings his bell, and he pours water onto the tape from above to loosen the adhesive. His intentions in both instances are unexplained.

These exchanges are interspersed with five musical spectacles featuring the woman downstairs lip-synching Grace Chang songs. In each case, there is some indirect trigger for the flight into song (the sight of a cockroach exiting the hole, a volley of indirect glances over the balcony in the hallway). There are thematic connections between the songs and the narrative context as well; a visceral sneeze, for example, launches into the song "Achoo Cha Cha," in which the singer describes her allergic response to the marriage proposals of her many suitors. These links are always somewhat tenuous, however, and are never clarified or resolved. Tsai, in an interview, attributes the musical sequences to the "interior world" of the woman, yet at the same time, they do not consistently begin or end at her provocation, nor do they appear to reflect what we might call her personal desires.[53] While Tsai focuses a great deal of attention on the intimate and personal actions and gestures of his characters, there is little in his work to suggest that the surface of the body belies a divisible interior.[54] Indeed, the richness of the corporeality he presents resists notions of interiority or of a mind–body split. The musical sequences in *The Hole* may be fantasies, but given their ambiguous relation to the remainder of the film, it may be more productive to view them as dreams in general, collective dream-images born from the connections between human bodies and the bodies of the spaces they occupy. Tsai himself complicates psychological readings of the musical spectacle when he states that "on another level, the musical numbers are weapons I use to confront the environment at the end of the millennium."[55] This environment, for Tsai, is explicitly linked to the economic, political, cultural, and environmental conditions of Taiwan.[56]

Tsai uses the musical spectacle to activate a complex interaction between real and fantastic spaces. These might not fully achieve what Deleuze would call a circuit between an actual image and its virtual counterpart, as elements of the musical fantasy suggest direct associations with the tropes of Hollywood and Hong Kong musicals in general, and with the icon of Grace Chang in particular. Yet the circulation that occurs here comes far closer to that state than the typical musical film would allow. The key distinction is that in *The Hole,* the musical number is an intervention that arises from the real, but rather

Yang Kuei-mei in *The Hole.*

than departing from it altogether, the spectacle serves to penetrate and transform that real space, creating a zone of indeterminacy where the real is falsified and burlesqued. Each musical number takes place within the cramped and dingy passageways of the apartment complex. Stairways and corridors are modified into stage sets, spotlights appear, and everyday objects such as strips of plastic sheeting and fire extinguishers become props for the dance. The woman, who in the real world of the film is always harried and exhausted, is glamorously styled and elaborately costumed. Yet the power and joyfulness of these spectacles springs from their failure to metamorphose convincingly. The apartment complex remains bleak and stifling, now rendered strange by the uncanny performance. Yang Kuei-mei's costumes, and those of the backup dancers that mysteriously appear in several of the numbers, are fantastically vivid, yet the overall visual effect is always just slightly off, as if the mise-en-scène aspires to something far grander than it is able to achieve. This effect is furthered by the obviousness of Yang's lip synching and by the awkward choreography. In the "I Want Your Love" ("Wo Yao Ni De Ai") number, for example, Yang lip-synchs the Mandarin chorus of the song but stops abruptly during the English-language verse and merely dances. Lee appears in this number as well, wearing a pompadour and a fifties getup in which he looks endearingly uncomfortable. His attempts to dance away from Yang's advances degenerate into delightful silliness as they toss a fire extinguisher back and forth and skip frenetically down the hallway.

The first musical number encapsulates many of the tensions that drive the film as a whole. Inside her dark apartment, Yang is applying egg whites to her face while listening to the radio. The announcer drones on for an inordinate time, shifting breezily from an update on the epidemic to an insipid report on how best to cook instant noodles. Yang stands silently in the middle of her living room, her face upturned as she waits for her facial to dry, when she is struck in the face by falling dirt. She gasps in horror as she watches a cockroach crawl out of the hole and into her apartment. The scene cuts abruptly to a long shot of the marble lobby of the apartment building. The elevator doors open to reveal Yang in a spangled evening dress and an elaborate red-feathered headdress. The battered beige laminate walls of the elevator that we saw earlier are now covered in black and illuminated by tiny white lights that blink off and on in clusters. Yang begins to sing and dance to a Latin-themed Chang song, "Calypso," lit by a strong circular spotlight. The camera begins a slow dolly across the floor of the lobby, revealing the broken doors on the mailboxes, the dirty walls, and the obvious artifice of the homemade light panels inside the elevator as it approaches.

The "Calypso" sequence in *The Hole*.

Yang mimes Chang's voice with enthusiasm as she dances inside the tiny elevator with abundant sensuality. The lyrics of the song describe the exuberant joy of singing the calypso, which Yang further enacts through her movements. Whereas her appearance earlier, captured off-guard within the intimate space of her apartment, had been somewhat dowdy and unpretentious, here Yang is stunningly groomed in a slinky dress slit to her upper thigh. Yet as the song shifts to a puzzling verse in which Chang compares her joyful dance to that of a "proud rooster," Yang begins jerking her head and flapping her elbows, movements that render her feathered headpiece suddenly ridiculous. Throughout the entire number, Yang remains within the confines of the cramped elevator.

The emotional outpouring of the song reverberates sharply against the harshness of the space that constricts it. "I twist and I turn with endless pleasure," Chang's voice coos, "to forget my hard day of endless labors." The sweet and somewhat futile hopefulness of this sentiment is echoed by the tensions contained by their visualization, the constriction and banality of the setting confronted by the abundant aspirations of Yang's performance. After reaching the elevator, the camera begins to slowly pull back. The overhead lights in the lobby are now extinguished, and Yang is isolated within the spotlight. The elevator doors close as the song ends, and the spotlight darkens. The next cut returns abruptly to the harsh florescent lighting of the "real" lobby, as this same elevator, no longer filled with twinkling lights, now opens to reveal the drunken body of Lee passed out on the floor.

The self-conscious nature of Tsai's musical numbers is an unusual combination of understatement and excess. The performances are humorous at times, yet utterly sincere and never ironic. While their insertion into the narrative of the film is more abrupt and gratuitous than in canonical musical films, perhaps these numbers echo more organically the actual experience of listening to pop music—the strange confluence of drama and spectacle with the banality of the everyday. Music transports and extends us, yet always within the same walls that remain oblivious to our transformation. If the musical spectacle, as Kracauer suggests, makes visible the contradictions inherent in the physical world, Tsai's musical numbers seem highly attuned to these paradoxes.

## The Body as History

The connection between *The Hole* and the types of spectacles found in the Esther Williams films is certainly not direct. Yet if we were to speak of the specularization of the female musical star as a refrain, there are some resonances between the two bodies of work. In each case, the singular female body is displayed as an object of fascination, a body marked by multiplicity, contradiction, and hybridity. In each case, the relation between the body and the outside is one of permeability and symbiosis. The body is subsumed in reactive environments and undergoes a process of corporeal transformation. Williams and Yang (as well as Grace Chang) are objects of fascination, yet their sexuality is distilled, contained, and indirectly expressed. Their relations with environments, objects, and animals often take precedence over veiled suggestions of romantic consummation. Williams, for example, is rarely shown engaging in acts of affection with her costars and is featured much more prominently within the ambiguous space of the pool.[57] The relationship between the woman and man in *The Hole*, while expressed in several sequences via romantic songs, is intentionally coded as asexual.[58] Yang performs musically in a way that Williams does not, as her physicality is directly linked to the nuances of the song. Yet the prevalent imperfections of playback in *The Hole,* much like in *Carmen Jones* and the jukebox film, raise issues of disembodiment and masquerade that supplant the direct corporeality of the performance. The musical spectacles in *The Hole* and in the Williams films are sonically strange, taking place in hermetic bubbles whose connection with the outside world is tenuous.

Indeed, the contradictions that exist in *The Hole's* musical sequences highlight the problematic tensions found in a Williams or Chang-style film. Music is an ambiguous entity in this formulation. It takes part in construction of female body as spectacle and commodity, through the lyrics and compositions as well as through the nature of the performance. The Grace Chang songs selected for these scenes exhibit a strange combination of overt Western musical structures and Mandarin lyrics and phrasing. The "Calypso" number plays with the popular fascination with "exotic Latin culture" in the 1950s, filtered through the Hong Kong Cathay studio's fascination with the exotic United States, further confusing notions of location, culture, and the commodification of style. If Tsai presents music as a counterbalance to the destructive forces at work in our culture, he is careful to demonstrate the interdependence of these elements. The joys of the musical spectacles he presents are never fully divorced from their banal points of emergence, and the escape they gesture toward is never complete.

Whereas the Williams spectacle ultimately respects, and perhaps even fetishizes, the boundaries of the female body as a unified entity, Tsai uses every tool at his disposal to dissolve distinctions between interior and exterior. If the woman that appears in the musical numbers is a spectacular double of the woman downstairs, her body is metamorphosed on another level as well. Coupled with these periodic flights into musical fantasy, the woman is gradually undergoing a much darker process of becoming. She begins exhibiting flu symptoms—hence the sneeze that launches her into the "Achoo Cha Cha"—and immediately recognizes that she has been infected with Taiwan Fever. This instant reflects the intersection of a number of simultaneous movements articulated through the conjoined bodies of the woman and of her environment. She is multiplied through her musical double at the same time that her body is wracked with illness and begins the process of becoming-insect. The flooding that crumbles her walls, too, is one and the same with the forces that have penetrated her own fragile surface.

The woman's relationship with her apartment is so tightly woven that the differences between them are indistinguishable. This is not merely a case where the environment serves as a metaphor for her inner state. The permeability of the apartment's ceiling and walls allows for the damp conditions and roach infestation that very literally make her ill. Moreover, the bodies of the apartment, of the complex, and of the city itself bear the marks of the historical conditions that brought them into being—the by-products of a technological, aspiring capitalist state that has overextended itself. The alienation being expressed here is very specific to contemporary Taiwan, the context of its strained relations with China, Japan, and the West, and the fallout of its economic boom. Rain and disease are present here as the very tangible results of housing crises, massive environmental problems, and more general class inequities. The centrality of disease in this film and its relation to the physical body and the body of the city is key here. Disease forges a link between the physical body and the body of the city—a thematic refrain that can be mapped throughout Tsai's larger body of work.[59]

The woman's body, too, is born from this history; her flaws and weaknesses, her flows and movements are all part of the nexus of forces that define a cultural moment. The alliance that is formed between the woman and her building is a dark and desperate one. The woman's attempt to preserve her boundaries is a battle for her survival, rendering the flooding and disintegration of her home that much more tragic. In one of the more poignant illustrations of her shared becoming with her building, the woman engages in an erotic telephone conversation—perhaps with her plumber. As she languidly pulls sheets of wallpaper from the wall, she tells the listener that she is "stripping . . . I'm undressing myself."

The presence of water as a dominating theme in his films points to this more global connection between bodies and spaces. Rain, rivers, and bodily fluids permeate all types of divergent bodies, eradicating the distinctions between them. As Jean-Pierre Rehm eloquently describes the use of water in Tsai, "Just as rain never appears in his films as a gift from some distant grandeur, but rather as a downpour where high and low are joined in the cramped space of a single horizon, tears and incessantly flowing water establish the final form of solidarity (a paradoxical one) between things and beings."[60] Rain is an invading force, fallout from the excesses of industrialization. Water flows from people as well, in the form of tears that express absolute alienation and piss, which in its excessive presence in Tsai's films often suggests drunkenness, fear, and illness. The woman in *The Hole* succumbs to her infection, scuttling across her wet floor on her hands and knees, drowning, in effect, in her own apartment. This is the becoming-fluid of Esther Williams through the looking glass:

the water that is the surfeit of Taipei's cultural conditions painfully disintegrates her body and her identity.[61]

If Tsai's musical presents a historical image, it can be located precisely within his reformulation of the body as open to the outside.[62] For Foucault, the body is central to any genealogical critique. The genealogical approach, rather than seeking the false objectivity of historical distance, examines that which is closest, the details of everyday existence. The body is shaped by social conditions, transected by vectors of power, while at the same time remaining a potent site for resistance:

> The body manifests the stigmata of past experience and also gives rise to desires, failings, and errors. These elements may join in a body where they achieve a sudden expression, but as often, their encounter is an engagement in which they efface each other, where the body becomes the pretext of their insurmountable conflict.[63]

One can read the descent of history through the excesses and anachronisms that mark both the bodies of beings and the bodies of spaces. The body is never a mere living fossil, however, but a conglomeration of contradictory forces that actively destroy that body:

> Descent attaches itself to the body. It inscribes itself in the nervous system, in temperament, in the digestive apparatus; it appears in faulty respiration, in improper diets, in the debilitated and prostrate body of those whose ancestors committed errors. Fathers have only to mistake effects for causes, believe in the reality of an "afterlife," or maintain the value of eternal truths, and the bodies of their children will suffer.[64]

Lee and the hole.

Marked by failure, decay, and the scars of the past, the body is history incarnate, a nexus point at once individual and global, personal and political. "The body is the inscribed surface of events," Foucault writes, "the locus of a dissociated Self . . . and a volume in perpetual disintegration."[65] Genealogical analysis, as such, must root itself in the historical nature of corporeality as well as in the corporeal nature of history.

Foucault describes the impact of history on the body as a destructive force. The conflicts, infections, and excesses that are articulated through the body, while inducing illness and suffering, at the same time pose a threat to the unity of the system that produces them. Grosz writes about Bataille's formulation of excess, which in many ways intersects with a genealogical approach:

> For Bataille, dirt, disorder, contagion, expenditure, filth, immoderation—and above all, shit—exceed the proper, what constitutes "good taste," good form, measured production. If the world of the proper, the system, form, regulated production, constitutes an economy—a restricted economy—a world of exchange, use, and expedience, then there is an excess, a remainder, an uncontained element . . . a world or order governed by immoderation, excess, and sacrifice, an economy of excremental proliferations.[66]

Grosz reads these superfluous and unnecessary excesses in the context of architecture, positing excess and ornamentality—those things that serve no clear functional purpose—as potential strategies for rethinking notions of space and for building spaces that would resist repressive systems.[67]

Disease, filth, rain, insects, and abandoned architectural spaces are the uncontained elements within the economy of *The Hole.* The resistance they present, however, is far from transcendent. They mutate the body through illness, through flooding, painful acts of becoming-insect and becoming-fluid that push the body to its absolute limits. While many of the things bodies can do relate to the suffering of "excremental proliferations," the body also acts as a conduit or catalyst for movement and transformation. Eleanor Kaufman writes of Klossowski's work on Nietzsche, "The experience of the body in its extreme states (sex, sickness) provides access to an otherwise inaccessible realm of lucidity, one where the distinction between body and thought, between matter and energy, is momentarily suspended."[68] I suggest that the musical body, the body engaged in the ornamental excesses of performance, enters into another type of extreme state. While this state is obviously quite distinct from that of sex or illness, the body-in-music is another type of becoming that explores the limitations of corporeality, dissolves distinctions between interior and exterior, and forges new alliances between the bodies of living beings, objects, and environments.

Tsai combines a proliferation of irresolvable corporeal processes (becoming-insect, becoming-building, becoming-fluid, becoming-Grace Chang) within the singular figure of the woman downstairs. Her multiplied and impossible body bears the marks of history, yet it is also a site of emergence. That the destruction of the woman's body is accompanied by her more ecstatic musical multiplications results in a highly paradoxical formulation—we find here two simultaneous movements, one toward infestation, dissolution, and death and the other toward music and pleasure. The hole in this context can be read not as a lack but as a site of exchange; encounters are not governed by a moral mandate but by chance and proximity, the creation of unnatural couplings, an ethics of alterity.[69]

In the finale of the film, the woman has been fully transformed by the virus. She slips on the water that has now permeated the floor of her apartment and crashes to the floor. She crawls madly about the perimeter of her walls, finally burying herself beneath a towering heap of bags of tissue paper. A bright light suddenly appears from above. The man upstairs, who has been watching, attempts to rouse her from her hiding place, banging on the floor with a hammer. He sobs uncontrollably. She eventually surfaces, returned, perhaps only momentarily, to her lucid self. She lies panting atop the pile of bags, and a hand descends from the hole, holding a glass of water, which she grasps and quickly consumes. The hand descends again, open; she hesitates, then grabs the arm with both hands and is lifted up, disappearing through the hole. The final musical number now begins, set in the man's apartment. The woman, in a red gauzy dress, and the man, in a white tuxedo, dance together, slowly, gazing into each other's eyes. They hold each other at some distance, with deep affection but not with a passion that could be called sensual. They listen silently to the music (no one is lip-synching here) as they rotate to its rhythm. "I don't care who you are," Chang sings, "Just hold me close." The film closes with a postscript title card from Tsai: "In the year 2000, we are grateful that we still have Grace Chang's songs to comfort us."

The hope that this ending might inspire is uncharacteristic for Tsai. The woman's rescue appears literally transcendent. To call Chang's songs comforting, too, is perhaps to suggest that music is a temporary (and ultimately futile) escape from the disease and alienation that define our contemporary condition. It is not necessary, however, to read music as it is presented here as merely escapist. Chang's songs are comforting, and they do inspire pleasure and hope, yet this is not to say that they are disconnected from the conditions of historical reality. Nor is it to say that the pleasure they provide is always one of regression, the soothing repetition of familiar formulas, false identities, and the

Yang passes through the hole.

certainty of a happy ending. Music here is created by the same system that destroys the body, but it also refuses to be contained. Popular media cannot be read as passive reflections of their historical conditions. The culture industry, in the process of churning out pop songs and films, generates excesses and by-products that, while colored by their origins, are not necessarily faithful to them. Popular music, as one of those by-products, bears the marks of its historical genesis within the structures of commodity culture. It relies on formulas and clichés that repeatedly assert the fixity of gendered and raced identities. Yet popular music is also irreverent and irrepressible, generating contradictions and differences that seep through the borders of those identities. Unpredictable, fickle, and elusive, music—and film—are nevertheless powerful forces that can, when actively engaged with, provoke transformation, disrupting and destabilizing unified models of time, space, and identity. The link, however, between the destructive becomings of infection and the productive becomings of music should not be read as one of transcendence. It would be an error to read either illness or the musical spectacle as a finale, for neither side can win without destroying the conditions necessary for existence itself.

For Nietzsche, if survival in the modern world is possible, the destructive thrust of the historical drive must be accompanied by the force of creation and a movement toward the future. He posits history as the "antithesis" of art, for history has only the power to destroy illusions and has no capacity to construct.[70] Art fabricates illusions, and these illusions may contribute to the metanarratives of a universalizing History. But when art is guided by an incisive, creative perceptiveness, when it grasps the details of existence outside the obscuring generalizations of a repressive History, art can generate the productive illusions that oppose reality, identity, and truth. In concert, then, with the genealogy of history, the creative tendencies of art penetrate the minutia that history unearths, and propelled by a similar resistance to teleological narratives, begin the work of crafting a new means of existence:

> If the value of a drama lay solely in its conclusion, the drama itself would be merely the most wearisome and indirect way possible of reaching this goal; and so I hope that the significance of history will not be thought to lie in its general propositions, as if these were the flower and fruit of the whole endeavour, but that its value will be seen to consist in its taking a familiar, perhaps commonplace theme, an everyday melody, and composing inspired variations on it, enhancing it, elevating it to a comprehensive symbol, and thus disclosing in the original theme a whole world of profundity, power, and beauty.[71]

The musical spectacle, as a historical image, has the potential to serve a similar function. Rather than escaping from its material conditions, the spectacle excavates the excesses and detritus that a more proper history would leave buried. Through its musicality, the spectacle keys into the durations of the everyday, transforming them into suspended refrains. These refrains, like a cracked crystal, lay bare the strata of the past contained in the present while rending that present open, at the same time, to the forces of the future.

# Conclusion

Perhaps the highest object of art is to bring into play simultaneously all these repetitions, with their differences in kind and rhythm, their respective displacements and disguises, their divergences and decenterings; to embed them in one another and to envelop one or the other in illusions the "effect" of which varies in each case. . . . Even the most mechanical, the most banal, the most habitual, and the most stereotyped repetition finds a place in works of art, it is always displaced in relation to other repetitions, and it is subject to the condition that a difference may be extracted from it for these other repetitions. For there is no other aesthetic problem than that of the insertion of art into everyday life.

—GILLES DELEUZE, *Difference and Repetition*

The musical film is a locus for a number of conflicting tendencies. The musical is rife with stereotype, cliché, habitual structures, and repetition. But it simultaneously allows for multiplicity, hybridity, chance, perversion; for assemblages between diverse types of bodies; and for a free-play of difference. Musicals are nostalgic; they obsess over the past and offer images of utopian futures that often only reassert the conditions of the present. Yet the musical film is also able to free itself from the strictures of chronology, to leap into the virtual past, creating fluid connections and disruptive juxtapositions that destabilize teleological histories. Musicals offer glimpses of dream-images, even of crystalline images of time, only to recuperate those moments into the sensory-motor logic of the movement-image. Musical films are marked by pulsed time, by plodding rhythms, as well as by territorialized categories of identity. At the same time, the exuberant excesses of the musical spectacle can also introduce disruption into the confines of the measure, departing into flights of nonpulsed, floating time.

Contradiction is not unique to the musical genre. The tensions that I outline here resonate with many artistic forms, and particularly with the range of media spectacles produced by an increasingly savvy entertainment industry. Yet the musical film is incredibly idiosyncratic, expressing its incongruities in a highly distinctive way. My project in these pages has been to explore these idio-syncrasies and incongruities, paying particular attention to moments of rupture, failure, discomfort, and inconsistency. The industrial conglomerates that produce audiovisual media have a vested interest in containing excesses and accidents, those differences that pose a threat to their dominance. There is abundant evidence that the differences that do surface within musical films are quickly recuperated and diffused, although these recuperations are never completely successful. By examining works that reside at the margins of the genre—jukebox films, novelty musicals such as Esther Williams's swimming vehicles, films such as *Carmen Jones* that perform disturbing and unconvincing corporeal substitutions, reinterpretations of the genre by filmmakers outside the Hollywood system such as Godard, Demy, and Tsai—the disruptive potential of the musical's excesses comes more sharply into focus.

In each film I have examined, these points of rupture tend to coincide with a musical moment, that instant when the swelling forces of melody and movement tip the scales away from linearity, causality, rationality, and self-same identity in favor of fluidity, multiplicity, irrationality, and the contradictory juxtapositions of the virtual past. Music, as such, appears to be particularly positioned to challenge linear rationality. I am not convinced it is possible or even desirable to arrive at a definitive explanation for music's potentials in this regard. I do not believe that this can be attributed solely to its form and structure, nor do I believe it is enough to simply say music is an abstract and non-representational medium. Clearly, the types of popular songs typically used in musical films are highly representational on a number of levels—lyrically, structurally, in terms of their visualizations, and in terms of their historical conventions. Nevertheless, music has a clear capacity to allow for the expression of contradiction, and it does so in a manner that often resists resolution. Even when a habitual resolution is suggested, it is rarely sufficient enough to contain the differences to which the song gives voice. This capacity is maximized in the musical moment, for the combination of image and music allows for an even greater range of contradictory compositions.

The musical film is a compromised form. But like the *tableau vivant* that contains paradoxical juxtapositions of motion and stillness, the uncomfortable negotiations of the musical moment create a productive realm of indeterminacy. Temporality is unhinged, and disparate historical events coincide with one another. Space is collapsed in such a way that surface and depth are indistinguishable; animate and inanimate bodies become part of one and the same movement. The conflicting gestures of the musical, which move toward differentiation and toward the repetition of the same, destabilize the very terms by which we normally make sense of a filmic text. The distinction between subject and object is obscured in musical films; people become one with the spaces they occupy, and the notion of agency is subsumed by a larger movement of world. Even when musical films assert the desirability of unified subjects who adhere to ideologically "correct" modes of behavior, they do so by forcing the subject to confront difference, to encounter a double or an alternative plane of existence that undermines that unity (e.g., Laurey's dream ballet in *Oklahoma!*). More often than not, the character will choose to retreat into the safety of self-same identity, yet the encounter alone is enough to suggest that these identities are far from inevitable and are highly unstable.

In discussing the political implications of cinematic works, it is essential to distinguish between actual, lived bodies, discourses that construct and control those bodies, and forms of artistic expression. While these forces intersect and interact with each other, the movements and trajectories of each are neither identical nor equivalent. Art can present a provocation, a shock, that makes thought possible. An artistic work that opens or dissembles the body, circulating images that can be read in light of the "body without organs" or "becoming-woman," is not asserting that actual bodies are irrelevant or that the discourses that control actual bodies can be easily dismantled. On the contrary, the embedded, pervasive nature of these discourses demands that artists and philosophers radicalize their means of expression—images, thoughts, and words—as weapons against those molar forces that territorialize and fix the body. The objective is not to arrive at a truer representation of the body or to offer a picture of utopia to which we should aspire. Such a project would not only be impossible, it would be antithetical to the projects of deterritorialization and becoming. Ideally, art will work to imagine new kinds of bodies and new alliances between bodies that can be actualized in new modes of thinking.[1]

To resist, for Deleuze, is to elude the transparency of communication, "to create vacuoles of noncommunication, circuit breakers, so we can elude control."[2] The creative act consists in falsifying the universalizing dictates of societies of control, creating new pathways of thought, and recognizing that which exceeds the realm of knowledge. If the cinema penetrates the past in a manner that resonates with a Bergsonian leap into the virtual past or with a Nietzschean descent into genealogical history, it does so in the interests of the future. Deleuze writes:

> We will then think the past against the present and resist the latter, not in favour of a return but "in favour, I hope, of a time to come" (Nietzsche), that is, by making the past active and present to the outside so that something new will finally come about, so that thinking, always, may reach thought. Thought thinks

its own history (the past), but in order to free itself from what it thinks (the present) and be able finally to "think otherwise" (the future).[3]

By delving into the realm of the personal—the individual romance, the domestic drama, the folk narrative—and by pressing against the limits of corporeality—asking what the body is capable of doing—the musical film sinks its teeth into the matter of the everyday. Yet the musical is not content to remain embedded in the present. It does not merely communicate information about the everyday as it is, for it jams the circuits of the present with pockets of incommensurability, with time out of joint. The everyday is opened to the outside in the musical spectacle, confronted by the paradoxes of the virtual past, and confronted, too, by the repetition and cliché that define everyday existence. The musical film repeats the past, repeats the cliché, but in a manner that discovers a difference that might allow us to "think otherwise."[4]

Some readers might question whether one can call the commercial Hollywood musical a work of art given Deleuze, and Deleuze and Guattari's, use of the term. Deleuze does discuss Hollywood musicals in relation to the dream-image in the *Cinema* books, yet he is also hostile to the notion that commercial products be considered art.[5] Deleuze's skepticism about commercial works is not a dismissal of the popular but a rejection of the closure and resolution offered by profit-making media. An advertisement might provoke us, but the problems it poses can always be solved through a purchase. The Hollywood musical is undeniably a commercial product, but my objective has been to demonstrate that the problems it poses are not so easily resolved. Many of the films I discuss in these pages—the jukebox film or the Esther Williams movie—are blatant moneymaking ventures that may fall short of Deleuze's parameters for a creative project. Yet their accidental stumblings, their monstrous bodies, their discontinuous images and sounds, and their impossible spaces all exceed and resist rationality, truth, and identity. If such works cannot be called creative works of art in their own right, they do produce that opening, that in-betweenness or zone of indeterminacy that engenders creation.

I have intentionally drawn on works that range from "low" to "high" to stress that the first stirrings of this refrain of resistance are present within even the most exploitative or rudimentary musical films. Music operates via resonances, harmonies, counterpoints, and dissonances, elements that appear to varying degrees in experimental compositions as well as popular songs. Dissonance is of course not exclusive to the realm of music, but this proclivity renders the medium that much more open to chance and contradiction. Deleuze and Guattari write:

In fact, the most important musical phenomenon that appears as the sonorous compounds of sensation become more complex is that their closure or shutting-off (through the joining of their frames, of their sections) is accompanied by a possibility of opening into an ever more limitless plane of composition. According to Bergson, musical beings are like living beings that compensate for their individuating closure by an openness created by modulation, repetition, transposition, juxtaposition.[6]

The popular musical film is an articulation of a refrain that is then picked up and transformed through new creative interventions. The chance hesitations and missteps that emerge in the Soundie, for example, may indicate a burgeoning refrain that will undergo further amplifications and mutations in the hands of Godard or Tsai. This is not to establish a hierarchy between the two articulations or to imply that the refrain will undergo a teleological evolution. My point is not that the more territorialized refrain might enable a more perfect work of art. I am suggesting, instead, that each articulation introduces a degree of discontinuity that has the potential to open pathways into the new. The musical's provocation may effect new kinds of filmic or musical expressions, new philosophical concepts, or perhaps its reverberations can be actualized into new kinds of material practices. The trajectory of the opening is entirely unpredictable, and there is no guarantee that the next recurrence of the refrain will continue the process of deterritorialization. But that potential nevertheless exists.

Art is effective when it engages with the demands of everyday life. The products of the culture industry, for Deleuze, are rarely able to approach the radical ideals toward which the true work of art should aspire. Yet given the complex negotiations of everyday existence, it would be a grave error to dismiss the expressions of the popular out of hand. Musicals, like all popular, commercial media, are inhibited by the interests of their creators, interests that are diametrically opposed to difference, becoming, and the line of flight. Perhaps the popular work is the best place to start imagining how real change can be introduced into our own highly compromised conditions. If the process of becoming starts by entering into alliances of proximity, it is not unreasonable to suggest that we begin looking for the first expressions of differentiation in the melodies that are closest to home. A variation in the refrain, this nascent step across the line from walking to dancing, from talking to singing, may be transitory and it may be ultimately recuperated. But if it is able to extract even the tiniest difference from the onslaught of the same, if it can introduce even the smallest stutter into the system, this variation may call forth profound, wholly new means of thinking differently, so long, that is, as we choose to listen.

# Acknowledgments

Many voices have contributed to this project throughout its long evolution. I express my deepest gratitude to David Rodowick, who first introduced me to Deleuze, and to Lisa Cartwright and Douglas Crimp, who provided guidance on these ideas in their earliest incarnations. Many thanks to Jason Weidemann at the University of Minnesota Press for his faith in this project and to Danielle Kasprzak, Nancy Sauro, and Davu Seru for their assistance during the editorial process. I am especially grateful for the thoughtful and thorough comments I received from Gregg Lambert and Steven Shaviro.

I am further indebted to many interlocutors who offered their insights on drafts or presentations of this work. These include Gillian Anderson, Margot Bauman, Zoe Beloff, Joe Bisz, Ian Buchanan, Jonathan Buchsbaum, Ed Chan, Julian Cornell, Ann Davies, Bridgett Davis, Elena Del Rio, Kelly Gates, Claudia Gorbman, Elizabeth Grosz, Narin Hassan, Heather Hendershot, Jennifer Hudak, Stuart Liebman, Laura U. Marks, David Martin-Jones, Rick Maxwell, Susan McClary, Joanna Mitchell, Gregory Pardlo, Kirsi Peltomäki, Zivah Perel, Chris Perriam, Patricia Pisters, Victor Manuel Rodriguez, Joan Saab, Timothy Scheie, John Talbird, Sandra Tarlin, and Carol Vernallis. Angela Gibson was particularly generous with her editorial advice and her friendship—thank you.

I thank the organizations that provided funding for my research: the Department of Art and Art History and the Susan B. Anthony Institute for Gender and Women's Studies at the University of Rochester; the Henry Luce

Foundation; the Department of Media Studies and the Division of the Arts and Humanities at Queens College, City University of New York; and the CUNY Faculty Fellowship Publication Program. Ed Stratman at the George Eastman House was incredibly accommodating in allowing me access to Eastman House film archives and their extensive collection of Soundies. Mark Cantor was generous with his knowledge of Soundies jukebox films, Bob Orlowsky with his knowledge of Scopitones, and Fred MacDonald with his assistance to access stills from his archives.

Robert and Kathlyn Herzog, my parents, have stood behind all of my various ventures and follies, offering unflagging confidence and encouragement. I owe them more than I could ever express. My grandfather, Gottfried "Slim" Herzog, instilled in me a deep love for philosophy, which for him was always tied to the art of living, and my grandmother, Mary Mihal, shared her life-long love of film, music, and dance: this project is dedicated to their memories. Binx has remained a patient and loyal friend throughout. And Peter Walsh has been steadfast in offering his insights, his expertise, and his love—none of this would have been possible without him.

# Notes

## Introduction

1. Jean-Paul Sartre, *Nausea,* trans. Lloyd Alexander (New York: New Directions Publishing, 1964), 175–76.

2. Steve Neale, *Genre and Hollywood* (New York: Routledge, 2000), 105.

3. For an extended study of this phenomenon, see Kay Dickinson, *Off Key: When Film and Music Won't Work Together* (New York: Oxford University Press, 2008).

4. The category of "integrated musicals" has been defined in varying ways but typically refers to musical and non-musical sequences that share an "internal narrative logic," and as such "dissolve the distinction between narrative and number" (Thomas H. Schatz, *Hollywood Genres: Formula, Film Making, and the Studio System* [New York: Random House, 1981], 194; Richard Dyer, "Entertainment and Utopia," in *Genre: The Musical,* ed. Rick Altman [London: Routledge and Kegan Paul, 1981], 185). Songs appear to arise "naturally," with or without the demand for plausible justification, and often serve a central purpose in the evolution of the plot.

5. Gilles Deleuze, *Negotiations: 1972–1990,* trans. Martin Joughin (New York: Columbia University Press, 1995), 125.

6. Claudia Gorbman, *Unheard Melodies: Narrative Film Music* (Bloomington: Indiana University Press, 1987).

7. Michel Chion, *Audio-Vision: Sound on Screen,* trans. Claudia Gorbman (New York: Columbia University Press, 1994), 80.

8. Ibid., 8.

9. Walter Murch, "Dense Clarity-Clear Density," from a talk given at the exhibition *Volume: Bed of Sound,* P.S. 1 Contemporary Art Center, Long Island City, New York (July–September 2000), http://www.ps1.org/cut/volume/murch.html.

10. Chion, *Audio-Vision,* 8–9.

11. See Gorbman, *Unheard Melodies,* 19–20.

12. See Jeff Smith, *The Sounds of Commerce: Marketing Popular Film Music* (New York: Columbia University Press, 1998) for an excellent discussion of the history and function of the compilation score, especially chapter 7.

13. For readings on a spectrum of such moments, see *Film's Musical Moments,* ed. Ian Conrich and Estella Tincknell (Edinburgh: Edinburgh University Press, 2007).

14. Tincknell and Conrich, in a similar manner, define the musical moment, in part, as "a particular point of disruption, an isolated musical presence . . . most notable for its potential to disturb the text through its unexpectedness or at times excessiveness" ("Introduction," in *Film's Musical Moments,* 1–2).

15. Rick Altman, *The American Film Musical* (Bloomington: Indiana University Press, 1987), 16–27.

16. Ibid., 17–19.

17. Ibid., 110.

18. Ibid., 322.

19. Ibid., 359–64.

20. Jane Feuer, *The Hollywood Musical,* 2nd ed. (Bloomington: Indiana University Press, 1993), 43–44.

21. Ibid., 90. See also Jane Feuer, "The Self-Reflective Musical and the Myth of Entertainment," in Altman, *Genre: The Musical,* 159–74.

22. Dyer, "Entertainment and Utopia," 183–84.

23. Ibid., 185.

24. Ernst Bloch, *The Utopian Function of Art and Literature: Selected Essays,* trans. Jack Zipes and Frank Mecklenburg (Cambridge, Mass.: MIT Press, 1993), 118.

25. Ernst Bloch, *The Spirit of Utopia,* trans. Anthony A. Nassar (Stanford, Calif.: Stanford University Press, 2000), 41.

26. Dyer, "Entertainment and Utopia," 177.

27. Ibid., 189.

28. Richard Dyer, "The Colour of Entertainment," *Sight and Sound* 5, no. 11 (1995): 28. Dyer's *Only Entertainment,* 2nd ed. (New York: Routledge, 2002), reprints this essay and "Entertainment and Utopia," alongside a contextual introduction and additional chapters on this dynamic. See also Kenneth MacKinnon, "'I Keep Wishing I Were Somewhere Else': Space and Fantasies of Freedom in the Hollywood Musical," in *Musicals: Hollywood and Beyond,* ed. Bill Marshall and Robynn Stilwell (Exeter, U.K.: Intellect, 2000), 40–46, which argues for the productiveness of combining Dyer's positive and critical positions.

29. Sean Griffin, "The Gang's All Here: Generic versus Racial Integration in the 1940s Musical," *Cinema Journal* 42, no. 1 (Autumn 2002): 21–45.

30. Matthew Tinkcom, *Working Like a Homosexual: Camp, Capital, Cinema* (Durham, N.C.: Duke University Press, 2002), 5.

31. Steven Cohan, *Incongruous Entertainment: Camp, Cultural Value, and the MGM Musical* (Durham, N.C.: Duke University Press, 2005), 338.

32. Many thanks to Gregg Lambert for pointing out the connections between habitus and questions of duration and differentiation within the musical moment. These relations will be explored in more detail in chapter 1.

33. Gilles Deleuze, *Difference and Repetition,* trans. Paul Patton (New York: Columbia University Press, 1994), 70.

34. Gilles Deleuze, *Empiricism and Subjectivity: An Essay on Hume's Theory of Human Nature,* trans. Constantin V. Boundas (New York: Columbia University Press, 1991), 69.

35. Deleuze develops his concept of the sensory-motor schema to describe structures and transitions that are governed by a linear, cause-and-effect logic. It emerges from Bergson's discussion of the faculties of perception and the actualization of images into action. In order to act upon its environment, a body must isolate from the undifferentiated flow that it perceives only those images that interest it in particular, upon which it can choose to act. The complex correlations between objects and images are thus reduced to causal (and spatial) links. Deleuze finds that the associations made between elements in the movement-image progress along a similar trajectory. For more on Bergson's theory of perception, see chapter 3.

36. Gilles Deleuze, *Cinema 2: The Time-Image,* trans. Hugh Tomlinson and Robert Galeta (Minneapolis: University of Minnesota Press, 1989), 41, 272.

37. Henri Bergson, *The Creative Mind: An Introduction to Metaphysics,* trans. Mabelle L. Andison (New York: Citadel Press, 1992), 106.

38. Henri Bergson, *Creative Evolution,* trans. Arthur Mitchell (Mineola, N.Y.: Dover Publications, 1998), 155.

39. Ibid., 176.

40. Gilles Deleuze, *Bergsonism,* trans. Hugh Tomlinson and Barbara Habberjam (New York: Zone Books, 1991), 32–33.

41. Bergson, *Creative Evolution,* 306.

42. Gilles Deleuze, *Cinema 1: The Movement-Image,* trans. Hugh Tomlinson and Barbara Habberjam (Minneapolis: University of Minnesota Press, 1986), 2.

43. D. N. Rodowick similarly notes, "Deleuze's reasoning is certainly weak here," for Deleuze, in his attempt to distinguish between film and natural perception, privileges the automated movements of the projector, eliding any involvement of "cognitive correction" in the perception of the filmic event and creating a "curious identity between movement and image." Rodowick, *Gilles Deleuze's Time Machine* (Durham, N.C.: Duke University Press, 1997), 22.

44. Bergson, *Creative Evolution,* 272, 273.

45. Gilles Deleuze and Félix Guattari, *A Thousand Plateaus: Capitalism and Schizophrenia,* trans. Brian Massumi (Minneapolis: University of Minnesota Press, 1987), 13.

46. Ibid., 12.

47. Ibid., 23.

48. Henri Bergson, *Matter and Memory,* trans. Nancy Margaret Paul and W. Scott Palmer (New York: Zone Books, 1991), 9. See chapter 3 for an extended discussion of Bergson's theory of perception.

49. Henri Bergson, *Time and Free Will: An Essay on the Immediate Data of Consciousness,* trans. F. L. Pogson (New York: Macmillan, 1959), 100, as quoted in Dorothea Olkowski, *Gilles Deleuze and the Ruin of Representation* (Berkeley: University of California Press, 1999), 121. Translation altered by Olkowski.

50. Olkowski, *Gilles Deleuze,* 114.

51. Deleuze, *Negotiations,* 164–165.

52. Rodowick, *Gilles Deleuze's Time Machine,* 176.

53. Ibid., 177.

54. Deleuze, *Negotiations,* 149.

55. Ibid., 148.

56. Henri Bergson, *The Two Sources of Morality and Religion,* trans. R. Ashley Audra and Cloudesley Brereton with the assistance of W. Horsfall Carter (New York: Henry Holt, 1935), 30–32, as quoted in Deleuze, *Bergsonism,* 110.

57. Deleuze and Guattari, *A Thousand Plateaus,* 265–67.

58. Ibid., 262.

59. Gilles Deleuze, "Sur la musique," transcription of a seminar on *Anti oedipe et Mille Plateaux* at the University of Vincennes, May 3, 1977, trans. Timothy S. Murphy. Both the original and translated versions available under *Les Cours de Gilles Deleuze,* "Anti Oedipe et Mille Plateaux" at http://www.webdeleuze.com/php/sommaire.html.

60. Deleuze and Guattari, *A Thousand Plateaus,* 267.

61. Ibid., 69.

62. See Ronald Bogue, *Deleuze on Music, Painting, and the Arts* (New York: Routledge, 2003), 24–31, for a thorough discussion of Messiaen in relation to Deleuze and Guattari and a cogent overview of Deleuze's work on music.

63. Deleuze and Guattari, *A Thousand Plateaus,* 305.

64. The bird sounds in Hitchcock's film were created electronically, and Messiaen's *Turangalila Symphony* (1948) made use of the Ondes Martenot analog synthesizer in its reformulation of birdsongs. See Elisabeth Weis, "The Evolution of Hitchcock's Aural Style and Sound in *The Birds,*" in *Film Sound: Theory and Practice,* ed. Elisabeth Weis and John Belton (New York: Columbia University Press, 1985), 298–311; and Andrew Murphie, "Sound at the End of the World as We Know It," *Perfect Beat* 2, no. 4 (1996).

65. See chapter 2 for an extended discussion of the refrain in relation to processes of territorialization.

66. Deleuze and Guattari, *A Thousand Plateaus,* 267.

67. Ibid., 263.

68. Pierre Boulez, *Boulez on Music Today,* trans. Susan Bradshaw and Richard Romney Bennett (London: Faber and Faber, 1971), 94.

69. Gilles Deleuze, "Le Temps musical," transcription of a 1978 conference at the Institut de Recherche et Coordination Acoutique/Musique, Centre Georges Pompidou, Paris, trans. Timothy S. Murphy. Both the original and translated versions are available under *Les Cours de Gilles Deleuze,* "Conférences," at http://www.webdeleuze.com/php/sommaire.html.

70. See Claire Colebrook's introduction to *Deleuze and Feminist Theory,* ed. Ian Buchanan and Claire Colebrook (Edinburgh: Edinburgh University Press, 2000), 1–17, for an excellent summary of the principal questions driving these debates. See also chapter 4 of the book in hand.

71. Deleuze, "Sur la musique."

72. Deleuze, "Le Temps musical."

73. Charles J. Stivale, "Summary of *L'abécédaire de Gilles Deleuze,*" summary of the series of interviews between Gilles Deleuze and Claire Parnet, filmed in 1989 and broadcast 1994–1995. From the section "O is for Opera," http://www.langlab.wayne.edu/ CStivale/ D-G/ABC3.html.

74. Deleuze, "Sur la musique."

75. Deleuze, "Le Temps musical."

76. The concept of fabulation is discussed in more detail in chapter 3.

77. Elena Del Rio presents an extended analysis of this scene in her excellent book *Deleuze and the Cinemas of Performance: Powers of Affection* (Edinburgh: Edinburgh University Press, 2008).

78. See Deleuze's chapter on style in *Proust and Signs,* trans. Richard Howard (Minneapolis: University of Minnesota Press, 2000), 161–69.

79. Ibid., 168–69.

## 1. Illustrating Music

1. Chion, *Audio-Vision,* 157.

2. Ibid., 158, 163.

3. There are several notable exceptions to this trend. Jeff Smith gives an excellent account of the development of the Scopitone and its impact on narrative film music in *The Sounds of Commerce.* Gregory Lukow also presents a well-researched discussion of both formats in his article "The Antecedents of MTV: Soundies, Scopitones and Snaders, and the History of an Ahistorical Form," in *The Art of Music Video: Ten Years After,* ed. Michael Nash (Long Beach, Calif.: Long Beach Museum of Art, 1991), 6–9. John Mundy links Soundies to other film and television formats in *Popular Music on Screen: From Hollywood Musical to Music Video* (Manchester, U.K.: Manchester University Press, 1999), 93–95. For discussions of Soundies in relation to the history of jazz and jazz on film, see Klaus Stratemann, *Duke Ellington Day by Day and Film by Film* (Copenhagen: Jazz Media, 1992); and Krin Gabbard, *Jammin' at the Margins: Jazz and the American Cinema* (Chicago: University of Chicago Press, 1996).

4. While this was the overwhelming case with early work on music videos, subsequent criticism has moved in new directions. For critical correctives, see Andrew Goodwin, *Dancing in the Distraction Factory: Music Television and Popular Culture* (Minneapolis: University of Minnesota Press, 1992); and Will Straw, "Popular Music and Post-Modernism in the 1980s," in *Sound and Vision: The Music Video Reader,* ed. Simon Frith, Andrew Goodwin, and Lawrence Grossberg (New York: Routledge, 1993), 3–21. For more recent work on the evolution of the music video, see *Medium Cool: Music Videos from Soundies to Cellphones,* ed. Roger Beebe and Jason Middleton (Durham, N.C.: Duke University Press, 2007).

5. Jody Berland, "Sound, Image and Social Space: Music Video and Media Reconstruction," in Frith, Goodwin, and Grossberg, *Sound and Vision,* 30.

6. "Personal Report on Movie Premiere," *Billboard,* October 5, 1940: 34. For the corporate history and complete Soundies filmography, I am indebted to Maurice Terenzio, Scott MacGillivray, and Ted Okuda, *The Soundies Distributing Corporation of America: A History and Filmography* (Jefferson, N.C.: McFarland, 1991), and to the updated version of the volume by MacGillivray and Okuda, *The Soundies Book: A Revised and Expanded Guide to the "Music Videos" of the 1940s* (Lincoln, Neb.: iUniverse, 2007).

7. Other companies promoting cinematic jukeboxes included Vis-o-Graph, Featurettes, Phonovision, Tonovision, Metermovies, Phonofilm, and Talkavision. See Terenzio, MacGillivray, and Okuda, *The Soundies Distributing Corporation of America,* 4–5; and "The Buyers Guide," *Billboard,* January 18, 1941: 80. In addition to the official Soundies films, I also consider shorts produced by rival companies during the same period. For the most part, these films do not differ widely in terms of their structure, tone, or execution, and I group them under the general name of Soundies (a practice that has become commonplace among collectors and other Soundies enthusiasts).

8. "Jimmy's Got It Again," *Look*, November 19, 1940: 14. The "Jimmy" in question is James Roosevelt, son of Franklin D. Roosevelt, one of the partners and principal promoters of the enterprise.

9. The reflected nature of the Panoram mechanism causes the image to be reversed from left to right. Thus, original Soundies reels, when projected normally, are flipped, including all titles and credits. After the Panoram became defunct, several companies purchased the rights to distribute existing Soundies for the home market. Often the backward titles were snipped from the originals and either replaced by new titles or left out altogether. This presents difficulties for researchers and collectors in attempting to identify obscure artists and songs.

10. Mark Cantor, e-mail correspondence with author, October 22, 2002. See also Terenzio, MacGillivray, and Okuda, *The Soundies Distributing Corporation of America*, 15.

11. Terenzio, MacGillivray, and Okuda, *The Soundies Distributing Corporation of America*, 10.

12. On the conflict between the Soundies Distributing Corporation and the American Federation of Musicians, see ibid., 12–13.

13. See David Hume, *A Treatise of Human Nature*, 2nd ed., ed. L. A. Selby-Bigge, with text revised and variant readings by P. H. Nidditch (Oxford: Oxford University Press, 1978), 197–203.

14. Deleuze, *Empiricism and Subjectivity*, 69.

15. Hume, *A Treatise of Human Nature*, 146–47.

16. Ibid., 147.

17. Deleuze, *Difference and Repetition*, 97.

18. Chion, *Audio-Vision*, 5.

19. Ibid., 167.

20. See Claudia Gorbman's discussion of orchestration in a scene from *Nights of Cabiria* (Fellini, 1957) in *Unheard Melodies*, 24–25.

21. Michel Chion, *Le son au cinema* (Paris: Cahiers du Cinema/Editions de l'Etoile, 1985), 183–84.

22. Many thanks to Gillian Anderson and Claudia Gorbman for their insights regarding the unusual visual and sonic composition of this scene.

23. Gilles Deleuze, "He Stuttered," trans. Constantin V. Boundas, in *Gilles Deleuze and the Theater of Philosophy*, ed. Constantin V. Boundas and Dorothea Olkowski (New York: Routledge, 1994), 28.

24. Ibid., 24.

25. Chion, *Le son au cinema*, 191.

26. Terenzio, MacGillivray, and Okuda, *The Soundies Distributing Corporation of America*, 17–24.

27. Lukow, "The Antecedents of MTV," 9.

28. Anna McCarthy, *Ambient Television: Visual Culture and Public Space* (Durham, N.C.: Duke University Press, 2001), 45.

29. See ibid., 29–62; and Terenzio, MacGillivray, and Okuda, *The Soundies Distributing Corporation of America*, 1–16, for outlines of the conflicts each technology faced in the public market.

30. Susan Sontag, "Notes on 'Camp'" (1964), in *Against Interpretation and Other Essays* (New York: Farrar, Straus and Giroux, 1966), 277, 282–84.

31. Ibid., 277. For anthologies providing an introduction to the debates surrounding camp, see Moe Meyer, ed., *The Politics and Poetics of Camp* (New York: Routledge, 1994); and Fabio Cleto, ed., *Camp: Queer Aesthetics and the Performing Subject: A Reader* (Ann Arbor: University of Michigan Press, 1999).

32. Steven Cohan's reading of camp in relation to MGM musicals has many resonances here, particularly in his discussion of the MGM house style as excessive, aggregate, and geared toward a multivalent audience *(Incongruous Entertainment)*. For a discussion of kitsch and cheese in relation to camp, see Annalee Newitz, "What Makes Things Cheesy? Satire, Multinationalism, and B-Movies," *Social Text* 18, no. 2 (Summer 2000): 59–82.

33. Although beyond the scope of this chapter, it is interesting to consider the contemporary status of Scopitones (and Soundies) as highly collectible, almost fetishized objects of curiosity. This status, along with a more generalized historical distance, has inevitably influenced my own reading of these formats.

34. Sontag, "Notes on 'Camp,'" 285.

35. Among the numerous titles in this vein are Sylvie Vartan, "Locomotion"; Les Surfs, "Si J'Avais Un Marteau"; Les Chats Sauvages, "Sherry Baby"; Les Baronets, "Twiste et Chante"; and Richard Anthony, "Itsi Bitsi Petit Bikini."

36. "Ad Tests for French Movie Juke," *Billboard,* September 11, 1961, 66.

37. Andre De Vekey, "Scopitone Seeking British Cooperation," *Billboard,* January 2, 1965, 32.

38. See Smith, *The Sounds of Commerce,* 141–46. Alternative histories are available on several Web sites. While there are some contradictions in terms of data, given the lack of academic work on the medium, they provide one of the best sources for researchers. For a well-researched historical overview, see Jack Stevenson, "The Jukebox That Ate the Cocktail Lounge—The Story of the Scopitone," 1999, http://hjem.get2net.dk/jack_stevenson/scopi .htm, reprinted in Stevenson, *Land of a Thousand Balconies: Confessions of a B-Movie Archaeologist* (London: Critical Vision, 2003, 31–46). Another valuable resource is Bob Orlowsky's "Scopitone Archive," http://www.scopitonearchive.com, providing one of the most complete Scopitone filmographies available and a discussion forum. Many of the films referenced in this chapter can be viewed at Scopitones.com, a blog featuring downloadable films, ephemera, and Scopitone news, http://www.scopitones.com.

39. French Scopitones did feature a limited number of United States and British artists, such as Paul Anka, Dion, Dionne Warwick, and Petula Clark. Germany also produced a number of titles, as did Britain.

40. Ray Brack, "Cinema Juke Box: Just a Novelty?" *Billboard,* July 10, 1965, 45+.

41. "Scopitone Puts Out Pics by Disk Artists," *Billboard,* July 10, 1965, 46.

42. Brack, "Cinema Juke Box," 48.

43. Gale Wald observes a similar scenario in a 1941 Rosetta Tharpe Soundie. Wald, "From Spirituals to Swing: Sister Rosetta Tharpe and Gospel Crossover," *American Quarterly* 55, no. 3 (September 2003): 387–416.

44. See Amy Herzog, "In the Flesh: Space and Embodiment in the Pornographic Peep Show Arcade," *Velvet Light Trap* 62 (Fall 2008): 29–43.

45. Steven Shaviro, *The Cinematic Body* (Minneapolis: University of Minnesota Press, 1993), 117.

46. Ibid., 117.

47. The blog at Scopitones.com provides a sampling of Scopitone-related events and

media references, http://scopitones.blogs.com. The HBO series *Flight of the Conchords* featured a Scopitone parody (in French) for the song "Foux Du Fafa" ("Girlfriends" episode, August 5, 2007).

48. Shaviro, *The Cinematic Body,* 110.

49. Gilles Deleuze, *Masochism: An Interpretation of Coldness and Cruelty,* trans. Jean McNeil (New York: George Braziller, 1971), 77, as quoted in Shaviro, *The Cinematic Body,* 111.

50. Steve Wurtzler, "'She Sang Live, but the Microphone Was Turned Off': The Live, the Recorded and the *Subject* of Representation," in *Sound Theory, Sound Practice,* ed. Rick Altman (New York: Routledge, 1992), 89.

51. Wurtzler, "'She Sang Live," 91. See also Rick Altman, "The Technology of the Voice, Part II," *Iris* 4, no. 1 (1986): 107–19.

52. Rick Altman, "Afterword: A Baker's Dozen Terms for Sound Analysis," in *Sound Theory, Sound Practice,* 250.

53. Berland, "Sound, Image, and Social Space," 25.

## 2. Dissonant Refrains

1. Deleuze and Guattari, *A Thousand Plateaus,* 312.

2. Number of film titles produced between 1894 and 2005, according to the archives at the Carmen Project at the Centre for Research into Film and Media, University of Newcastle, published in the annotated filmography and bibliography *Carmen on Screen,* ed. Ann Davies and Phil Powrie (Woodbridge, U.K.: Tamesis, 2006). For a thorough discussion of *Carmen's* history on film, see Phil Powrie, Bruce Babington, Ann Davies, and Chris Perriam, *Carmen on Film: A Cultural History* (Bloomington: University of Indiana Press, 2007).

3. Peter Robinson, "Mérimée's *Carmen,*" in Susan McClary, *Georges Bizet, Carmen* (New York: Cambridge University Press, 1992), 1.

4. McClary, *Georges Bizet, Carmen,* 115.

5. See ibid.

6. See Marvin D'Lugo, "Historical Reflexivity: Saura's Anti-*Carmen,*" *Wide Angle* 9, no. 3 (1987): 52–61, for a discussion of Saura's use of *Carmen* to critically explore notions of "Spanishness."

7. Alice Craven similarly points to "Godard's refrain technique," though her theorization of the refrain is drawn from literary theory and genre criticism. "Jean-Luc Godard's Refrain and the Question of Genre," *Discourse Social/Social Discourse* 1, no. 3 (Winter 1988): 301–16.

8. Phil Powrie, "Godard's *Prénom: Carmen* (1984), Masochism, and the Male Gaze," *Forum for Modern Language Studies* 31, no. 1 (1995): 65.

9. Bogue, *Deleuze on Music, Painting, and the Arts,* 17.

10. See ibid., chapter 1, for a lucid summary of Deleuze and Guattari's work on music, rhythm, and territorialization.

11. Linda Hutcheon, *A Theory of Adaptation* (New York: Routledge, 2006), 150–51, 158. *Carmen* serves as one of Hutcheon's key examples of an adapted, and adaptive, text.

12. For an elaboration of the various Beethoven quartets referenced in *Prénom Carmen,* see Miriam Sheer, "The Godard/Beethoven Connection: On the Use of Beethoven's Quartets in Godard's Films," *Journal of Musicology* 18, no. 1 (Winter 2001): 173, 181–87.

13. See discussions of this aspect of the film by Powrie, "Godard's *Prénom: Carmen,*"

68; and Verena Andermatt Conley, "A Fraying of Voices: Jean-Luc Godard's *Prénom Carmen*," *L'Esprit Créateur* 30, no. 2 (Summer 1990): 69.

14. Evlyn Gould, *The Fate of Carmen* (Baltimore, Md.: Johns Hopkins University Press, 1996), 13–14.

15. Gould, *The Fate of Carmen*, 113.

16. Susan McClary notes that most contemporary "revisionist readings of *Carmen*" similarly devote the majority of their attention to questions of gender. McClary, *Georges Bizet, Carmen*, 125.

17. David Wills, "Carmen: Sound/Effect," *Cinema Journal* 25, no. 4 (Summer 1986): 33–43. Also note that Bizet's opera entered the public domain in 1981, allowing for unrestricted, royalty-free interpretations of the work. It was at this point that Preminger's *Carmen Jones* was first shown in France, having previously been banned in the country by Bizet's estate. See Ann Davies, "High and Low Culture: Bizet's Carmen and the Cinema," in *Changing Tunes: The Use of Pre-existing Music in Film*, ed. Phil Powrie and Robynn Stilwell (Burlington, Vt.: Ashgate, 2006), 51.

18. McClary also identifies class as one of the primary conflicts that Godard examines through his reworking of the Carmen narrative. See "*Carmen* as Perennial Fusion," in *Carmen: From Silent Film to MTV*, ed. Chris Perriam and Ann Davies (Amsterdam: Rodopi, 2005), 205–16.

19. McClary notes that in Bizet's original opéra comique version, Carmen's defiance is further emphasized by her sung response to the spoken questions; the act of singing in itself works to undermine the logic of the legal authorities. McClary, *Georges Bizet, Carmen*, 85.

20. On the centrality of Preminger's film to *Prénom Carmen*, see H. Marshall Leicester, Jr., "Discourse and the Film Text: Four Readings of 'Carmen,'" *Cambridge Opera Journal* 6, no. 3 (November 1994): 249–50.

21. In this regard, Carmen X might be read alongside Sally Potter's *Thriller* (1979), in which the heroine interrogates and deconstructs her own position as the Mimi character in Puccini's *La Bohème*.

22. Micaëla does act in an expository capacity in Bizet's opera; she travels from Don José's village to bring a message from his mother and acts as a marker for this past and the unfulfilled future (the safety of a socially acceptable marriage) against which we evaluate Don José's actions for the remainder of the opera. She remains firmly linked to this one significatory function, however, within the world of the narrative, whereas Mérimée's archeologist and Godard's Claire speak from the outside, offering a metacommentary that Micaëla could not provide. *Prénom Carmen*'s extensive use of female voice-over, in this regard, is key.

23. Powrie, "Godard's *Prénom: Carmen*."

24. Godard stated in an interview that "the real subject of Carmen is the music and the body, and the script comes from that realization—the lovemaking between music and body." His inspiration for this realization was *Carmen Jones*. Colin MacCabe, *Godard: A Portrait of the Artist at Seventy* (New York: Faber and Faber, 2005), 286.

25. Susan McClary, *Feminine Endings: Music, Gender, and Sexuality* (Minneapolis: University of Minnesota Press, 1991), 57–58; and *Georges Bizet, Carmen*, 74–77.

26. Wills, "Carmen" 42.

27. Ibid., 40.

28. See McClary, *Georges Bizet, Carmen*, for a discussion of the representational function

of music in opera, especially chapter 4. Interestingly, McClary also notes that Bizet cites Beethoven as his greatest idol (48). McClary specifically addresses Bizet's "German" leanings and their implications in *Prénom Carmen* in "*Carmen* as Perennial Fusion."

29. Godard has drawn heavily from Beethoven's string quartets throughout his career, especially those from the composer's late period (opp. 131, 132, 133, and 135), featuring them in several of his films, including *Le nouveau monde* (1962), *Une femme mariée* (1964), and *Deux ou trois choses que je sais d'elle* (1966). See Sheer, "Godard/Beethoven Connection."

30. Maynard Solomon, "Beethoven: Beyond Classicism," in *The Beethoven Quartet Companion,* ed. Robert Winter and Robert Martin, (Berkeley: University of California Press, 1994), 59–75.

31. See McClary, *Feminine Endings.*

32. See Susan McClary, *Conventional Wisdom: The Content of Musical Form* (Berkeley: University of California Press, 2000).

33. Leon Botstein, "The Patrons and Publics of the Quartets: Music, Culture, and Society in Beethoven's Vienna," in Winter and Martin, *The Beethoven Quartet Companion,* 93.

34. Ibid., 100.

35. Christopher Reynolds, "From Berlioz's Fugitives to Godard's Terrorists: Artistic Responses to Beethoven's Late Quartets," *Beethoven Forum* 8, no. 1 (2000): 163.

36. Franz Schubert, diary entry of June 16, 1816, from *Schubert: A Documentary Biography,* ed. O. E. Deutsch (London, 1946), 64, as quoted in Solomon, "Beethoven," 69.

37. See MacCabe, *Godard,* 285–86; and Richard Brody, *Everything Is Cinema: The Working Life of Jean-Luc Godard* (New York: Metropolitan Books, 2008), 445.

38. That *Carmen Jones* had been banned in France until 1981 may have shifted the perception of the film there, granting it an enhanced, renegade status. In an interview, Anna Karina recalls traveling with Godard to London to view the film. See Jeffrey Gantz, "Une histoire d'Anna" (interview with Anna Karina), *Boston Phoenix,* September 5–11, 2003, http://www.bostonphoenix.com/boston/movies/reviews/documents/03132795.asp.

39. Andrew Sarris, *The American Cinema: Directors and Directions, 1929–1968* (New York: DeCapo, 1996), 74, 104–5.

40. John Orr, "Otto Preminger and the End of Classical Cinema," *Senses of Cinema* 40 (July–September 2006), http://www.sensesofcinema.com/contents/06/40/otto-preminger.html.

41. Jacques Rivette, "The Essential" ("L'essentiel," *Cahiers du Cinéma* 32, February 1954), trans. Liz Heron, in *Cahiers du Cinéma: The 1950s: Neo-Realism, Hollywood, New Wave,* ed. Jim Hillier (Cambridge, Mass.: Harvard University Press, 1985), 133.

42. See Jeff Smith, "Black Faces, White Voices: The Politics of Dubbing in *Carmen Jones,*" *Velvet Light Trap* 51 (Spring 2003): 39.

43. Ibid., 32.

44. McClary, *Georges Bizet, Carmen,* 133.

45. Marsha Siefert, "Image/Music/Voice: Song Dubbing in Hollywood Musicals," *Journal of Communication* 45, no. 2 (Spring 1995): 60. The lead singers in *Porgy and Bess,* Adele Addison and Robert McFerrin, were both African American opera performers. The question of the "racing" of vocal performances is an extraordinarily complex one. Tonal color and other performative qualities (the racial coding of the voice) appear to be privileged over the racial identity of the playback singer in films that utilize vocal substitution.

46. Smith, "Black Faces, White Voices," 41.

47. Chris Fujiwara, *The World and Its Double: The Life and Work of Otto Preminger* (New York: Faber and Faber, 2008), 162–63.

48. Ibid., 163.

49. Donald Bogle, *Dorothy Dandridge: A Biography* (New York: Amistad, 1997), 277, quoting from Stephen M. Silverman, "That Black 'Carmen,'" *New York Post,* July 16, 1986.

50. Otto Preminger, *Preminger: An Autobiography* (New York: Bantam, 1978), 159.

51. Prosper Mérimée, *Carmen and Other Stories,* trans. Nicholas Jotcham (New York: Oxford University Press, 1989), 339.

52. Mladen Dolar, *A Voice and Nothing More* (Cambridge, Mass.: MIT Press, 2006), 80–81.

53. Preminger, *Preminger,* 162.

54. Julie Dash's *Illusions* (1983) presents a moving interrogation of the politics of dubbing, with a particular focus on the racism endemic to voice substitution in classical Hollywood musicals.

55. See Siefert, "Image/Music/Voice," 47–48. Siefert links practices of voice replacement with the political economy of the film industry and the marketing of soundtracks. See Carol Clover, "Dancin' in the Rain," *Critical Inquiry* 21 (Summer 1995): 722–47, for a reading of voice replacement in relation to anxieties about accountability, race, and gender in *Singin' in the Rain* (1952).

56. Chion, *Audio-Vision,* 63.

57. Ibid., 63.

58. Michel Chion, *The Voice in Cinema,* trans. Claudia Gorbman (New York: Columbia University Press, 1999), 130.

59. Chion, *The Voice in Cinema,* 156.

60. Dolar, *A Voice and Nothing More,* 80.

61. Ibid., 81.

62. Rick Altman, "Moving Lips: Cinema as Ventriloquism," *Yale French Studies,* no. 60, Cinema/Sound (1980): 67, 79.

63. See Smith, "Black Faces, White Voices." On blackface and the larger history of the musical, see Michael Rogin, *Blackface, White Noise: Jewish Immigrants in the Hollywood Melting Pot* (Berkeley: University of California Press, 1996). Again, I would note that readings of blackface in *Carmen Jones* and *Porgy and Bess* become even more tangled in the cases when the operatic playback singers are themselves black.

64. Smith, "Black Faces, White Voices," 33.

65. Ibid., 36.

66. See Deleuze, *The Movement-Image,* 87–101.

67. See Smith, "Black Faces, White Voices," and McClary, *Georges Bizet, Carmen,* 134.

68. Maria Callas, *Carmen,* by Georges Bizet, cond. Georges Prêtre, Orchestre du Théâtre National de l'Opéra de Paris, EMI Classics 5 56283 2 (compact disk).

69. James Baldwin, "Life Straight in De Eye," *Commentary* 1 (January 1955): 74.

70. Metered time, in Deleuze and Guattari's formulation, appears to be analogous to pulsed time. See the introduction to the book in hand.

71. Kaja Silverman, *The Acoustic Mirror: The Female Voice in Psychoanalysis and Cinema* (Bloomington: Indiana University Press, 1988), 164.

72. Hutcherson's race is rarely noted in criticism of *Carmen Jones,* although I would argue this fact significantly complicates the politics of the film. According to Marilyn Horne,

Hutcherson was a tenor, "but he spent his entire life pushing his voice down to sing the role of Porgy because he was black and that was the only job he could get. It was a true American tragedy." Michael Portantiere, "Horne Aplenty," interview with Marilyn Horne, *TheaterMania* .com, http://www.theatermania.com/content/news.cfm?int_news_id=4322.

73. Preminger discusses the overtly fantastical nature of the film, although he does so in response to criticism regarding the image of African American culture he presents. See Gerald Pratley, *The Cinema of Otto Preminger* (New York: A. S. Barnes, 1971), 110–11.

74. Chion, *The Voice in Cinema,* 151.

75. See Rodowick, *Gilles Deleuze's Time Machine,* 149–51. The concept of fabulation is discussed in greater detail in chapter 3 of the book in hand.

76. Chion, *Audio-Vision,* 36.

77. Ibid., 38.

## 3. En Chanté

1. Bergson, *Matter and Memory,* 133.

2. Eleanor Ringel, review of *The Umbrellas of Cherbourg, Atlanta Journal and Constitution,* June 21, 1996, 22P.

3. Terrance Rafferty, "Jacques Demy: A New Wave Auteur without the Rough Edges," *New York Times,* November 11, 2001.

4. Demy confirms this in an interview when he states that what one might call distanciation in his films, "ça n'est pas Brechtien comme principe." Michel Caen and Alain Le Bris, "Entretien avec Jacques Demy," *Cahiers du Cinéma* 155 (May 1964): 7.

5. See the introduction to the book in hand for an overview of the concept of fabulation as it is utilized in Deleuze's writings.

6. See Peter Kemp, "Stingin' in the Rain: *The Umbrellas of Cherbourg,*" *Senses of Cinema* 16 (September–October 2001), http://www.sensesofcinema.com/contents/01/16/cteq/umbrellas.html.

7. Caen and Le Bris, "Entretien avec Jacques Demy," 8, my translation.

8. See the introduction to this book. See also Ronald Bogue, *Deleuze on Cinema* (New York: Routledge, 2003), chapter 1, for an excellent summary of Bergson's theory of perception in relation to Deleuze.

9. I am much indebted to Dimitris Papanikolaou and Bennet Schaber for pointing out the connection between this sequence and Bergson's formulation of time. My reading of *Les parapluies* was further enriched by Papanikolaou's "Opening an Umbrella Term: Meta-Musicals," presented at the conference Film Musicals, University College Cork, Cork, Ireland, September 19–20, 2003.

10. This opening perhaps makes reference as well to René Clair's *Sous les toits de Paris* (1930), a film with which *Les parapluies* shares many affinities.

11. Deleuze, *The Time-Image,* 67.

12. Ibid., 119.

13. Bill Marshall and Sylvie Lindeperg, "Time, History and Memory in *Les parapluies de Cherbourg,*" in Marshall and Stilwell, eds., *Musicals: Hollywood and Beyond,* 98–106.

14. American Film Institute, American Film Institute Seminar with Jacques Demy, held November 16, 1971, at the Center for Advanced Film Studies (Beverly Hills, Calif.: American Film Institute, 1978), tape 1, p. 10–11.

15. Deleuze, *The Time-Image,* 124.

16. Stuart Klawans, "Candy-Colored Sadness," *The Nation,* April 29, 1996.

17. I am relying on the translation of the verse provided in the subtitled, restored version of the film released on DVD by Miramax films in 2003.

18. Ronald Bogue, "Fabulation, Narration, and the People to Come," in *Deleuze and Philosophy,* ed. Constantin V. Boundas (Edinburgh: Edinburgh University Press, 2006), 204–5. See also Bergson, *The Two Sources of Morality and Religion.*

19. Bergson, *The Two Sources of Morality and Religion,* 195.

20. Bogue, "Fabulation," 208.

21. John Mullarkey, "Life, Movement and the Fabulation of the Event," *Theory, Culture, and Society* 24, no. 6 (2007): 59.

22. Bogue, "Fabulation," 209.

23. Gilles Deleuze, *Negotiations, 1972–1990,* trans. Martin Joughin (New York: Columbia University Press, 1995), 174.

24. Rodowick, *Gilles Deleuze's Time Machine,* 159–60.

25. See Bogue, "Fabulation," 215.

26. For a well-researched discussion of the history of Donkey Skin tales, see Marina Warner, *From the Beast to the Blonde: On Fairy Tales and Their Tellers* (New York: Farrar, Straus and Giroux, 1994), 319–69; and Louis Marin, *Food for Thought,* trans. Mette Hjort (Baltimore, Md.: Johns Hopkins University Press, 1989), 29–38.

27. "The Old Flea-Bag," for example, included in Andrew Lang's *Green Fairy Book* collection (published as "The Dirty Shepardess" in the first edition, 1892), reproduced the narrative of *Peau d'âne* almost exactly yet without the threat of incest or the magical donkey. The editor of the 1978 edition of the collection attributes the story to Paul Sébillot, *Littérature orale de la Haute-Bretagne* (Paris, 1881), who in turn claims to have heard the story told by a teenage farm boy in Liffré in 1878. Andrew Lang, *The Green Fairy Book,* Brian Alderson, ed. (New York: Viking Press, 1978).

28. While English translations of the story describe the first dress as being the color of the sky or of the heavens, the French *temps* used in Perrault's original verse and in Demy's film can be translated either as weather or time. The dressmaker in Demy's film uses the dual meaning for a comic wordplay when he receives the order. The impossible presence of a dress the color of time seems entirely consistent with the wild anachronisms and temporal anomalies that punctuate the film. There is a further, perhaps coincidental, connection among this dress, film, and temporality. In a documentary on Demy, Catherine Deneuve recalls that the dress was constructed out of the same material used to make movie screens, such that colored lights and images of clouds could be projected onto it. See *L'univers de Jacques Demy* (Varda, 1995).

29. See "Images of Thought and Acts of Creation" in the introduction of this book for a summary of Deleuze's work on the cinema in relation to these questions.

30. Eleanor Kaufman, "Deleuze, Klossowski, Cinema, Immobility," *Film-Philosophy* 5, no. 33 (November 2001), http://www.film-philosophy.com/vol5-2001/n33kaufman.html.

31. Ibid.

32. Ibid.

33. Pierre Klossowski, dialogue from *La monnaie vivante* (Paris: Losfeld, 1970), 84, quoted in Kaufman, "Deleuze, Klossowski, Cinema, Immobility."

34. See Kaufman, "Deleuze, Klossowski, Cinema, Immobility"; and Deleuze, *The Movement-Image*, 56.

35. Deleuze, *The Time-Image*, 114.

36. Gilles Deleuze, "Klossowski or Bodies-Language," Appendix II in *The Logic of Sense*, trans. Mark Lester with Charles Stivale, ed. Constantin V. Boundas (New York: Columbia University Press, 1990), 280–301. References to this article, reprinted from *Critique* (1965), will be cited separately from the main body of the text.

37. Demy, when asked about Aimée's appearance in both films, replied, "I felt there was a certain beauty in seeing the ten-year spread between *Lola* and the *Model Shop*. . . . You could feel that Anouk Aimée was a different person." American Film Institute Seminar with Jacques Demy, tape 1, p. 8.

38. Deleuze, *Difference and Repetition*, 287.

39. Ibid., 287.

40. Deleuze, *Logic of Sense*, 1.

41. Deleuze, "Klossowski," 282–83.

42. Eleanor Kaufman, "Klossowski or Thoughts-Becoming," in *Becomings: Explorations in Time, Memory, and Futures*, ed. Elizabeth Grosz (Ithaca, N.Y.: Cornell University Press, 1999), 146–51.

43. Deleuze, "Klossowski," 289.

44. Ibid., 283.

45. Ibid., 280.

46. Ibid., 281.

47. See chapter 4 for further discussion of the Berkeley-style spectacle.

48. Deleuze, *Logic of Sense*, 237.

49. Carol Clover offers a similar reading of the Final Girl who serves as the protagonist in slasher films, providing the androgynous double to the similarly androgynous killer. The Final Girl triumphs in the end by establishing her subjectivity and the law via the phallus used against the killer. "Her Body, Himself: Gender in the Slasher Film," *Representations*, no. 20 (Autumn 1987): 187–228. Clover makes a provocative link between the double of the horror film and the double of pornography that could extend to the doubles of the musical and fairy tale.

50. Deleuze, *Logic of Sense*, 237.

51. Ibid., 237.

52. Brian Massumi, *A User's Guide to Capitalism and Schizophrenia: Deviations from Deleuze and Guattari* (Cambridge, Mass.: MIT Press, 1992), 81.

53. Ibid., 81.

54. Gilles Deleuze, *Foucault*, trans. Seán Hand (Minneapolis: University of Minnesota Press, 1988), 98. See also Rodowick, "The Memory of Resistance," in *Gilles Deleuze's Time Machine*, 194–210.

55. Michel Foucault, *The Order of Things: An Archaeology of the Human Sciences* (New York: Vintage, 1994), 326.

56. Deleuze, *Logic of Sense*, 238.

57. Ibid., 238.

58. Ibid., 304.

59. Deleuze, "Klossowski," 283.

60. Deleuze, *Logic of Sense*, 10.

## 4. Becoming-Fluid

1. Siegfried Kracauer, *The Mass Ornament: Weimar Essays,* trans. Thomas Y. Levin (Cambridge, Mass.: Harvard University Press, 1995), 75–76.

2. Ibid., 75.

3. Ibid., 75.

4. Ibid., 81.

5. See Catherine Williamson, "Swimming Pools, Movie Stars: The Celebrity Body in the Post-War Marketplace," *Camera Obscura* 38 (May 1996): 4–29; and Esther Williams, *Million Dollar Mermaid,* with Digby Diehl (New York: Simon and Schuster, 1999).

6. Coincidentally, Chang also appears in a striking adaptation of *Carmen, The Wild, Wild Rose* (Wong, 1960), giving an electrifying performance as an ill-fated lounge singer. DVDs of many of her films are available via http://www.hkflix.com.

7. Williams's work is not unique in this, as I would locate this tendency, to greater or lesser degrees, in all backstage musicals, particularly in the impossible fluid spaces of the Busby Berkeley–style performance.

8. Steven Cohan provides an extended reading of this scene and of Williams as a star figure in general, in *Incongruous Entertainment.* He stresses as well the centrality of race and ethnicity in the Williams vehicle, particularly the inclusion of Latin American performers and music in *Bathing Beauty.*

9. Martin Rubin, *Showstoppers: Busby Berkeley and the Tradition of Spectacle* (New York: Columbia University Press, 1993), 180.

10. Deleuze, *The Time-Image,* 60–61.

11. Ibid., 61.

12. Ibid., 59.

13. Siegfried Kracauer, *Theory of Film: The Redemption of Physical Reality* (Princeton, N.J.: Princeton University Press, 1997), 41. See also D. N. Rodowick, *Reading the Figural, or, Philosophy after the New Media* (Durham, N.C.: Duke University Press, 2001), especially "The Historical Image," 141–69.

14. Rodowick, *Reading the Figural,* 164.

15. Ibid., 183.

16. Ibid., 189.

17. Michel Foucault, "Nietzsche, Genealogy, History," in *Language, Counter-Memory, Practice: Selected Essays and Interviews,* trans. Donald F. Bouchard and Sherry Simon (Ithaca, N.Y.: Cornell University Press, 1977), 162.

18. Ibid., 146. Rodowick offers a revised translation of this passage in *Reading the Figural,* 190.

19. My argument here is indebted to András Bálint Kovács, "The Film History of Thought," trans. Sándor Hervey, in *The Brain Is the Screen: Deleuze and the Philosophy of Cinema,* ed. Gregory Flaxman (Minneapolis: University of Minnesota Press, 2000), 153–70.

20. See Kovács, "The Film History of Thought," 163–67.

21. Bergson, *Matter and Memory,* 127.

22. Deleuze, *The Time-Image,* 41.

23. Ibid., 273.

24. Ibid., 273, emphasis added.

25. Ibid., 273.

26. Williamson, "Swimming Pools," 15; Williamson provides a thorough account of the cross-marketing strategies attached to Esther Williams as an icon.

27. Altman, *The American Film Musical,* 19–27.

28. See Tinkcom, *Working Like a Homosexual;* Cohan, *Incongruous Entertainment;* and Leonard J. Leff, "'Come on Home with Me': *42nd Street* and the Gay Male World of the 1930s," *Cinema Journal* 39, no. 1 (Fall 1999): 3–22.

29. Tinkcom, *Working Like a Homosexual,* 46.

30. D. A. Miller, *Place for Us: Essay on the Broadway Musical* (Cambridge, Mass.: Harvard University Press, 1998), 2.

31. Lucy Fischer analyzes this scene in detail in "The Image of Woman as Image: The Optical Politics of *Dames,*" in Altman, *Genre: The Musical,* 81.

32. See Lucy Fischer, "The Image of Woman" and "Designing Women: Art Deco, the Musical, and the Female Body," in *Music and Cinema,* ed. James Buhler, Caryl Flinn, and David Neumeyer (Hanover, N.H.: Wesleyan University Press, 2000), 295–315; see also Patricia Mellencamp, "Sexual Economics: *Gold Diggers of 1933,*" Pamela Robertson, "Feminist Camp in *Gold Diggers of 1933,*" and Linda Mizejewski, "Beautiful White Bodies," all anthologized in *Hollywood Musicals: The Film Reader,* ed. Steven Cohan (New York: Routledge, 2002).

33. Rubin, *Showstoppers,* 179.

34. Deleuze, *The Movement-Image,* 79.

35. Ibid., 80.

36. Williamson, "Swimming Pools," 10.

37. Kyle Crichton, "Big Splash," *Colliers,* September 26, 1942, 13, as quoted in Williamson, "Swimming Pools," 10.

38. Williamson, "Swimming Pools," 10.

39. See Williams's rather dishy account of the difficulties this caused her with Gene Kelly and Stanley Donen on the set of *Take Me Out to the Ball Game* (Berkeley, 1949). Williams, *Million Dollar Mermaid,* 168–71.

40. Williams's autobiography begins with a fascinating anecdote that adds a personal dimension to her fluid identity. She recounts being treated for anxiety with psychotherapeutic LSD and coming to the realization that the death of her teenaged actor-brother early in her childhood had spurred her decision to "take his place" supporting her struggling family. After leaving her doctor's office, while getting ready for bed, she had an "afterglow" vision: "When I looked in the mirror . . . I was startled by a split image: One half of my face, the right half, was me; the other half was the face of a sixteen-year-old boy. The left side of my upper body was flat and muscular, like the chest of a boy. I reached up with my boy's large, clumsy hand to touch my right breast and felt my penis stirring. It was a hermaphroditic phantasm that held me entranced as I discovered my divided body" (Williams, *Million Dollar Mermaid,* 17).

41. Deleuze and Guattari, *A Thousand Plateaus,* 258–59. See also Massumi's discussion of this passage in *A User's Guide to "Capitalism and Schizophrenia,"* 93–96.

42. Given the criticism Deleuze and Guattari received for their reliance on male authors in their discussion of becoming-woman, it is perhaps relevant to note that Deleuze's partner, Fanny Deleuze, translated the work of Lawrence and Carroll and was an active interlocutor in the production of *Capitalism and Schizophrenia* volumes. It seems reasonable to suspect that her work contributed to their interpretations of these authors. See Félix Guattari,

*The Anti-Oedipus Papers* (New York: Semiotext(e), 2006); and Charles Stivale, *Gilles Deleuze's ABCs: The Folds of Friendship* (Baltimore, Md.: Johns Hopkins University Press, 2008).

43. See Elizabeth Grosz, "A Thousand Tiny Sexes: Feminism and Rhizomatics," in Boundas and Olkowski, *Gilles Deleuze and the Theater of Philosophy*, 206.

44. See Luce Irigaray, *This Sex Which Is Not One,* trans. Catherine Porter with Carolyn Burke (Ithaca, N.Y.: Cornell University Press, 1985), 140–41. Dorothea Olkowski presents an excellent overview of the range of feminist responses to Deleuze and Guattari in her chapter "Can a Feminist Read Deleuze and Guattari?" in *Gilles Deleuze and the Ruin of Representation.* See also Elizabeth Grosz, "Intensities and Flows," in *Volatile Bodies: Toward a Corporeal Feminism* (Bloomington: University of Indiana Press, 1994), 160–83; and "A Thousand Tiny Sexes," 187–210.

45. Alice A. Jardine, *Gynesis: Configurations of Woman and Modernity* (Ithaca, N.Y.: Cornell University Press, 1985), 217.

46. Massumi, *A User's Guide to Capitalism and Schizophrenia,* 87.

47. Grosz, *Volatile Bodies,* 180–82.

48. Massumi, *A User's Guide to Capitalism and Schizophrenia,* 104.

49. See Tsai's director's notes included in the DVD edition of *What Time Is It There?* (Wellspring Media, 2004).

50. *Rebels of the Neon God,* Tsai's first feature film, has a recurrent, minimalist musical theme, a score that apparently was added at the insistence of a producer. See Danièle Rivière, "Scouting," interview with Tsai Ming-liang, trans. Andrew Rothwell, in *Tsaï Ming-liang,* by Jean-Pierre Rehm, Olivier Joyard, Rivière, and Tsai (Paris: Editions Dis Voir, 1999), 111.

51. While I am not able to include *The Wayward Cloud* in my analysis here, it provides an intriguing extension of Tsai's fascination with water, alienation, sexuality, and the musical moment in film. In this work, severe drought leads to the eroticization of watermelons, which become frequent props in the film productions of the protagonist, a pornographic actor. The film is punctuated with wildly colorful musical numbers that are almost completely divorced from the narrative.

52. That solitary customer is played by Maio Tien—the actor who often plays his father—who leaves the shop wordlessly when he discovers the bean paste he is searching for has been discontinued.

53. David Walsh, interview with Tsai Ming-liang, *World Socialist Web Site,* October 7, 1998, http://www.wsws.org/arts/1998/oct1998/tsai-007.shtml.

54. Tsai, in a later interview, describes his work as limited to the surface of the body: "But more and more now I think that my observation can only be restricted to appearances, and never reach the inner character." Rivière, "Scouting," 83.

55. Walsh, Tsai interview.

56. Ibid.

57. In *Dangerous When Wet,* Williams's conflicted feelings about a suitor (Fernando Lamas) are diverted into a fantasy sequence where she swims with the cartoon characters Tom and Jerry before relinquishing herself to the tentacles of an animated French octopus.

58. Tsai states in an interview, "I deliberately used an actress much older than the actor in order to prevent a heterosexual love from developing." While the lack of overt romance complicates the dynamic of the film in provocative ways, I find this statement curious (the age difference was not obvious or insurmountable to this viewer) and disappointing, especially given Tsai's openness to intergenerational, interfamilial, and other "unnatural"

couplings in films such as *The River*. Shelly Kraicer, "Interview with Tsai Ming-liang," *Positions* 8, no. 2 (Fall 2000): 582.

59. See especially his 1997 film *The River* and his 1995 television documentary *My New Friends*, a series of interviews with young, gay, HIV-positive men.

60. Jean-Pierre Rehm, "Bringing in the Rain," trans. J. Ames Hodges, in *Tsaï Ming-liang*, 24.

61. Perhaps it is not anecdotal to note here that *la fuite* of *la ligne de fuite* can refer to a flight as well as to a leak. See John Rajchman, *The Deleuze Connections* (Cambridge, Mass.: MIT Press, 2000), 12.

62. Rey Chow speaks in very similar terms about *The River:* "I would propose that what Tsai has undertaken is a production of discursivity, one that is not exactly geared toward a centralizable and thus summarizable logic, but that operates in the manner of an archeological excavation. What is being excavated? The *remnants of social relations,* which are presented by Tsai as *images with little or no interiority—*in the form of bodies, gestures, movements, and looks." Rey Chow, "A Pain in the Neck, a Scene of 'Incest,' and Other Enigmas of an Allegorical Cinema: Tsai Ming-liang's *The River,*" *CR: The New Centennial Review* 4, no. 1 (2004): 123–42.

63. Foucault, "Nietzsche, Genealogy, History," 148.

64. Ibid., 147.

65. Ibid., 148.

66. Elizabeth Grosz, *Architecture from the Outside: Essays on Virtual and Real Space* (Cambridge, Mass.: MIT Press, 2001), 153.

67. Grosz, *Architecture from the Outside,* 155. Grosz reads Bataille with and against Irigaray in her theorization of "architectures of excess," contrasting Irigaray's femininity with Bataille's excrementality as an alternate excess that architecture fails to contain. While I am unable to pursue this line of questioning here, Grosz's formulation suggests a provocative means of reading the gendered nature of the excesses produced within the space of the musical in general and *The Hole* in particular.

68. Kaufman, "Klossowski or Thoughts-Becoming," 151.

69. I am also particularly interested in the correlations between *The Hole* and Tsai's *The River*. Here, the body of the male lead is infected through his encounter with water, and he is ravaged by an inexplicable pain in his neck, a pain that cripples and contorts his body. There is no musical comfort to be found in *The River,* however, and the young man's journey leads him to a far darker site of exchange—an incestuous sexual encounter with his own father.

70. Friedrich Nietzsche, "On the Uses and Disadvantages of History for Life," in *Untimely Meditations,* ed. Daniel Breazeale, trans. R. J. Hollingdale (Cambridge: Cambridge University Press, 1997), 95.

71. Ibid., 92–93.

## Conclusion

1. See Gilles Deleuze, "Having an Idea in Cinema (On the Cinema of Straub-Huillet)," trans. Eleanor Kaufman, in *Deleuze and Guattari: New Mappings in Politics, Philosophy, and Culture,* ed. Eleanor Kaufman and Kevin Jon Heller (Minneapolis: University of Minnesota Press, 1998), 14–19. See also Rodowick, *Gilles Deleuze's Time Machine,* 194–210; and Bogue, *Deleuze on Music, Painting, and the Arts,* 191–95.

2. Deleuze, *Negotiations: 1972–1990,* 175.

3. Deleuze, *Foucault,* 119.

4. See Rodowick, *Gilles Deleuze's Time Machine,* 202–10.

5. Emphasizing the distinction between the creative and the commercial in an interview, for example, Deleuze states, "There is no commercial art: that's nonsense." Deleuze, "The Brain Is the Screen: An Interview with Gilles Deleuze," trans. Marie Therese Guirgis, in *The Brain Is the Screen: Deleuze and the Philosophy of Cinema,* ed. Gregory Flaxman (Minneapolis: University of Minnesota Press, 2000), 369.

6. Gilles Deleuze and Félix Guattari, *What Is Philosophy?* trans. Hugh Tomlinson and Graham Burchell (New York: Columbia University Press, 1994), 190.

# Index

**Amy Herzog** is assistant professor of media studies at Queens College, City University of New York.